Through the History of the Cold War

The Correspondence of George F. Kennan and John Lukacs

Through the History of the Cold War

The Correspondence of George F. Kennan and John Lukacs

EDITED BY JOHN LUKACS

PENN

University of Pennsylvania Press

Philadelphia | Oxford

Published by
University of Pennsylvania Press
Philadelphia, Pennsylvania 19104-4112

Printed in the United States of America on acid-free paper
10 9 8 7 6 5 4 3 2 1

Library of Congress Cataloging-in-Publication Data

Kennan, George F. (George Frost), 1904–2005.
Through the history of the Cold War : the Kennan-Lukacs corresapondence / George Kennan and John Lukacs
    p.   cm.
ISBN 978-0-8122-4253-9 (acid-free paper)
1. United States—Foreign relations—1945–1989—Sources. 2. United States—Foreign relations—Soviet Union—Sources. 3. Soviet Union—Foreign relations—United States—Sources. 4. Cold War—Sources. 5. Kennan, George F. (George Frost), 1904–2005—Correspondence. 6. Lukacs, John, 1924—Correspondence. I. Lukacs, John, 1924–. II. Title.
E840.K383   2010
909.82'5—dc22   2010003406

Contents

Introduction

I wrote and sent my first letter to George Kennan on September 3, 1952. He answered it on October 13. His last letter was dictated for me on August 27, 2003. I wrote to him my last letter on January 25, 2004. This exchange of letters went on through more than 50 years—a reciprocal correspondence amounting to almost 400 letters containing more than 1,000 typed or handwritten pages.[1]

There are, I think, three reasons why this correspondence should have more than routine interest to many people, and not only to scholars. One obvious reason is George Kennan (and, in my opinion, the potential increase of his posthumous reputation). Another important reason is that this correspondence went through almost the entire cold war, and then for more than a dozen years thereafter—and our views of the cold war, more precisely: the relations of the United States and the Soviet Union, are the subjects of many, though of course not of all, of our letters to each other. I write "our views"—which may be the third, and unusual

---

[1] Approximately 179 letters from George Kennan to me; approximately 186 letters from me to George Kennan.

value of these letters—because throughout the cold war, Kennan and I felt the need to express views and perspectives and opinions about its participants that were (and perhaps remain) different from the ideas held and professed by the great majority of its politicians or commentators, whether "conservatives" or "liberals." Allow me, for once, to exaggerate: we have been—often—a minority of two.

Here I am compelled to sum up but two of these minority views. Both Kennan and I believed that the reaction of the United States to Soviet aggressiveness had come not *too soon* (as many liberal and radical historians and other intellectuals argued, at least in the 1960s) and not even at the right and proper time (as is the now orthodox consensus) but, regrettably, *too late*: that the division of Europe and the geographical limits, the conditions of a Russian occupation of Eastern and Central Europe, should have been a principal concern of the U.S. government at least after August 1944. More important, and more enduring, were his (and my) concerns no longer with political and intellectual illusions about communism and Russia but with their very opposite: with the enormous popular rise of an ideology of anticommunism having become a substitute for a decent American patriotism—regrettably obscuring (and eventually protracting) the very nature of the cold war, which involved the relations of states rather than of ideologies; of America and Russia, rather than of capitalism and communism, or of "totalitarianism" and "freedom." In my *George Kennan: A Study of Character*, I wrote about George Kennan in 1946: "Here was a handsome and impressive man, still young, a superb speaker who awoke his nation about the dangers of communism, not a liberal or internationalist, not one of the New Deal crowd: what a prospect of a public career stood before him in and after 1946! But that never tempted George Kennan, it never occurred to him— just as he never thought then, or even in retrospect after many years, that there was any inconsistency between his anticommunism and what may be called his anti-anticommunism."[2]

I had sensed this as early as in 1952—indeed, even earlier. And that was the impetus and the inspiration for this then twenty-eight-year-old foreigner, a beginning historian, an unknown and unknowable recent refugee from Hungary, for his presumption to address a letter, his first

---

[2] John Lukacs, *George Kennan: A Study of Character* (Yale University Press, 2007), 129.

to George Kennan, ambassador of the United States in Moscow—which then he chose to answer quite soon after its receipt, in the midst of a personal crisis, the stunning shock in his career, when he was suddenly forbidden to return to Moscow.

In 1952 the writing of letters (beyond routine notes of business or courtesy) was still not uncommon, though its practice had already become less and less frequent even among academics and literary people.[3] This decline of letter-writing accelerated fast, even before the advent of fax and e-mail and universal telephony. In our case the frequency and the extent and the size of our letters grew in converse ratio to this deterioration debouching into e-mail or even less.[4] The main reason for this was that, in different ways, both of us were compulsive writers. Both of us, I think, would have agreed with T. S. Eliot, who once said that the motive to write is the desire to vanquish a mental preoccupation by expressing it consciously and clearly. And the subjects of our preoccupations, about the cold war, and about his native and my adopted country, were often similar. But there was a difference, especially in the beginning. George Kennan was a superb writer: a great, and often exceptional master of English. I was, I admit, in love with the English language—but no master.[5]

An example of our preference for the written word occurred in 1996 when Richard Snow, editor of *American Heritage*, suggested a recorded interview with Kennan, conducted by me, for the fiftieth anniversary of Kennan's famous "X" article: what had led up to it? Kennan and I then decided to discuss this important subject in the form of three exchanges of letters between ourselves. The resulting six letters were published by the University of Missouri Press in 1997, with my introduction. (I do not include these six letters in this book.) This was, I think, the only example of his private letters to me that exist in print. (In *A Study in Character* I chose not to quote or include anything from his letters to me.)

---

[3] A coincidence: my article "On Literary Correspondence" appeared in *Commonweal* on February 20, 1953.

[4] Neither of us acquired e-mail. During the last years of our correspondence Kennan had a fax machine that his secretary would occasionally manage, not he. By that time not only our letters but our telephone conversations too had become lengthier.

[5] "Our language is a sulky and inconstant beauty and at any moment it is important to know what liberties she will permit" (Cyril Connolly).

Having now said something about (our) motives for writing letters, I am compelled to say something about their purposes. George Kennan and I were two very different men: of different ancestries and backgrounds and temperaments and ages (twenty years). I wrote before that we had certain things in common, to which I may now add one more: I do not think that either of us wrote letters with posterity in mind. Nor were our letters meant to be read by other people—whence some of the special value of their, often unusual, authenticity and sincerity.

Much of the same is true of Kennan's diaries. Their motive, too, was to unburden his mind by describing his recent impressions and thoughts consciously and clearly. He was an inveterate diarist: he began writing a diary at nineteen and kept writing diaries, intermittently, into his nineties. After about 1980 he sent me, on occasion, copies of pages of his diaries for me to read. At that time many of them were descriptive ruminations of his travels. I found them exceptionally telling and beautiful. Consequently it was I who convinced him to put some of them together and have them published. His agent then submitted his selection to a publisher, who printed them in 1989 under the dun title *Sketches from a Life*.[6] It turned out to be one of his best-selling books.

Ten years later, in 1999, I was contemplating what to work on. Many years before I had developed a great admiration for the writing of Harold Nicolson (another compulsive writer and diarist). I was impressed with the success of the three volumes of selections from his *Diaries and Letters* published by his son Nigel. I proposed to try something of the same for Kennan, going through his diaries and most of his letters (not those addressed to me) and composing such a volume of selections. He gave me permission to find and read them in his office and in the still closed portion of his papers in the Mudd Manuscript Library at Princeton University. After some months, however, I was (and felt) compelled to abandon this work.

That did not affect our friendship: rather the contrary. During the last four years of his life my wife and I drove to Princeton often to visit him. The last time I saw him was about a month before he died. Two years later, mostly on the urging of a friend, one of the finest American historians, I decided to write the aforementioned biographical study of George Kennan. Putting everything else aside,

[6] George Kennan, *Sketches from a Life* (Pantheon, 1989).

I wrote it during six pulsating months. It was published in 2007 by Yale University Press.

For the present volume I had planned to reproduce every one of Kennan's letters to me, from 1952 to 2003, in their entirety (excluding only routine notes by him or his secretaries informing me of mundane matters, such as changes of the day when we were supposed to meet). There are about 180 of his substantial letters to me, many of them handwritten, some amounting to several long pages. My letters to him (of all of them I have kept carbon or Xeroxed copies) I thought best to much abridge or excerpt. So I do. The main reason for this is that, especially in our early correspondence, my letters are often verbose and too long—hence their substances are less valuable than his. Yet now, having reread our entire correspondence, I chose to exclude or abridge some of his letters too; and not just for the stake of making this book more readable. In some instances I saw no need to include pages in which he, so carefully and precisely, corrected or commented upon what I had sent him from page to page, line to line, point by point. But my omissions and abridgments of some of his letters are not because of their length. I chose to do so in order to concentrate on the main subjects of our correspondence: the cold war, and history, and—perhaps—philosophy from time to time. The result is a total of 202 letters, 104 written by him and 98 by me.[7]

As the years went on, our relationship slowly changed. One milestone may have been 1960, when I sent him the manuscript (or were they the galleys?) of my *A History of the Cold War*: I was stunned and exhilarated to receive a three-page, closely typed, extensively annotated and approbatory letter from him (see pages 28–29 below). After about 1970, his letters to me were longer and longer. By 1980, we had become close friends.[8] His last letters to me (not included in this volume) were

---

[7] Elisions in the texts of the letters printed in this volume are marked by three dots: . . . The dates of letters are reproduced always. Their salutations are not. (It was not until later in our correspondence that Kennan chose to address me as "John"; I responded accordingly, not without some reluctance, years later.)

[8] He and his wife Annelise were very fond of my wife Stephanie. (Once he said to her that I understood him better than had anyone else.) They visited us from time to time. By January 2003 he was no longer mobile; yet I had to dissuade him from leaving his bed and be driven to Stephanie's funeral.

models of clarity as late as in the spring of 2003, into the one-hundredth year of his life.

There are more than a dozen studies of George Kennan, of whom a full and extensive biography is yet to be written. That will be a very difficult endeavor—not because of the complexity of his character but because of the very opposite: the evidence of his personality in the enormous mass of written heritage he left behind. His friendship for me has enriched my life. So I am grateful to his children too, who now have given me permission to do whatever I may wish with his letters to me.[9]

I owe a very special debt to Mrs. June Weiland, of Phoenixville, because of her exceptional care and intelligence in typing many of these letters and then collating them. Her help was invaluable.

John Lukacs
"Pickering Close," near Phoenixville, Pennsylvania

---

[9] Our entire correspondence is in four large files in my private library. They will be eventually transferred either to the Mudd Library at Princeton University or to another university library.

I

The Cold War Begins
Containment or Liberation

LETTERS, 1952–1954

I arrived in the United States in 1946, having fled Hungary in the same year when George Kennan arrived in Washington, called back from Moscow, to become a high officer on the bridge of the American ship of state. The cold war was about to begin. I hoped that the United States would take a determined stand against the Soviet Union, perhaps even leading to the eventual liberation of my native country. A year later I read Kennan's "X" or "Containment" article* with mixed sentiments. I was pleased with his lucid description of Soviet conduct; but I was also disappointed that he said nothing about challenging the Russian occupation of Eastern Europe. A few years passed: and the more I read of Kennan (including his first book, American Diplomacy, 1900–1950 *(1951) the more impressed I was with him. I was an assistant professor of history but, like most refugees, still obsessively concerned with the fate of my native country and with the political conditions of the cold war in Europe. An article dealing with Europe and Russia, sent to* Foreign Affairs *was not published. I had begun to write for* Commonweal, *the Catholic intellectual weekly, including two articles about "containment" published in their August 28 and September 5, 1952, issues. I took the liberty of sending them to Kennan, now ambassador to Moscow, with the following letter.*

*"The Sources of Soviet Conduct," *Foreign Affairs* (July 1947).

J.L. to G.K.

3 September 1952

Mr. George F. Kennan
American Ambassador to the U.S.S.R.
Moscow
c/o Foreign Service Mail Room
Washington, D.C.

Dear Mr. Ambassador:

I am a diplomatic historian and have read your writings with much interest and often with admiration. You are surely aware about the present and somewhat obscure debate which is developing in this country about the applications of "containment" and it is a mere coincidence that an article of mine dealing with this subject appeared presently in two successive issues of *Commonweal*.

Articles, however, have strange case histories. I wrote this article a year ago upon the request of *Foreign Affairs*. They deemed some of my arguments as difficult to substantiate and I could not rewrite it in the way they have requested. Now it [has] appeared in another magazine in a somewhat mutilated and edited form. Edited, that is, just enough to give the impression that it was the original "containment" thesis and not its application which I criticize. This is one of the reasons why I am taking the certainly unusual liberty of sending you the original manuscript, also enclosed.

My main reason is, however, that I feel very strongly about my thesis and I also feel very strongly about your unusual diplomatic acumen; hence my decision to thrust my professional views upon you, Mr. Ambasssador, as there is truly no one else whom I would rather have read and perhaps consider my views.

Believe me, Mr. Ambassador,

Very sincerely yours,

Kennan's prompt answer to this letter by an unknown young man was extraordinary. On September 19, irritated by a silly question by a reporter at an airport in Berlin, he said that the treatment of foreign diplomats in Moscow was nearly comparable to the treatment when he had been interned in Germany for a few months during the last war. Two weeks later the Soviet government chose to forbid his return to Moscow, expelling him from his ambassadorship there. In the midst of the crisis Kennan found the time and effort to answer my letter.

G.K. to J.L.

HICOG Box 700 APO 80
(Bad Godesberg)
October 13, 1952

Dear Mr. Lukacs:

I have received and read with interest the article submitted to me with your letter of September 3. The subjects you discuss are of course serious ones, as are the views you put forward; and I would like to be able to comment on them. Unfortunately, the position I hold with the Government makes it simply impossible for me to enter into this sort of discussion at the present time. I can only say that I welcome your article as a contribution to the exchange of views on this subject and hope that some day I will be in a position to do more than I can do at present to answer the many comments and questions that have been brought forward publicly concerning the views I have stated in my own articles.

Very sincerely yours,

George F. Kennan

In 1953 my respect for Kennan grew to admiration. Both of us deplored that the United States had not attempted to concern itself with Russia's Central and Eastern European ambitions earlier. But by now both of us were acutely aware of the threatening presence of an ideological crusade of "anticommunism," compromising American decency and traditional patriotism, a second Red Scare that, because of its popularity and because of its international consequences, was more dangerous than the first. Against it Kennan delivered a profound address at the University of Notre Dame on May 13, 1953.

The time of this speech is significant. Kennan spoke when Senator Joseph Mc-Carthy's power and influence were at their highest. President Dwight Eisenhower chose not to oppose McCarthy in public. His secretary of the army and other members of the cabinet, as well as most senators and representatives, thought it best to show that they agreed with McCarthy's anticommunist purposes and with many of his means. Polls, whatever their value, reported that at least half of the American people agreed with McCarthy. (Kennan was still one month away from his official retirement. He still had a desk somewhere in John Foster Dulles's State Department.)

Around the same time a number of books and articles appeared criticizing Kennan. Best known among them were those by James Burnham and William Henry Chamberlain, Containment or Liberation. *(I reviewed the latter in* Commonweal, *October 16, 1953.)*

J.L. to G.K.

October 31, 1953

All of my students have been requested to read your noble speech at Notre Dame. I had addressed myself to a similar theme, and I am sending you a copy of these three lectures that I gave a year ago to a group of graduate students at the University of Pennsylvania and at Bryn Mawr. These lectures [not found] are, I think, but more rambling, and less lucid expositions of the same profound tendencies to which you addressed yourself at Notre Dame. . . .*

*At the end of 1953, having become then a frequent contributor to *Commonweal*, its editors included me in their "Critics' Choice for Christmas" issue (December 4), where I listed my four book choices, and then added: "While it perhaps does not belong in a Christmas Book List, I feel I should be remiss in my duties as a critic if I failed to remind readers of that terse, manly, and courageous address given by Mr. George Kennan at the University of Notre Dame on May 13, 1953, and which, in my opinion, is the best, and noblest example of American public prose since the Gettysburg Address." Fifty-four years later I chose to reprint that entire speech in the appendix of my *George Kennan: A Study of Character* (Yale University Press, 2007).

G.K. to J.L.

The Institute for Advanced Study
Princeton, New Jersey
November 6, 1953

I have received and read with interest your letter of October 31 and its enclosures. . . .*

I am always at a loss to know what to say in those relatively rare instances when I agree deeply with others who write on problems of foreign affairs. I can only send a sort of distant signal of understanding and sympathy. I could not agree more deeply than I do with the five points listed on pages 3–4 of your letter of April 3 to N.N., and you would be amazed to know how often I have urged these things behind the scenes. In particular, I have spent years trying to make our people understand that what is involved in our conflict with the leaders of the Soviet Union is outstandingly the problem of territory and its inhabitants—the problem of who shall exercise police power over whom, and where. If I have not advanced these views publicly, it is because my position in these recent years has made it difficult for me to do so without appearing to attack and undermine men with whom I had myself been associated and toward whom I felt a bond of personal obligation and loyalty despite all differences of view.

I have now detached myself wholly from the world of contemporary international affairs and I am fully absorbed in the study of certain limited areas of our own diplomatic history. Insofar as I have any thoughts about what is going on today, I usually have them only when I peruse the *New York Times*, and they are very gloomy ones indeed. It seems to me that if we manage to survive these coming years without a new catastrophe that would really set civilization back to a disheartening degree, it will not be because of ourselves but despite of ourselves: by virtue, that is, of the fact that we have so little, rather than so much, control over the course of events, that the stuff of human reactions is so obstreperous and so little understood that our efforts to affect it have only a sort of coincidental result.

*I cannot reconstruct what these enclosures were.

I suppose that in the course of time I shall be moved to participate in the debate in some way and at some stage. But for the present, I am bound to say that it seems idle to me. Until there is a rather fundamental re-education of the influential strata of the American public, reasonable and realistic words will continue here to fall on deaf ears. It reminds me of what Goethe said about the fools:

"Wenn sie den Stein der Weisen hätten,

Der Weise fehlte dann dem Stein."*

For this reason, I see no way to be useful but by the laborious process of attempting to improve the teaching and understanding of history, leaving in the lap of the gods the question as to whether we will all survive long enough for this to have any practical value.

One thing I would like to say to you. You had your doubts about the early policy of containment. I assume you are referring here to the X article. I can assure you that the frame of mind from which the article was written was not characterized by any lack of interest in Eastern Europe. I regarded this as a matter which had been settled, for the time being, by the events of 1945, and in a most disastrous way. The last thing that ever entered my mind was that the line of conduct I was suggesting should embrace an acceptance of the permanence of Soviet control in Eastern Europe. But I saw no way of getting at that problem but by first restoring something of the health and strength and self-confidence of Western Europe. As early as 1948, as soon as the first beneficial fruits of the Marshall Plan had been reaped, I urged a line of policy that would have aimed at the separation, gradually or otherwise, of Soviet and American forces on the Continent and the emergence between them of an area dominated by neither, uncommitted militarily, and capable of taking some of the edge off of the unhealthy situation of "bipolarity." I know of no other way, even today, to approach the question of the liberation of the Eastern European countries without bringing on another military calamity.

As you know, this line of thought has never been accepted, either here or in Britain and France. Today everyone seems in resounding agreement that the Russians do not want to discuss the German problem and that it would be utterly impossible to arrive at any

---

*The stone of wisdom they did not have, / Nor was there wisdom in the stone.

compromise with them in this area. Perhaps this is right—but how do we know? I am not aware that any effort has ever been made to achieve a realistic exchange of views with Moscow on this subject—and by realistic I mean an effort made quietly and through suitably informal channels to our people that if we want to help the Russians retire from Eastern Germany, which would probably be the beginning of their retirement from large portions of Eastern Europe, and especially if we wish them to do this peacefully and without danger of a world war, then we must help them to do it in such a way as not to shatter their prestige too fatefully and abruptly. What we have proposed publicly would mean for them a political rout—a smashing humiliation and shaking of their world position. This they are certainly not interested in discussing. . . .

Kennan's answer to a personal letter where I (at undue length) asked for his advice about the prospects of a writing and/or teaching career.

G.K. to J.L.

The Institute for Advanced Study
Princeton, New Jersey
November 18, 1953

The problem about which you asked me is a personal one, and in such matters I am afraid no one can help any one else very much.

I wonder whether you are not expecting too much of life and yourself and underrating the possibilities that lie in your present undertakings. My own impression is that youth in this country, while often badly disoriented by social environment and parental influence, is still eager and impressionable, and that the voices being raised in favor of a more realistic and useful comprehension of international realities are not entirely crying in the wilderness. The real rewards of the teacher always lie in developments remote from the present and confused with a host of other origins, but that should not detract from the dignity of the profession or the satisfaction to be gained in it.

II

The Cold War at Its Peak
The Soviet Union Redux

LETTERS, 1954–1964

In 1955 the new "post-Stalin" Soviet regime of Nikita Khrushchev and Nikolai Bulganin started to retreat. They agreed to remove their occupation troops from Austria. They relinquished their bases in Finland; they made up with Tito's Yugoslavia; they received West German Chancellor Konrad Adenauer in Moscow; they gave official recognition to the West German government without demanding reciprocal Western recognition of the East German Communist government. Kennan and I were distressed by how the Eisenhower-Dulles administration and most of American public opinion failed to recognize the significance of all of this.

J.L. to G.K.

28 October 1955

After some hesitation, I am sending this to you and thus I impose again on your privacy for one, predominant reason: I should like to know whether you agree with what I tried to phrase in that last part; whether you agree with this definition of what I see as a great, and growing, national dilemma. Foreign affairs are such an integral part and parcel of this kind of thing they ought not be treated as separate disciplines or techniques. I think that the American character is changing, and that virtually none of the existing intellectual hypotheses of divisions:

Conservative vs. Liberal, Republican vs. Democrat, Isolationist vs. Interventionist, inner-directed vs. outer-directed, &c., &c. are even approximately correct. I think that the division, unfortunately, exists, but that it exists along an entirely different line. . . .

His answer to my letter of October 28 and to the long paper I had attached to it.

G.K. to J.L.

The Institute for Advanced Study
Princeton, New Jersey
October 31, 1955

As you yourself noted, the questions touched on in your paper are tremendous ones, and I find it difficult to comment on them with the brevity which my own circumstances, at the moment, make necessary.

What you have said in this paper probably finds a greater measure of understanding in my mind than in that of almost anyone else you could have approached, in this country. I, too, consider Europe still the decisive theatre of world happenings. To me, too, the great problem seems to be to arrange for an acceptable long term delimitation of Russian influence on the Continent. I believe that such an arrangement should be possible, but only if the alternative to Soviet control in the areas from which Soviet influence may be withdrawn is not inclusion into an American military bloc but membership in some sort of a continental group or community which is not associated with either Russian or American military power. Finally, I find myself more and more favoring a policy of extensive withdrawal, not from our existing formal obligations in the world, but from the somewhat vainglorious and unrealistic pretenses which underlie our words and activity with relation to wide areas of it. To my mind, the British Isles, Iceland, Canada, and Portugal with the Azores, are vital to our security, as, of course, are the littoral states of the Caribbean. I would consolidate our alliances within this area, and would insist, in addition, on the effective neutralization of a zone further afield, to embrace Scandinavia, Formosa [Taiwan], the Japanese and Philippine archipelagoes, also

parts of Africa, and as much of the continent as could be freed for this
purpose. Beyond that I would like to see this country learn to mind
its own business, to adopt toward others policies similar to those of
the Swiss, to recognize the uniqueness of its national experience and
the irrelevance of many of its practices for the problems of others, to
address itself to the ordering and sanification of its own life—to find, in
other words, its own soul, and to cultivate, with dignity and humility,
the art of self-improvement, asking of others only respect, not love or
understanding.

I don't know whether this answers your question. It will be enough,
I think, to show that we are not far apart.

J.L. to G.K.

9 November 1955

Sometime during the Nineties an English Conservative writer,*
contemplating some sort of pending legislature proposed by the
Conservatives themselves, exclaimed: "But we are all Socialists now!"
The results of this development were not always salutary. In this
country one might cry: "But we are all internationalists now!" Perhaps
what we would need is some good isolationists of the Beard type, not
of the type whose isolationism amounted to xenophobia, and unilateral isolation from Europe though not from Asia. But all this suggests
is that the Isolationist vs. Internationalist dichotomy was, really, never
true, and that it may have been an intellectual oversimplification
stemming from the quite erroneous technical and progressive view of
history. . . .

---

*He was William Harcourt, not a Conservative but a Liberal.

G.K. to J.L.

The Institute for Advanced Study
Princeton, New Jersey
July 11, 1956

It was some time ago that I read your excellent paper on "the great Russian-American dilemma"* and I am sorry that circumstances have prevented me from acknowledging it sooner. I need not tell you that I read the paper with a large measure of agreement—an experience which becomes increasingly rare in these years of general public confusion.

I am grateful to you for making it available to me, and I hope that it will find a hearing.

J.L. to G.K.

21 August 1956

I am concerned with the extraordinary public misconception of your principles and opinions. And it occurred to me that you may, one day, wish to clarify these vulgarized interpretations of your principles. I have heard learned people misconceive your principles as being those of a "soft liberal" or, alternately, those of an American *Machtpolitiker*. . . .

Are Wilson, Kellogg, Dulles really American *moralists*; are they not, rather, really, American *ideologues*? About the second proposition: Is it not, really, true that Americans are excessively rather than inadequately enamored *nowadays* of ideas? Is it not true that we are frequently enchanted by new ideas and looking for more and more idea-men but that during this process we are drawing further and further away from our *principles*? I am not concerned with picking a semantic issue around definitions; I am, as I think you yourself are, concerned with the sad state of mental confusion wherewith we have come to confuse morality with ideology and ideas with principles—and not only in politics.

My conviction is strong that what you are trying to do is a reestablishment of a moral hierarchy but not to teach Americans *Machtpolitik*

---

*Kennan's response to another—unpublished—article I had sent him.

at all—the difference between yourself and certain American professors of refugee origin.* It is a *moral* difference; and hence the deep sadness which comes over me when I see your intentions and your very propositions misconstrued. . . .

You are accused of denying the place of morality when what you are trying to do is to distinguish sham political morality from true morality—ideologies from principles. . . .

I have recently run across a conversation in which the retired Metternich explains this to the Spanish diplomatist and thinker Donoso Cortes very clearly. "They [principles and ideas] are difficult to distinguish" says Metternich. "An idea," says he, "ist wie eine Kanone, die hinter einer engen Maueröffnung aufgestellt ist. Niemand hat von dieser Kanone etwas Schlimmes zu befürchten, der sich etwas auf die Seite stellt und der direkten Schussrichtung aus dem Wege geht. Grundsätze dagegen sind mit einem Geschuss zu vergleichen, das um die eigene Achse drehbar ist und, in freien Gelände aufgestellt, sich unbehindert bewegen, das Feuer nach allen Richtungen ausspeien und den Irrtum überall treffen kann." . . .**

His answers to my two questions: 1) about Wilson and Kellogg (note that he refrained from writing about Dulles) and 2) about the differences between sham moralism and authentic morality.

G.K. to J.L.

The Institute for Advanced Study
Princeton, New Jersey
September 6, 1956

My answers to your questions are, in brief, that Wilson, as I see it, was an ideologue; Kellogg was an unhappy man, hounded by American

---

*I was thinking of professors of International Relations such as Hans Morgenthau and Robert Strausz-Hupé, who were beginning to establish their influence (1956–1957 was also the beginning of Henry Kissinger's career, whose name was unknown to me then).

**"An idea is like a siege gun behind a narrow opening in a wall. Anyone not standing in its straight trajectory has nothing to fear. Principles, on the other hand, are like a cannon on a rotating platform, capable of firing in any direction, hitting errors anywhere.

do-gooders into talking a lot of nonsense. As for ideas: I am sure you are right that I have not made myself plain. Of course there are many of them in our country, and there are still circles—thank God—where they are received at their true value. But a very great and influential part of our society would be unreceptive and hostile, today, to any ideas that did not fit in with the prevailing preconceptions concerning our society.

I hope what you say about my attitude toward moralism is correct. I do indeed believe in morals, but as a matter of individual faith, conscience, and principles. What I detest is moralistic posing and the attempt to clothe in the garments of virtue functions and undertakings that are very much a product of the ambitions and appetites and necessities of this world. While a Presbyterian, I fear that I share in high degree the ancient Christian principle that the worldly power— Caesar—has nothing to do with the Kingdom of God. In any case, I regard the role of government as something irrelevant to Christian ethics, and greatly dislike seeing the exercise of worldly power (and foreign policy is only a part of this) masked as a spiritual purpose.

We did not exchange letters during and after the Hungarian revolution of October 23–November 4, 1956; but he as well as I thought that the crushing of the revolution was neither entire nor enduring, and that Moscow had a shock from which it would not fully recover.

J.L. to G.K.

17 January 1957

I have just finished reading your "Russia Leaves the War"* and my sentiments compel me to compose this letter to you. . . .

It even may be said that this is a new kind of book, eminently suitable as a prime example of how diplomatic history should be written in this new age of democratic diplomacy. It is obvious that, with the passing of the classical and bourgeois type of diplomatic intercourse, the very record of modern diplomatic relations must necessarily be

* *Russia Leaves the War* (Princeton University Press, 1956).

affected by that passing. It is no longer possible to reconstruct the relations of nations by a main reliance on the archives of their respective
Foreign Offices . . .

I cannot close without two immediate remarks provoked by your
book. One is that very profound footnote on p. 13 about Americans
being conservative at home, and radical advocates abroad. I do not
know whether you know that the same sentiment about Russia is
expressed somewhere in Dostoevsky's *Diary of a Writer*, though
I cannot now recall where. There are, indeed, so many curious
similarities—but only similarities—between American and Russian
national tendencies: I have always felt that the only country where the
Slavophiles had a similar counterpart was the U.S.—I am thinking of
the Populists in the 1890's. . . .

G.K. to J.L.

The Institute for Advanced Study
Princeton, New Jersey
January 25, 1957

I need not tell you that I have read with deepest appreciation your kind
and thoughtful letter of January 17. What you have said about the task
of writing history of diplomacy in modern times is most penetrating
and I can endorse it with enthusiasm. Very few people have had the
perspicacity to see that this first volume was an attempt to describe the
way diplomacy works in our own age and particularly as it is practiced
by a political system such as ours. Some of the British reviewers, very
thoughtful in other respects, have raised the reproach that the subject
of this book was unworthy of the effort. It is a question in my mind
whether that would be true even if all that was concerned was the
immediate historical content; but it seemed to me, in writing it, that
something much greater was concerned: namely, the huge limitations
and handicaps that rest upon the very effort to transact international
business by such concepts and in such a manner. These limitations are
no less real, and no less fateful, today than they were then.

I am now completing the second volume, which I hope will be an
improvement on the first; and I am finishing it with a chapter of discus-

sion on these wider problems. I hope this will be of interest to you
when it appears. . . .

---

*In 1957, while at Oxford, Kennan gave six weekly lectures for the BBC, the
so-called Reith Lectures, about the cold war but especially about the division of
Europe. Their audience as well as their repercussions were surprising and stunning, especially in Britain and elsewhere in Western Europe—though not in the
United States. The Central Intelligence Agency and the United States Information
Service made strenuous efforts to organize entire scholarly and public confer-
ences refuting Kennan and his arguments. I was shocked by this.*

J.L. to G.K.

2 December 1957

Your voice does not yet have that echo in this country which it
deserves. . . .

The confusion of the intellect which, to me, seems to be a prominent mark of the history of our age has, as you only too well know,
overwhelmed the so-called "liberal" elements in this country for so
long now that their opposition to the follies of our present foreign
policy is, by necessity, weak, ineffectual, purposeless, and wrongly
directed. You, therefore, occupy a unique place between what may
be considered two overlapping, and inchoate bodies of American
opinion. . . .

There are, at this very moment, still powerful elements among
the older and established groups of the American social and financial
and political and senatorial elite who are, I believe, in strong potential
agreement with what you propose. But it is due to the dreadful nature
of this age of "mass communications"—a dreadful term in itself—that
inarticulate agreement, however potential, is largely useless. There
were times when one could feel that one did one's duty by uttering
the warnings. Now, when these times seem to have passed, it may be
defeatism to assume that the setting up of microphones is the technical
task of others. I do not say that you should storm the microphones; I
only say that behind the many padded doors, the microphones are kept

by people who might surrender them easier than we are inclined to think. . . .

G.K. to J.L.

7 Merton Street, Oxford

28 December 1957

The question which you raise in your letter of 2 December is an extremely serious one, the implications of which—as you know—reach far beyond anything connected with my own person. I wish I knew the answer to it.

I am quite aware that there are limits, and probably decisive ones, on what one can do outside the established framework of political life. I also realize that nothing effective has ever been accomplished politically which did not involve a great deal of compromise with the less worthy aspects of political organizations; the selfishness, the cupidity, the personal ambition, the thirst for popularity, etc.

On the other hand, it is difficult for me to believe that either of our great political parties could provide a suitable vehicle for what little I have to offer. Neither is in a position to give leadership in winning acceptance for new ideas; their function is only to compete in the representation of such old ideas—or more often old clichés—as they feel have already found popularity. It seems to me that a political organization, to be useful in our country today, would have to have a devotion to the truth, as a starter, and it would then have to place this devotion, and its dictates, ahead of the desire to have its people elected to office. It would have to reconcile itself, in other words, to the probable role of a minority party, able to teach and to criticize but not to rule.

In the absence of such a party, I can see nothing else to do but be what I am today—an individual voice; and I see no satisfactory background for such a role other than the academic profession. The greatest source of strength I now enjoy is, I believe, my complete independence—the fact that I am beholden, intellectually, to no-one, speak for no-one but myself, and have no institutional connection, loyalty to which would prevent me from saying what I believe. A truly individual voice is a rarity in this day and age. All this would be lost if

I were to associate myself with either of the present political parties. Some day I may do so; for I regard myself now as expendable in any good purpose, and if the possibilities of usefulness seem at any time to be greatest within that harness, I will accept it. For the moment, it does not seem to me that this is the case . . .

J.L. to G.K.

8 January 1958

/1/ Would you, on an eventual future occasion, consider including Hungary with Poland and Czechoslovakia?* There are political, historical, geographical, &c. reasons for the inclusion of my native country in this group, while leaving Bulgaria, Rumania in another. I shall not go into details.

/2/ I still do not think that your Reith Lectures have the echo in this country which they deserve. . . .

J.L. to G.K.

11 March 1958

I tried in vain to place a detailed review article of your new book. . . .

Thank you, indeed, for having Princeton University Press send me the IInd volume of your Russian diplomatic history** which I read with the greatest interest and pleasure . . .

Then I also read your Reith Lectures*** and the concluding, superb essay. I agree with about every word you say which is not an empty phrase . . . The only point where I may have a *slightly* different opinion from yours is that though I believe that no sane American today

---

*In the same year as Kennan's Reith Lectures, Polish foreign minister Adam Rapacki made a surprising public proposal for a nuclear-free zone in Central Europe that would include both Germany and Poland. There was no response to this from the West. What Kennan had suggested was a reciprocal partial withdrawal of the Russian and the American military occupation zones from the two Germanys (as had occurred in Austria in 1955) and Poland and Czechoslovakia.

**This was *The Decision to Intervene* (Princeton University Press, 1958).

***The Reith Lectures were published in the United States in 1958 as *Russia, the Atom, and the West* (Harper), with a conclusion added by Kennan. I proposed to write an article-essay about them for the *New Yorker*, which proposal was unanswered.

believes in preventive war, there does exist an important minority who, through a misapplication what to them seem ethical principles, believe rigidly that any compromise with Soviet Russia would be impractical as well as unethical. This sort of thinking cuts across party lines and it is unfortunately dominant within the so-called "new conservative"* movement, an intellectual reaction against the more extreme follies of the "progressive" school. . . .

I found Kennan's proposals so important for my native country that I took the trouble to translate the pertinent Reith Lecture into Hungarian and sent it to a Hungarian newspaper (Nemzetőr) published in Munich (with a considerable readership after the 1956 Hungarian revolution). My translation was refused with a short note, referring to George Kennan as an appeaser of the Soviets. . . .

J.L. to G.K.

11 January 1959

I am now trying to convince the editors of the principal Hungarian newspaper published in Europe by the young men of the 1956 Revolution to translate and print your article in its entirety. . . .

You say that "the present Western position appears to demand a simple unilateral Soviet retirement from Eastern Europe." You also speak of a "Western community which had nailed its flag to the mast of an unconditional capitulation of the Soviet interest in Central and Eastern Europe." You also say that for certain people ten years ago "the purpose of the building of Western strength was not the creation of bargaining power with view to eventual compromise but the achievement by Western Europe of a political and military posture so powerful and so eloquent that recalcitrance would melt before it and Europe would eventually find its unification automatically on *our* terms . . ." I do not think that this is the case. I believe, instead, that Western and American statesmanship has not given any conscious or serious consid-

*Written twenty-five or more years before the public appearance and influence of the "neo-conservatives."

eration to the problem of Eastern Europe for a long time. I believe that
the rhetorical question asked by you on page 206 of your article is fully
warranted, that the basic presuppositions of NATO *were* predicated
on a vague but also invariable belief that the problem *was* to contain
militarily, in permanence, the Soviet empire on the Elbe (and Enns)
line. I know that this was not *your* belief; I know it not only now but
ever since in 1952 you answered a letter and an article of mine, criticizing "containment" with a thoughtful letter. Yet I suggest that this was
and still is official American policy (whatever these last words exactly
mean) nevertheless. . . .

Eight or nine years ago, I wrote that future historians may well say
that the first five years of the great American-Russian crisis were due to
a fundamental, mutual misunderstanding: the United States believed
that, after their conquest of Eastern Europe, the Russians were ready
to push into and conquer Western Europe, which was not the case; the
Russians believed that the Americans were ready to intervene and upset
their realm in eastern Europe, which was neither the case. . . .

You speak about "a lack of any assurance that a Hungary released
from the Warsaw Pact would not promptly join the Atlantic one"—but
the revolutionary government did give such an assurance two or three
times, and with perfect sincerity. The model of the Hungarian revo-
lutionists was the situation of Austria, and not of any NATO nation.
On the other hand, you are very right—and it must be repeated over
and over again—that the continued presence of American forces in
Germany played a paramount role in Russian decisions at that time.
(You may be interested to know, for instance, that during and after
the revolution, Soviet military and security organs in Hungary were
extremely sensitive not about the presence of Western, and even American persons but about anybody who may have been West German.)
I also believe that at that time there existed a singular opportunity for
an American-Russian settlement in Europe but that, notwithstanding
the Soviets' treachery and brutality in Hungary, the American administration will be condemned, too, by history for its attitude during that
crucial episode. It is really such a tragic paradox that the death of Stalin
almost coincided with the first inauguration, and the Hungarian crisis
of 1956 with the reelection of the present President. . . .

G.K. to J.L.

The Institute for Advanced Study
Princeton, New Jersey
January 16, 1959

Thank you for your comments on my *Foreign Affairs** article, all of
which I have read with interest and respect. Time does not permit
me to go into them in detail at this moment. Let me just say that I
very much welcome the things you had to say, in particular about the
Munich crisis, and regret that they were not published.

G.K. to J.L.

The Institute for Advanced Study
Princeton, New Jersey
April 5, 1959
Handwritten

Words written from the depths of one's intellectual conscience call for
no thanks from others—for they are only the fulfillment of a duty to
one's self. But I cannot refrain from saying that I was deeply moved
by your article in *The American Scholar.*** Nobody else has said these
things; and they are all deeply true.

I am about to write an address to be delivered before the Executive's Club in Chicago some days hence, on the Berlin crisis. It will
be the first public statement I have made on this subject. Your article
gives me new courage for this ordeal—for an ordeal it is to attempt to
enter usefully in the course of some 30 minutes of speaking time, into a
discussion as confused and unreal as any I can recall in history. I shall
see that you get a text of the result.

---

*"Disengagement Revisited," *Foreign Affairs* (January 1959). Both Kennan and I (at that time
alone and contrary to most scholars, and even to Churchill in his *Memoirs of the Second World War*,
volume 1), thought for some time that before and during the Munich crisis in September 1938,
Stalin and the Soviet Union, despite their commitments to their alliance with France and Czechoslovakia, would *not* have gone to war for Czechoslovakia.

**My article, "The American Imperial Disease" was published in *American Scholar* (Spring
1959). Later, in May, my "Ten Misconceptions of Anti-Communism" were printed in the *United
States Naval Institute Proceedings*.

In May 1959, Khrushchev was at last permitted to visit the United States. He was received by President Eisenhower in a spirit of indifference and even cold disdain.

J.L. to G.K.

10 February 1960

I feel I am compelled to jot down some of my thoughts that were gener-ated by my accidental reading of your articles in Foreign Affairs and in the American Historical Review. . . .*

Don't you think that when we speak about historical truths we are faced with an especial difficulty on the part of the Russians—I say Russians, not Communists? I have for some time come to the conclu-sion that history as a form of thought (or, in other words, the historical character of truth), is something unique and special for Western, and particularly, European civilization. I do feel that a difficulty exists here in any dialogue with Russians, and this includes Dostoevsky's, not only Lenin's Russians. They have a different concept, and perhaps even a different feeling, of truth. . . .

It is especially because history as a form of thought is such a precious, unique, but endangered thing of our heritage that history has now become too serious a thing to be left to the professional histo-rians. Do not be misled by their respectful attitude toward you. There are many excellent persons among them; but their excellence stands in a direct ratio with their appreciation of the limits of *professional* historianship. . . .

Ten weeks after this letter, an American U-2 spy plane was shot down over the Soviet Union, with considerable embarrassment, for Eisenhower meeting in Paris when Khrushchev (loudly) revealed this during a "summit."

---

*"Peaceful Coexistence: A Western View," *Foreign Affairs* (January 1960); "Soviet Historiogra-phy and America's Role in the Intervention," *American Historical Review* (January 1960).

G.K. to J.L.

The Institute for Advanced Study
Princeton, New Jersey
February 26, 1960

What you say about the concept of history by which the Russians
are inspired is quite true. They do indeed have a different feeling of
truth. However, many Russian scholars and scientists are increasingly
aware of the conflict between the pursuit of truth for genuinely scholarly purposes and the exploitation of factual material for purposes of
political argument. What I said in the AHR article was, I am sure, what
many Soviet historians—outstandingly the very old and the very young
ones—would themselves like to say and couldn't. In other words, I feel
that there is a chance of eroding the Soviet addiction to the political
exploitation of historical material. But even if I am wrong about this, it
seemed to me that it was necessary to tell the Soviet historians that if
they are going to cling to this manner of using historical material, they
cannot at the same time ask to be accepted on equal terms by western
historians.

One could, of course, argue about World War II as well as about
World War I; and to some extent one should. But remember that it was
outstandingly the intervention of 1918–1920 which is used by Soviet
ideologists as the basis for the claim that the capitalist world was always
hostile and bent on the destruction of Soviet power. There is no griev-
ance of comparable moment with regard to World War II—only the
charge that we stimulated the Nazis to attack Russia in the first place,
and that we secretly wished for a Nazi victory at all times. Certainly
there is some room for good historical polemics on these subjects, too.

---

*In late 1959 I proposed to write a book about the cold war to my then publisher
(Doubleday, which had published my introduction and translation of some writings of Tocqueville the year before). They accepted my proposal in December.
Consequently, I wrote* A History of the Cold War, *with its emphasis not on
ideology but on the evolving history of Russian-American relations. I was spurred
to write this because of the persistent and protracted shortsightedness of Amer-*

ican opinions and sentiments about the powers of Communism and Russia. A summary of the history of these relations I followed by a historical survey of its components—ideological, social, political, national, intellectual, etc.— consequent to my conviction about the hierarchy of these. I do not recall whether I had sent Kennan the manuscript or the galleys. The book was published in early January 1961.

G.K. to J.L.

November 4, 1960

I have now read (in fits and snatches, for life has not given me the privilege of any sustained application to anything in these past weeks) the proof of your book.

What can I say to you about it? Although it is always hard for an author to judge his own work, I think that you, with your exceptional detachment, know as well as I what, essentially, you have done. This is obviously a major effort of reflection on the causes and nature of the Soviet-American *Gegensatz*: the deepest and most important effort of this sort that has been made anywhere to date, to my knowledge. It abounds with things which to my mind need saying; many of them things I have tried to say myself, but never so comprehensively; others—ones that I have dimly realized but never pushed to the point of formulation; still others—insights that had never occurred to me, but the validity of which I instantly recognize. The book strikes me, in other words, as a really great work of philosophical-critical analysis, addressed to the most recent, the most grandiose; and perhaps the most fateful of history's great political conflicts.

What the reaction will be on the part of the public, I cannot say. Looked at in detail, the material is always interesting and often brilliant. But to embrace the entire book, to apprehend and to react critically to its general outlines of thought: this is something of which only the most thoughtful will be capable, and for which, in our present hectic age, when everything militates against sustained attention to anything, only those will have the time who do not stand in the thick of contemporary life and whose voices, therefore, are not apt to be widely heard. From such people as the daily reviewers of the large papers, you can expect little. The best you can hope, in my opinion, is that the reviewers of the American weeklies, dimly aware after perusing it that they have been looking at something quite exceptional, will give it bewildered and not very discriminating recognition. In England, and perhaps in Germany, the book will find some really competent critics. A number of serious readers, tucked away in the oddest places, will see it, read it, and profit from it, like myself. For the general public, it will seem, initially, to pass along and out of sight like so many other contributions that drift along that swift river of publication, so full of flotsam and jetsam, on the banks of which we all reside; but there will be a few who will remember it and search for it in after years, and you will no doubt have the consolation of being rediscovered by the thinkers of a later age: a consolation which gives little sustenance for the ego in its more superficial contacts with the present life, but represents one of those satisfactions which— as you say—precisely because they make it easier to die, also make it easier to live. In any case, you have my own heartfelt congratulations, and my admiring recognition for the effort, the dedication, and—if this is intelligible—the loneliness, that the writing of such a book must have implied.

Now a few trivial points. . . .*

G.K. to J.L.

The Institute for Advanced Study
Princeton, New Jersey
November 11, 1960

There is one matter I neglected to mention in my recent letter. Somewhere in the course of the manuscript (I failed to find it on searching for it the second time) you mentioned Parvus** and his activities. I felt that the reference to him was somewhat inaccurate. We now have a more detailed picture, from the German documents, of what the Germans did during the war in the line of financing opposition groups

---

*There followed three and a half pages of his single-spaced typed comments on details of my text.

**Parvus (one sobriquet of Alexander Israel Helphand) was a self-appointed agent between some people in the German government and some of the Bolsheviks, in 1917–1918.

in Russia. As far as the Bolsheviki were concerned, it seems to boil down to the fact that (a) in the earlier years of the war some money was placed at the disposal of an Estonian agent in Switzerland who claimed that he could get it into the hands of Russian revolutionary groups, including the Bolsheviki; whether he ever did is not known; and (b) during the summer of 1917 the Germans dispatched, through clandestine channels, funds which they thought were reaching the Bolsheviki and were used to finance the publication of the *Pravda*. It is very likely that one of the links in the chain of people handling this money was Ganetsky, who lived in Scandinavia and was, I believe, associated with Parvus. The best evidence today appears to indicate that Ganetsky was actually Lenin's spy on Parvus, and detailed to Copenhagen for this purpose. Lenin, in any case, had no personal confidence in Parvus and refused to approve direct dealings with him on the part of any of his major associates. There is no direct proof, to my knowledge, that Parvus ever sent money to the Bolsheviki or had any direct dealings with Lenin. He was of course deeply interested in promoting the revolution in Russia and evidently received large sums from the German government for this purpose.

In September 1961 President John F. Kennedy appointed Kennan American ambassador to Yugoslavia, where he spent about two years. During a European trip in 1962, I visited him in Belgrade in July, on my way to a short, anonymous, and incognito furtive visit to Budapest to see my ninety-year-old grandmother.

J.L. to G.K.

28 November 1962

There is one thing that impressed me in Hungary (and, perhaps, even during the fleeting few hours that I spent in Belgrade). This is the powerful endurance of German cultural forms. I have come around to believe that, so far as the historic geography of Europe goes, perhaps the most important consequence of the Second World War was the elimination of German (and Jewish) minorities all through Eastern Europe. But despite this physical absence of living Germans, there is something very German in the entire cultural atmosphere and in the cultural aspirations of the new bureaucracy, *including* the anti-Communist (or, rather, post-Communist) intellectuals. I thought of telling you this as I re-read my travel diary: "The serious, camera-toting, Baedekerish amateur professants of music and of art, men with Serkin and Klemperer faces, women putting out innumerable strong cigarettes in ceramic ashtrays, and brushing their hair back in a grey bun before fifty, like leading German actresses who survived Brecht. I shall not disdain them; I shan't snub them. Their basic European culture has already survived the brutal and barbaric attempts at Muscovite Russification. Leipsic and Dresden opera, Marxist humanism, textile and ceramics, Hauptmann and Brecht. The establishment of Russian rule in Eastern Europe, including Hungary, resulted in a culture whose best accomplishments are Weimar-Leftist, East-German. This is an historic condition; and it is inseparable from the great social change, from a perhaps irrevocable loss". . . .

J.L. to G.K.

12 May 1963

I am writing on the spur of the moment, because I just heard on the radio a lengthy news commentary by [CBS News correspondent] Daniel Schorr from Belgrade in which Schorr, among other things, talked of a sermon that Mindszenty gave last Sunday—he said, in English—in the chapel of the American Legation in Budapest . . .*
According to him, Mindszenty gave an extremely forceful anti-Communist sermon, saying, among other things that "the prisons of Hungary are too good for the present rulers of Hungary," etc. Schorr's conclusion was that Mindszenty has not only been bypassed by events, but that Mindszenty, in contrast to Pope John XXIII, thinks of Commu-

---

*Cardinal József Mindszenty took refuge in the American Legation (soon to become an Embassy) in Budapest on November 4, 1956, in the first hours of the Russian military suppression of the Hungarian revolution. His refuge was arranged and supported by the CIA. A radio news story about an alleged speech by Mindszenty there in 1963 was reported by Daniel Schorr that I found questionable. He removed from the embassy only in 1971, at the request of the Vatican.

nism and of the world struggle in the same terms he had thought fifteen years ago, the last time he was free. . . .

My first reaction to Schorr's news story was a kind of disbelief. Of course, *his* story *may* be essentially correct. But if that is so, we are in face of an interesting and melancholy psychological devolution. The seven years that Mindszenty spent in Communist prisons obviously contributed much to his judgment and political maturity. If Schorr's story is true, then during the next seven years, which he has spent between American walls, Mindszenty's judgment must have considerably deteriorated—in spite of (or perhaps because?) the information and the free press organs at his disposal. In that case there is, after all, a melancholy morale to this.

G.K. to J.L.

Belgrade, Yugoslavia
May 29, 1963

I have your letter of May 12. As you know, this is not a subject which relates to my immediate responsibilities; but I respect your opinion, and I shall try to see that it becomes known to others who are more responsibly involved.

I would only say that I have good reason to know that Mindszenty has had access to a wide and ample segment of the world press throughout this recent period; and if it should be true that his present views are extreme and unrealistic, it could not be attributed to his being deprived of this sort of information.

G.K. to J.L.

The Institute for Advanced Study
Princeton, New Jersey
30 April, 1964

I have held your note of the 19th for several days, hoping that I could surprise you by undertaking to read the manuscript. . . .*

*Of my *Decline and Rise of Europe* (Doubleday, 1964)

I have begun to doubt whether anyone, including even my own relatives, will ever understand the curious accumulation of pressures which drive in on me from a whole series of quarters. It is the despair of my life, because so many of them are worthy in themselves, and are ones that one ought to try to meet. And yet I am reluctant to yield to the suggestion, which hits me in at least a dozen powerful ways, every day of my life, that the best thing I can do with my time is to fragment my energies in an endless number of directions.

How History Should Be Written

LETTERS, 1964–1983

My writing of Decline and Rise of Europe *and also of* A History of the Cold War *were interruptions of my work on my most ambitious book,* Historical Consciousness, *which went on intermittently for almost thirteen years. I had not yet succeeded in finding a publisher for* Historical Consciousness *when I sent the manuscript to Kennan in 1966. I knew that I was burdening him with that; yet by that time I had become convinced that he and I had similar views not only about the cold war or Russian-American relations but about the very nature of history and of its reconstruction.*

G.K. to J.L.

At Sea
June 17, 1966
Handwritten

I am reading your manuscript on the ship and I shall note detailed comments first, as I go along, leaving general observation to the end.

(1) pp. 9–10. You speak here of the impossibility of studying history scientifically. I would rather say "of studying history *only* or even *primarily* scientifically," but basically, I strongly agree. I also agree with your reason—that historical information is incomplete. But here, I would go a bit further. Generally speaking, those sciences

that do, as you say, involve study of human beings by human beings (anthropology, sociology, etc.) are ones that draw their observations and conclusions from the behavior of human beings *en masse*; whereas history is distinguished by the fact that it has to deal primarily with the individual in all his uniqueness. There is, however, no wholly objective platform from which the human individual can be judged. Such a judgment—and this is its beauty and its richness—is always a product of the interaction of two personalities, the judged and the judger, and it is as much a reflection of, and a commentary on, the latter as on the former. To analyze the personality of another individual and to depict his behavior is something not entirely separable from our own personality and behavior: to understand these things is, in some degree, to understand ourselves and therewith to rise above ourselves. Historical cognition, in other words, is in part a form of self-knowledge. But self-knowledge is a matter of the will as well as of the mind. To be a great and valuable historian demands a sort of self-transcendence—of *selbstüberwindung*—which is an act of character and not just of the curious, ingenious and morally irresponsible mind (which latter, of course, is all that is required for abstract science).

(2) The above was written, obviously, before I came to p. 44. But what you write there leads me to an additional comment. It has to do with objectivity. There could, of course, be no greater fraud than the pretense of a total detachment and objectivity in the writing of history. There is no more *a* view of the past from *every* side than there is a view of the moon, or of an apple, from every side. When we use the word "view," we imply the viewer and the point in space or time— the perspective, in other words, from which he sees something, is as important a component of the view as is the object itself. There is, in other words, no historical truth—at least not in any sense useful to us—independent of the eye and the position of the viewer. Every historical treatise represents not the reconstitution of some detached, abstract historical truth, but rather a way of looking at something behind us in time; and there are as many ways of looking at that "something" as there are historians, just as in the world of the visual arts there are so many ways of seeing and apprehending an object as there are artists.

I say all of this only to emphasize that I deplore the fear of subjectivity which obviously assails our brethren in the social sciences. There is nothing wrong about the fact that every historical treatise is as much a commentary on the author and *his* time as it is on the period of which he writes. What is important is that the commentary should be an enlightened, generous and revealing one, marked by an impressive degree of that overcoming of self that I mentioned above. Gibbon is a good example. His *Decline and Fall* is perhaps more revealing and more valuable as a commentary on XVIII century England than as a commentary on ancient Rome. So what? XVIII century England also deserves its testimonials, its great witnesses. And one way of bearing witness to one's own age is to use it as a platform for writing about another.

(3) pp. 37–38. I believe I agree with what you say about Russia. Historical understanding in that country was always to be found in this "establishment," not in the revolutionary movement. This crudity of historical understanding did not begin with Russian Marxism; it was a pre-condition to it. It was, if anything, even more marked among the earlier Populists. An interesting revelation of this I found in the testimony given by Lenin's older brother, Alexander, to the investigating judges, just before his execution. One finds here a pathetic mixture of a naïve faith in the power of abstract science to provide the answers to all human problems, coupled with an utter absence of any historical understanding or even interest. Like Dostoevsky—simply no sense of continuity. There is more historical depth in a single page of Tocqueville, or even of his counterpart Custine who treated the Russian scene in the same period, than in all the literature of the Russian revolutionary movement—excepting only the later Kadets, who were, after all, only partially, and unhappily, a revolutionary party.

(4) p. 46. You speak of your memory being precisely *your* memory. In writing my books on the early period of Soviet-American relations, I was struck many times by the realization that all that I wrote had to pass through the filter of *my* imagination. My book could be no stronger than *my* capacity for envisaging, for imagining, for placing myself in the positions of other people. So great, as it seemed to me, was the role of imagination that sometimes I asked myself whether

it was not really a work of fiction, a sort of historical novel, or was writing rather than a record of literal reality. The difference was only that I was seized up and pinned from time to time, to demonstrable historical fact by the necessity of citing with all possible scrupulousness from the documents of the 1917–1918 period. My doubts were relieved only by the later assurances of eye-witnesses to the scene and period in question—assurances that what had passed through this filter of the imagination was indeed a reasonable approximation of the spirit and atmosphere of the time: *"wie es eigentlich gewesen war."**

(5) On the question of the relationship of literature to history, I am going to ask my secretary to send to you in the event you have not seen it, the text of some remarks I once made to the Penn Club in N.Y. on this subject.

(6) I would just like to add one word about time. There is nothing I trust less than our subjective sense of time. Time is, obviously, a relative concept—as is (I suppose) space. I am not even sure that time is the same to any two people or even to the same person in varying circumstances. We all know the dragging moments, as we all know the fleeting ones. But this means that the barriers that separate us from the past may be less real than we commonly suppose. Sometimes I wonder whether it might not be possible, with sufficient concentration, seriousness and imagination, to pierce this unreal barrier and to identify, if only momentarily and in flashes of insight, with what has been, rather than what is. I had a curious experience, some years ago, when I chanced to drive, alone, through my native city of Milwaukee, on a sultry summer afternoon, to see and contemplate the house— now neglected, blighted and forlorn—in which I was born and then, driving on to the vast Forest Home Cemetery, on the southern edge of the city, to walk directly as though by some divine guidance, among tens of thousands of graves, to those of my honored parents, which I had never seen before. In both places—before the old house and there on the grass before my parents' graves—I became aware of having a wholly altered sense of time. The intervening years lost reality. We were all, it seemed to me, part of one long afternoon. They—the house and

*The German historian Leopold von Ranke's famous desideratum for historians: to write it "as it actually was."

the graves—were now mute. They had lost their ability to respond.
The imaginative effort of understanding was up to me. But we were
not far apart. The intervening years seemed of small reality—of small
significance. I say all this only to illustrate and reinforce your statement
that historical truth touches our mind & senses otherwise than does
scientific truth. . . .

So much for the detailed comments. I read the paper with pleasure
and appreciation. What you say strikes me as profoundly observed,
new, and important. I am a poor judge of public reaction, or chances
of publication. What I have read has enriched *me* and I have no doubt
that it would enrich thousands of others if they would read it. That the
exercise of writing it may be a lonely, and hence a discouraging one, I
could well understand. It may be that what you are doing will never be
adequately understood or appreciated in your time. This, in any case,
seems to me to be a possibility. You should not, I think, let it bother you
too much. Should things be this way, you would be in good company,
historically. Please accept, in any case, my congratulations, and the
assurance of my high respect for what you have done.

J.L. to G.K.

13 July 1966

Your letter, in any event, gives me a great deal of encouragement, of
which I am in great need. . . .

You and I, twenty years apart in age, thousands of miles apart in our
respective places of birth and upbringing, with our different temperaments and backgrounds, seem to have reached astonishingly similar
conclusions about a great variety of things, including some rather deep
matters of personal philosophy. I am both pleased and proud of this:
and I am indebted to you for letting me know some of it. But what are
the reasons for this, somewhat extraordinary, coincidence of views?
Certainly one of the "reasons" must lie within our mutual interest in
modern and contemporary history, and particularly in our mutual
interest in the motive factors of the international behavior of nations.
Another, deeper "reason" must lie, however, in our separate but conver-
gent awareness of the inadequacy of contemporary philosophies (I am

using, of course, "philosophies" in the broadest sense of the term) of human nature. If, then, one meditates upon this, one becomes aware that such convergences are not as extraordinary as they might seem at first sight: because—and this is an aphoristic, shorthand statement—the road to certain truths leads through the graveyard of untruths . . .

The following idea has crystallized in mind some time ago: there may be a considerable identity in our experiences as we travel through space and through time. By this I mean that the principal pleasure in arriving in a place where we haven't been before but about which we already know something consists in the flashes of constant comparison between images and realities which then spark back and forth in our minds. We say to ourselves: "yes, this is the way I thought it would be"; "yes, why didn't I think of *this*"; "how surprising; I didn't expect *that*; but of course!" (I am leaving aside that if we could travel through time as we do through space—to, say, 1766 or 1866 in the way we *can* travel to, say, Portugal or Constantinople—our experiences would be rather similar. We would instantly recognize things that we had—consciously or sub-consciously—expected; and through the general, though incomplete, cohesion of our impressions the unexpected, too, would make sense within its context. But, of course, we do travel through time as well as through space; 1966 New York is not the same as 1966 Lisbon.) On a less profane level I think you would agree with St. Augustine's statement to the effect that God had not created time in the sense that it preceded the world but that he created time and the world together—wherefrom we may conclude that we are not merely the "creations" of time but, in a way, the "creators" of time, too. (All of this, of course, militates strongly against the philosophical concomitants of Darwinism.)—I must stop now. It is late at night. Once more, I must thank you for your generosity, sympathy, interest. . . .

The first volume of Kennan's Memoirs *appeared in 1967. I was exhilarated reading it. The* New Republic *accepted my proposal to write a review. Beyond that writing and my reading the* Memoirs *I wrote many notes for myself that I am adding.*

J.L. to G.K.

14 October 1967

Whether they will publish my review as is I do not know: I certainly hope so. I read your *Memoirs* very intensely, in one sitting. . . . I marked many passages and made many notes. Many of the thoughts that this kind of reading provoked would not properly belong in a review. Sometime during the reading I thought that I would write them down and eventually give them to you. Now I am sending them. Perhaps they will interest you. . . .

October 1967—KENNAN NOTES

Kennan and Nicolson. The comparison in my review is not forced. N. more feminine than K. But K. has been influenced by N. Did he take this excellent practice of short biographical sketches in the form of footnotes from N., who used to do this in some of his books? I suspect so. (But I miss some of N.'s saturnine character-sketches at their end.)

There is a kind of instinctive perfection in some of the diary sketches, of which I could only cite one in the review. Example (minor): in the Giesebrechtrasse sketch he wrote of the chorus of radios, etc. . . . playing church music and Wagnerian operas "mixed with strident gramophone jazz." For some reason this word *gramophone*—instead of "phonograph"—strikes me as absolutely perfect.

Neither T. Wolfe nor *any* Am. Writer of the Thirties that I know of was capable of certain snatches of insight comparable to what is implicit in the Wisconsin notes of K., circa 1936.

There is perhaps only one thing in the book that I cannot understand. It occurs at the end of the long paragraph on page 21. This "emotional distance" is unconvincing. The entire book proves that K. is not afraid of certain emotions; more, that his reason knows how to draw upon them. Of course, I do not know him well. How does this jibe with his otherwise implicit admiration for the kind of bearing which is expressed in the German patrician admonition "Mehr sein als scheinen" [To be more than to seem]. (Perhaps it is nothing but an expression of the practicability of self-discipline.)

In spite of his professed ambivalent feeling towards Germans and of his admiration for things British, there are qualities of his mind, and perhaps also character, that are Ger. Rather than Br.

But since these are all among the *good* German qualities, this is all to the good. Indeed, to me there is something v. satisfying, and encouraging, in the knowledge that K. came from the Midwest. Less congenial but warmer than the New England form of thinking. I feel that, like Santayana and myself, K. deep down has a profound antipathy for the New England Mind.

And yet there is an icy streak once in awhile, in spite of the frequent warmth of feeling. He is, I believe, too tough on the unfortunate Baltic republics. It was, after all, neither natural nor preordained that they should again become absorbed by Russia. And in his superb entry about 15 March 1939 in Prague, the Jewish man in the Legation who, in the afternoon, "decided to face the music and went home." It is all true and just but *cold.*

I have a feeling—and it is not much more than a feeling—that K. has (as I have) certain very unorthodox opinions on the meaning of the Fascist and Nazi attempt in European history (and perhaps even on the role of certain Jewish influences, less in the politics as within the culture of certain Western democracies). This does not mean that he has any inclination to sympathize with the Nazi regime; but it implies a particular kind of *insight.* I write insight rather than understanding only because understanding would suggest *comprendre,* and *comprendre c'est pardoner* (the horrors of the Nazis are not pardonable).

The sentence on Hitler on the bottom of his pp. 116–117 reveals an understanding of the man that many of his biographers have missed.

The design of this book is v. curious. The page design and the type-face are old-fashioned. That is all right, but then the dustcover is singularly unimaginative and unattractive. Altogether it looks like a book out of the late '20's or early '30's. Did the designer think that he was facing the memoirs of an oldtimer?

Another comparison w. Nicolson. N. more urbane, more worldly. Of course. But this had not done him too well in some of his judgments, perhaps except for his admirable French sensitivities. After everything is said, N. was an intellectual snob, and there were certain Blooms-buryish illusions of the British Lib-Lab people from which he simply could not liberate his mind. Examples of this appear in the last volume of his Diaries & Letters: N. was taken in by people like Benes, Maisky, Jan Masaryk, Alvarez del Vayo. Etc. Kennan would not have been.

Curious for me to write this, when N. was my idol (literary) when I was setting myself to write good English fifteen years or so ago.

P. 323 "To this day I am uncertain as to the origins of this persistent American urge to the universalization or generalization of decision." Certainly this is one of the great differences between the British and the Am. Mind. Let me attempt a hypothetical answer. The Am. Mind is intellectual rather than pragmatic, all superficial evidences to the contrary notwithstanding. (The Br., save for intellectuals, the opposite.) This originated in the Puritan, and esp. in the New England tradition (with all of its underlying pessimism and despair.) Added to this the peculiar American way of rhetoric, using speech for different purposes from any other people that I know. (How stupid and shortsighted are American intellectual historians such as Curti and Hofstadter who write long and famous books on "Anti-Intellectualism in American Life!")—Even when anti-intellectualism seemed rampant Kennan understood it better in his Notre Dame speech of 1953.

P. 408. I do think that Europeans, in 1947–49, had reasons to fear a sudden relapse into some kind of isolationism on the part of the Am. People. Eurs. wanted something like an Atlantic Alliance in order to reassure themselves against a Republican reaction which some of them saw coming. But this is a minor point. More important is my disagreement with K. about the danger of the spreading of Communism to new areas of Europe in 1946–1949. The danger was, rather, the massive presence of the Russians in Central Europe. Agree with K. that the Russians were not about to advance further to the west, or south. But their presence was nevertheless ominous and frightening. I believe that Am. Foreign policy during those years should have striven first of all to correct this condition of principal importance. This should have had a primacy even before the economic sanification of Western Europe.

P. 433. The *only* note—the one of the opinions of the German refugee, by then an Am. citizen—which was not worth including.

I am much taken with K.'s Latin-American memoranda. I, too, have felt this kind of impatience and despair about that part of the world— without ever having been there. . . . It is not so much their hopeless incompetence as the unreal, Indian rather than Hispanic, character of their rhetoric which infuriates me on occasion. I, too, have become more mellow toward them, as I have come to appreciate the inherent and instinctive virtues of Latin civilization—of ANY Latin civiliza-tion—in spite of all of its faults. Yet I am v. pessimistic in the long run about the relations of the US with Latin America, for a number of reasons which are too long to write about here save for one thing. I believe that the nervous skittishness of the State Dept. in face of the Kennan memo may have been attributable to the basic insincerity of American attitudes toward Latin Am., as indeed toward most "under-developed" peoples. It is that Americans will not *openly* admit and entertain the idea of the inferiority of these peoples, as long as they can patronize them. This patronizing ideology is a wonderful American mental gimmick in lieu of a self-confident feeling of superiority— for the latter would mean responsibilities, and also sympathies, of a different quality. But all of this may be changing now.

As I am writing this I suddenly recall a photo in the second vol. of the Eisenhower presidential memoirs which for some reason impressed me profoundly, as it reflected—surely against Eisenhower's wishes—ALL of the falsity of Americans' relations with South Americans. There are certain photographs that do this kind of thing for you. One should look at them often. This one is on the bottom of p. 480 (I just looked it up again), even the caption is telling: "Dr. Milton S. Eisenhower meets some Costa Rican citizens."

G.K. to J.L.

The Institute for Advanced Study
Princeton, New Jersey
19 October 1967

I would be leaving you under a misimpression if I did not say that I was much moved by the review of the book which you were kind enough to send me. More than that, however, I think I should not say at this point, for I would not like to feel that I had in any way influenced you in the review.

In an address at Swarthmore College in December 1967, Kennan (again so much earlier than other disappointed "liberals" or "conservatives") spoke strongly and directly against the radical and "revolutionary" ideas—and behavior—of the young and immature students of the 1960s.

3 December 1967

I should very much like to read your Swarthmore address. I know something about the college, since I served as a history examiner in their honors' program on three occasions. Their president, whom I met in passing years ago, struck me as something more than a young administrator, he had some of the marks of a man of letters—this now old-fashioned category. The history department, too, has its share of old-fashioned American scholars with broader cultural interests than their professional specialties. The students impressed me less last time (1966) than before. I met a few of them, true: but the honors' program calls for an extensive oral colloquium. I have the impression that while they are less irresponsible and radical than the bright (?) young things on other campuses, their prevailing philosophy is of the London School of Economics kind, if this makes sense to you at all. . . .

My review of the Memoirs *was published in the* New Republic *on October 28, 1967. Among other things, I wrote, "this political philosophy is, in an important sense, profoundly conservative. I am using this now often meaningless adjective in its original and traditional sense. History, tradition, the existence of national character, the constants of human nature, and the uniqueness of European civilization are pillars of Kennan's personal beliefs. He thinks little of science, technology, planning, One World, mass democracy, economic determinism. Liberals and progressives will not like this book, and not only because of Kennan's granite refusal to entertain illusions about the Soviet system." A man by the name of Evett attacked my review and my estimate of Kennan.*

G.K. to J.L.

The Institute for Advanced Study
Princeton, New Jersey
7 December 1967

I am returning herewith your correspondence with Mr. Evett, and thank you for letting me see it. Since he has apologized, I shall not pursue it; otherwise, I really think it would have been necessary to call the magazine to account for such a letter.

G.K. to J.L.

The Institute for Advanced Study
Princeton, New Jersey
3 December 1968

I want to tell you with what great appreciation I read your piece in *Commonweal* on violence and savagery in this country.*

---

*"America's Problem Is Not Violence but Savagery," *Commonweal*, November 15, 1968. The mention of *Historical Consciousness* probably refers not to his letter of June 17, 1966 (see earlier) but to the published book (by Harper and Row) that I had sent him.

I never heard from you after sending you my belated reaction on your *Historical Consciousness* last summer. I hope you are not offended, or too grievously disappointed, by what I said.

G.K. to J.L.

Crans-Sur-Sierre, Switzerland
March 27, 1969
Handwritten

I am normally living and working at Oxford, these months, my center of activity being All Souls College. I am not accomplishing much of anything, and was obliged, actually, to forfeit my usual salary to make possible this absence from Princeton. But I am glad to be away from my own country, almost every encounter with which pains me these days, and it is giving me a valued opportunity to stand off and consider whether there is anything useful I can do with the remaining years of my active life. (Thus far, I must say, I have not been able to discover anything; but I welcome the chance to think about it.)

J.L. to G.K.

13 April 1969

You say that thus far you have not been able to discover "anything useful" you could do in the next few years. Yet I have thought for some time that you may wish to give serious thought to another—and not merely a continuing, second—volume of your Memoirs. To me, your Memoirs are your finest book. . . .

Even in your histories, the best portions are those where you take a step back from your magisterial descriptions of "wie es gewesen," where you contemplate either the meaning of it all for the sake of shedding a kind of personal, and inimitable light on the problems of human nature itself, or on the ephemeral nature of human institutions (profoundly aware as you are of the nowadays very unfashionable truth along which the influence of human character on institutions is far longer and deeper than the reverse). The personal quality of your historianship is,

of course, reflected, too, in the excellences of your style, in your illuminating reconstructions of certain scenes, and in the maxims that you
can bring to the writing of diplomatic history from your own experiences. But your Memoirs reflect something more, too: they are the kind
of writing that is perhaps *the proper genre* for *your* genius. . . .

One of your principal themes in the Memoirs shows up the inadequacy of many American governmental institutions in dealing with
the affairs of the world. At that time American leadership consisted,
largely, of a class of people whose grip on the direction of statecraft
has now been weakening. By now the development of a meritocracy is
in full swing among us; and you have lived close to many intellectuals
for nearly two decades now; and you, of all people, are exceptionally
qualified to point out some of the principal shortcomings of mind (and,
alas, of character) that are rampant among this arrogant but essentially
unsure new class—again, for the sake of the future. Perhaps you yourself may have pondered at times whether this is not your duty now. All
of this may seem and, indeed, be presumptuous: but I could not keep
myself from writing it to you. . . .

G.K. to J.L.

All Souls College
Oxford, England
April 20, 1969
Handwritten

Thank you for your warm and encouraging letter. It will relieve you
to know that I do indeed expect to begin, at the end of this year, the
preparation of a second volume of the memoirs. It will present greater
difficulties than did the first, for it tends to run close to the present.
Nevertheless, I do have some things to say, particularly with relation to
the 1950's, which are in a sense necessary to complete the picture begun
in the first volume and I look forward to the work.

I have had opportunity in these weeks here at Oxford, to stand off
and look at my own situation a bit. I have satisfied myself, by this reflection, that it is not to be given to me to complete, in these remaining
years of active life, any further major work of scholarship; that I cannot

escape the role in which chance or providence has cast me; namely, that
of an occasional commentator on current international affairs; and that
I may as well yield to this necessity & make the best of it. I have no illusions about being able to affect the course of events and do not propose
generally to take my initiatives along this line. But I think I owe it to
self-respect to try to assure that in those instances (& they seem to
occur regularly) where I cannot avoid talking about such matters, I at
least do it with some competence and authority. For this reason I have
begun again to try to read seriously & systematically on contemporary
affairs, which for some years I had not done—I feel quite crushed in
spirit over what I read about student disorders in our universities—&
not so much the disorders themselves but even more the failings of
academic administration that have produced them, & the timidity
that has failed to check them, once begun. I think this is the end—for
a long time to come—of any real higher education in our country.
Perhaps only some of the Catholic colleges have a possibility of filling
the resulting gap. Depressing as Oxford sometimes is, I look at it today
with a kind of awe, reflecting that it is now probably the only place in
the world where one could still obtain a real liberal education. The great
continental universities are, as you know, for the most part quite paralyzed, & I fear that they, too, will take years to recover.

J.L. to G.K.

22 July 1969

In your last letter you made a passing remark to the effect that in this
country perhaps only some of the Catholic colleges might bridge
the gap that has now opened between the more-or-less traditional
standards of humanistic higher education and the present practices
that threaten their very existence. I wish this were so. I am not very
confident since the administrators and many of the younger teachers
in Catholic Institutions, too, are not exempt from the terrible itch to
prove that they are not less progressive than are others. Still, some of us
try. . . .

G.K. to J.L.

The Institute for Advanced Study
Princeton, New Jersey
20 August 1970

How kind you were to send me the two encouraging reactions about my *Memoirs.** They came at a particularly opportune time; for I am about to start, I hope, within a matter of weeks, on a second volume of some sort, and such reactions give me heart for the effort. I say "of some sort," because a great deal has happened since the first volume was written, and I cannot be sure that what I will now want to write will be an exact counterpart of it.

In preparation for this coming task, I have made an effort which seems to me little short of heroic, to free myself from peripheral involvements and to give myself time to think and write. I hope this respite will also give me time to come together once again with yourself and to take new stock of the matters that interest us both.

G.K. to J.L.

Princeton, New Jersey
November 15, 1970

I am writing—with some hesitation, because letters of this sort are always so inadequate—to tell you that I have read with highest admiration and a sense of genuine intellectual excitement your *Passing of the Modern Age.*** I don't know whether it has officially "appeared," or who else has seen it, or whether it has been reviewed; but in my opinion it is the highest and finest order of thought that has been addressed by anyone to the problems of this present age; and if the book is received with anything resembling the attention it deserves (and I am not at all

---

*An answer to my letter to him (August 14 and not included): the two letters praising his *Memoirs* were by Professor Ross Hoffman ("perhaps the best authority on Edmund Burke in this country") and Professor James Ward of Notre Dame.

**Published that month by Harper and Row. This letter, dear to me, was written the day my wife Helen died. I received it the day of her funeral.

certain that it will be), I think you will be remembered as one of the greatest, if not the greatest, of American historical philosophers.

I literally rejoiced at your ranking of justice below truth. I would also place it, I think, below duty. If I can remember, tomorrow (I am writing this at home at night), I may send you the text of a sermon—a layman's sermon—that I delivered a year or so ago, which has a certain bearing on that subject. . . .

G.K. to J.L.

The Institute for Advanced Study
Princeton, New Jersey
14 April 1971

I am particularly sorry not to have seen you at this time because I wanted to put to you a query which would have been better put orally than this way. It is simply whether you would have any interest in coming to this Institute for one academic year, or for a single term, in 1972–73 or 1973–74. It would be something to be considered only if you had specific work for the completion of which you would need such privacy and other amenities as the Institute can provide. I cannot give you the faintest assurance that an invitation could be issued even if you should wish to come. Applications for the succeeding academic year are screened each year in December. They are always more in number than we can accept; and the decision in any given case depends primarily on the disposition of my colleagues. But I merely wanted to say that if you would wish to apply, I would be happy to sponsor and support your application. I myself expect to be absent (at Oxford) in 1972–73, but here again in 1973–74, which will be my last year before retirement.

The Institute term runs only from beginning of October to mid-April. You could expect to receive, if you came here, a stipend of $4,000 for a single term, or $7,500 for an entire academic year, in addition to cheap housing in the Institute's settlement, and regular access, of course, to its cafeteria, library, etc.

J.L. to G.K.

12 May 1971

Thank you for your thoughtfulness and for the kindness of your suggestion. I do not quite know what to do. I have a sabbatical coming up in '72–'73 which would accord with a year spent at the Institute. On the other hand one of the attractions of the potential invitation—I know that it is merely potential not actual—would be your presence in Princeton, and in 1972–73 you say you will be in Oxford. . . .

    I read your Custine in *The New Yorker* with the greatest of interest.* I read C. years ago: but your exposition of the wider and deeper meaning of his preoccupations touched me acutely. You are quite right in suggesting the significant parallel of C. and Tocqueville. I am sure that they knew each other. (The Marquis de Brézé was a legitimist friend of T.; Custine to Brézé in 1831, in which C. is very critical of the United States. This about six months before T. left for America.) At that time, T.'s mind was more open: he was much less contemptuous of the Louis-Philippe kind of parliamentary regime than were some of his aristocratic intellectual friends. One minor detail: while C. surely read the first volume of *Democracy in America* (published in 1835), he may not have read the—in retrospect, more important—second volume which appeared in 1840 but the reception of which did not come close to that of the first. Having done some detailed work on Tocqueville years ago, I have a vague recollection that C. knew [Joseph-Arthur, comte de] Gobineau, who volunteered to help Tocqueville with some of his researches in 1843. (Much later, in the 1850's, Tocqueville wrote down a few astonishing insights about Russia in some of his private letters; and I wonder whether C. knew that extraordinary woman, Mme. Swetchine** who had a *very great* influence on Tocqueville at that time?). . . .

---

*"Custine," *New Yorker*, May 1, 1971.

** Madame Anne-Sophie Swetchine was a very intelligent Russian lady living in Paris, a converted Catholic, friend of Tocqueville, who in 1856 wrote her a very important and sensitive letter about his religious beliefs.

G.K. to J.L.

The Institute for Advanced Study
Princeton, New Jersey
20 May 1971

I was pleased that you read what you did of the Custine piece, but
sorry that you read it in the *New Yorker*; for this was only a portion of
the book, and the latter is much richer and better.* I shall try to see
that you get a copy of the book in the near future. It is due to appear
on June 15. You will see that in Chapters 2, 3, and 6, which the *New
Yorker* did not publish at all, as well as in certain passages of the other
chapters and the totality of the footnotes, all of which they omitted, a
great deal more is told about the origins of Custine's journey and about
his Russian contacts. There is also much more about his relations with
Tocqueville, and the influence of the latter's work on his own. My recollection is that Custine knew Mme. De Swetchine very well—that he was
in fact one of the habitués of her salon; and I have the impression that
it was probably there, or chez Mme. Circourt, that he met [the Polish
Romantic poet Adam] Mickiewicz. There are still, as you will see from
the book, many remaining mysteries concerning Custine's connections
and his relations, in particular, with various Russian and Polish figures.

Professor Gleb Struve, of the University of California, was very
disconcerted, I fear (as were a number of my Russian-Orthodox
friends), over the fact that I had chosen to write about Custine, and
particularly about Alexander Turgenev and [Pyotr] Vyazemski, at all;
and I omitted, out of consideration for his feelings, certain documentary material suggesting that Alexander Turgenev was receiving, while
in Paris, clandestine subsidies, presumably from some source in the
Russian government. This is another circumstance that causes me to
suspect that there was more to Custine's experience, and to his relations
with this little coterie of Russians in particular, than met the eye. Some
day I should like to pursue the various loose threads to the end.

P.S. [Philosopher Pyotr] Chaadayev, incidentally, corresponded
regularly with Mme. de Swetchine (as well as with her friends, the

---

The Marquis de Custine and His "Russia in 1839" (Princeton University Press, 1971)

Circourts); and Vyazemski was sent by his friend Turgenev to see her, when he was in Paris in 1838. All these people, it would appear, knew each other very well.

G.K. to J.L.

The Institute for Advanced Study
Princeton, New Jersey
18 January 1972

Thank you for sending me your article on pornography.* You are of course deeply right, as you are about so many things. This sort of thing is an expression of a dreadful sort of decadence; but whether it is the decadence of the American people at large or only of scoundrels who like to make money in this way and of people in the mass media who lack the good taste and firmness of character to refrain from exploiting a vogue of this nature I do not know. Here is a point at which one misses the restraining influence which upperclass respectability was once able to exert in the cultural field.

G.K. to J.L.

The Institute for Advanced Study
Princeton, New Jersey
7 February 1974

I have read with much appreciation your fine piece on Lenin and Wilson in *The National Review* [February 15, 1974]. Lest you see an abbreviated and perhaps (who ever knows?) distorted version of it in *Time* magazine, I enclose a full text of [my remarks]. I was filling in for Hubert Humphrey at a dinner commemorating Wilson's death, with members of his family present. That observation is not an apology for what I said; but it will explain why I did not dwell on my own disagreement with so much of his philosophy.

---

*My article, "Pornography and the Death Wish," was published in the magazine *Triumph* on January 11, 1972.

G.K. to J.L.

Princeton, New Jersey
March 8, 1974
Handwritten

I read the review of the Vatican documents* with interest and respect. The truth is, I fear, that for the Pope, having, as Stalin observed, no divisions, there was really not much he could do except to try, as he did, to moderate the conflict wherever a possibility presented itself and to try to save the structure of the Church for the continued exercise of its mission in the future. Easy as it sounds, it was really a very complex task. It is no wonder some mistakes were made.

G.K. to J.L.

Washington, D.C.
September 23, 1974
Handwritten

Being a visitor for one night at a daughter's home in this city and having an extra hour or two to spend, I picked up, on her bookshelf, a copy of your *Passing of the Modern Age* and have just been reading it once more. What a delight! I know how hard it must be for you to know that you have so much to say and yet to live in what must appear to you as a world of the deaf. But I hope it gives you some inner satisfaction to know, as I am sure you must know, that you stand in the very highest rank of Western thinkers and philosophers of this century—and with no peer in this particular country and generation. Forgive this strong language. I am not flattering.

I retired as an active professor on July 1, and am in the process of moving to Washington to take up (as you probably knew), an appointment as a visiting scholar at the Woodrow Wilson International Center for Scholars—a part of the Smithsonian Institution. The purpose?

---

*Referring to the first of my series of reviews in *Catholic Historical Review* (1977, 1979, 1983) of the very important eleven volumes of Vatican documents, *Actes et documents du Saint Siège relatifs à la Seconde Guerre Mondiale* (*Records and Documents of the Holy See Relating to the Second World War*) (Stalin stole this famous aphorism from Napoleon).

Partly to break the rhythm and habit of an increasingly sterile and
trivial existence in Princeton—answering letters, receiving visitors,
reading people's manuscripts, etc. Partly—and mainly—to get on with
my work on the Franco-Russian Alliance of 1894, a work which I hope
will some day commend itself to you, for it will find no better critic.
Partly, finally, to see what I can do in the way of creating a national
center for Russian (not Soviet) studies, with a view to raising this field
of inquiry out of the rigidities of academic bureaucracy and doing for it
what cannot be done for it in this age, in its homeland. To pursue these
interests here in Washington and to combine them with the intensive
social life which I know residence here will involve, is not going to be
easy; but somehow I face it with good heart, content in the hope that I
may, in this way, be doing for a future generation or generations what I
don't seem to be able to do for my own. . . .

J.L. to G.K.

10 October 1974

I am happy to learn of your progress on the 1894 book. You write that
it will find no better critic than I. This is unduly generous: even though
I received my principal training in diplomatic history, the period is not
one of my particular fields of detailed knowledge. Still I am looking
forward to your book with acute interest: first, because I read everything you write with the keenest kind of anticipation. Second, because
from what you told me about it, I sense that this will go beyond the
standard confines of diplomatic history, toward something that I, too,
believe to be very important, toward what I like to call inter-national
(note the hyphen) history, involving the relations not only of foreign
ministries and statesmen but of all kinds of political and social and
intellectual elements, in sum, the relations of entire national states. (I
hope that you will say something about the sentimental and cultural
Francophilia of the liberal Russian aristocracy—as contrasted with the
often different inclinations of the state bureaucracy; and I am sure that,
conversely, you will mention, if even in passing, the often insubstantial
and illusory but nonetheless fervent sudden Slavophilia of the French,
or at least of some of them. I am certain that you will tell us many

things about the corruptions & the vagaries of the press, not to speak of many unofficial agents dabbling in intelligence and statecraft. . . . My fascination is crystallizing as I write this.

You asked me about myself. In May I remarried, three and a half years after I had lost my unique wife. For the second time, I am blessed in having found a charming, warm-hearted, intelligent woman, sparkling with *esprit* who consented to share the rest of my life. You met Stephanie during that agreeable Easter Sunday in '72 when you and Mrs. Kennan stopped to lunch here. Not everything is smooth: she has four children, and many of their standards & preferences are rather different from mine. But, as the great Bernanos once wrote: "Le bonheur, c'est toujours un risque" ["Happiness is always a risk"]. And God will provide—I hope that he provides, above all, more calm equanimity and tolerance . . . on my part. . . .

I want to correct your impression suggested by your sentence: "how hard it must be for you to know that you have so much to say and yet to live in what must appear to you as a world of the deaf. . . ."

I have always known that the more-or-less original thinker (there is no such thing as a wholly original thinker) has a lonely and a hard row to hoe, and for many years I have reconciled myself to this. Part of this inner reconciliation has been the result of learning, part of it came with increasing maturity, (I hope), part of it—and this is not a superficial expression of gratitude—has been my contentment with the fact that, after all is said, I, a refugee and an unorthodox writer and academic, have been able to secure for myself private conditions of existence in this country that are beyond the dreams of my former countrymen, and without having had to sacrifice my intellectual independence in the bargain. . . .

What I cannot reconcile myself to are the conditions of intellectual narrowness *and* irresponsibility (a strange compound, this) rampant in this country (as also in other portions of the Western world), now. They amount to the rapidly increasing breakdown of communications. . . .

G.K. to J.L.

4/3/75

Re your note of the 6th: please forgive this laconic reply. I finished
my first tour of residence in Washington on March 31, and am about
to leave (day after tomorrow) for some weeks of archival work in
Europe—mostly in Vienna. Will be back at the end of May. Would
much like to see what you have written about Solzhenitsyn,* but don't
know where to suggest you should send it—if you send it to me, c/o
the Institute for Advanced Study, it should be held there for my return;
and that would perhaps be the best solution. The Vienna address is:
Pension Wiener, 16 Seilergasse, 1010 Wien.—So far as Indo-China is
concerned, I think our people have taken leave of their senses. There is
now nothing for us to do but to retire, keep our mouth shut, and try to
live it down.

G.K. to J.L.

Princeton, New Jersey
August 24, 1975

Thank you for sending me your article on Solzhenitsyn. I received it on
return from some months in Europe, a few days ago, and have now read
it—with the usual measure of wide satisfaction and approval. And this,
although I think Solzhenitsyn has been talking a lot of mischievous
nonsense in this country, not to mention the fact that I have a higher
opinion than you do of Isaiah Berlin.

    S., in my opinion, is going to go down in Russian history as the
greatest moral leader of this century—to date—a commanding figure in
that grand Russian tradition that sees the Dichter not just as entertainer
but as responsible teacher and helper to those who read him. What
impressed me most about *Gulag*, as you may have noted if you read the
review in the N.Y. Review of Books, was his humility in recognizing
the insidious character of the spiritual corruption that has permeated

---

*Kennan had been instrumental in bringing Solzhenitsyn from Switzerland to the United
States. My article, "What Solzhenitsyn Means," appeared in *Commonweal*, August 1, 1975.

Russian society under the Bolsheviki, and confessing the extent to which, as he now realizes, it once affected himself; but also his recognition that the greatest crime of the Russian Communists has been their contempt and disregard for the truth, and that the regeneration of Russian society will not begin until it learns to try to look soberly and honestly at its own past—which is only another way, of course, of saying what you said in your article about the essentiality of history,— of honest, thoughtful history—as the basis for a proper view of human society.

I am still struggling, whenever life gives me the odd moments of leisure for the purpose, with my own history of the origins of the Franco-Russian Alliance of 1894—love it and am inwardly quite excited over what I am doing—and hope that some day, when it appears, it will meet with your approval. It is my own way of writing history—not quite like any other; but it is honest, and I think it has value. . . .

On August 30, 1974, in a letter I wrote Kennan, I stated that "I have been thinking about the sorry developments in Portugal (where a mild authoritarian government had given way to a democratic-socialist regime). . . . I have been heartened by the popular failure of the Communists . . . while disheartened by the tragicomic behavior of their opponents. . . ."

G.K. to J.L.

The Institute for Advanced Study
Princeton, New Jersey
19 October 1975

I, too, am not at all happy about Portugal. Things have gone somewhat better, politically, than they bade fair to do, one month or so ago; but the best we can hope for is a species of Yugoslav solution, with a continually depressed economy and the gradual atrophy of all that made Portuguese life colorful, interesting, and attractive.

It seems to me that we are seeing, these days, the pattern of the future throughout the West: a grey, egalitarian uniformity going under the name of moderate socialism—the product of an outlook in which jealousy—jealousy of excellence no less than jealousy of a higher standard of living—is the dominant motif, and in which people are content to accept a colorless shabbiness and dreariness of life, comforted by the reflection that no one lives better or more attractively than themselves, rather than to live better, with the knowledge that someone else lives better still.

J.L. to G.K.

20 November 1976

Last August I spent three weeks in Norway. I returned with many strong impressions. The land was less majestic but more mystical and melancholy than I had imagined beforehand. I liked the people very much, and not only because of their evident strong qualities but also because of their provincialism. (I am putting this in a kind of intellectual shorthand.) If I were a Norwegian I, too, would have voted against joining the Common Market. On the surface their young people seem to behave and to adorn themselves and to mouth ideas that are indistinguishable from the habits and the public ideas entertained by other young people everywhere, including very much this country. Upon closer acquaintance I found that they are quite different, and that they *think* quite differently, in more than one way. Same thing about democracy and socialism in Norway. International democracy is a thin nothing, international socialism is a myth. There is only national democracy, and different national *social*isms. The world is becoming standardized, like a big airport, but only on the surface. . . .

G.K. to J.L.

Princeton, New Jersey
December 11, 1976

You did me the kindness to write me on a Saturday evening in November. I am responding, in kind, in December—and gladly so.

First: one or two details. The observations on Churchill-Roosevelt-Stalin, to which you referred, did appear in *Survey*. I do not have here (I am writing at home) the number of the issue; but I think it might have been about a year ago.

Secondly, if you are going to write about William C. Bullitt, you will, I suppose, have seen the volume of his correspondence with F.D.R. published two or three years ago by his brother; and in this case you will have seen the foreword I wrote for it.* Poor Bullitt: a member of the talented generation of Hemingway-Fitzgerald-John Reed; full of charm and vivacity; also brilliant; but deeply unhappy, a species of Midas of the spirit, in whom all the golden qualities turned to stone because he never loved anyone as much as himself.

If I can find a few paperback copies of my *Memoirs*, perhaps I could send them to you and some of them, someday, might be returned. Or no?

Now to other things:

I am glad you had a chance to see Norway. I have been going there for 45 years, and we continue, as you know, to spend our summers there. I liked it much more 45 years ago than I do now. Up to the 1920's the Norwegians had been, as Frederick the Great said of his soldiers, *grossgehungert* [lean and hungry]; and they were a marvelous people: strong, simple, earnest, and dignified. Now, they have been swept off their feet by the automobile and all that goes with it—even worse than we were. Their youth, as you say, seems indistinguishable from our own—although I have discovered, from the example of our more intimate Norwegian friends, that one must be careful in this judgment: the ones you see on the motorcycles, in the blue jeans, are not all there is—there are also, in the better families, more thoughtful, sensitive, and decent ones. One of the great troubles with the Norwegians is that they are, for all their outward jolliness, a very shy and troubled people, who combine, curiously enough, pride, on the one hand, with a certain lack of social and intellectual self-confidence, on the other. They are better people, actually, than they know how to show. But when they come to this country they seem, in their bewilderment, to lose the qualities they had in their home land; they sink back into the colorless lower middle class of Brooklyn or the south side of Chicago and come to talk English with an accent as vulgar, and as self-condemning, as any you could find.

---

*I had mentioned my plans to write on Bullitt in a previous letter.

My congratulations (or should I say, commiseration?) on your election as head of the American Historical Association.* I had not known
of this. I have been unhappy about the Association. I wished it would
interest itself more in history and less in questions of professional
advancement in the teaching profession. I am coming to think that it is
best when history is written by dilettantes—or at least by people who,
even if they may teach, write history for dilettantish motives, as you
yourself do, and as Gibbon did. Good history flows only from love of
subject, rarely, if ever, from the principle of *publish or perish*. I, incidentally, shall be delivering one paper at the December meeting of the
AHA. Perhaps I shall see you there.

As for myself: I labored, whenever I could get time, on my study of
the origins of the Franco-Russian Alliance, up to about one month ago.
(I had by that time completed some 20 out of what I expect to be 23 or
24 chapters.) Then, in some desperation, I laid it aside and undertook
to try my hand at a small book on contemporary problems of American
foreign policy. I did this (a) because I felt the moment to be a very
crucial one, and was concerned for the future of my children, and other
people's children; (b) because I had the feeling that what I had had to
say on this subject in the past had always been said in fragments, in
articles or speeches composed in response to the initiatives of others,
and that I ought at some point to try to put it all together, as a coherent
and rounded philosophy of American foreign policy; and (c) because I
had the feeling it was now or never—that, already 72 years of age, I was
not getting any younger, and had better try to say it now, while I still
might have the energy, than to suppose that I could say it later. A risky
undertaking: this. I find the task a difficult one, and do not know how
good the product will be. But at last I am making the effort. I hope to
complete it by mid-winter, then to go briefly to Paris and complete the
research for the final chapters of the other book.

As for the country: I am, as usual, for the long term pessimistic.
I do not have as mistrustful an attitude towards the President-elect
as you do. He has, I suspect, the provincial virtues—presumably also
the provincial weaknesses; but by and large I much prefer him to Mr.

---

*It was the American *Catholic* Historical Association (we both withdrew from membership in
the American Historical Association a few years before, I think).

[President Gerald] Ford. On the other hand, I doubt that he will be able to dispell the military fixations which govern our policy towards the Soviet Union; and I expect to see us go farther and farther on the path of wildly redundant military preparations. For a number of reasons, the Cold War has become an addiction of this society. We could not live without it, and would not want to. In this pattern of attitudes, there is obviously no place for anyone who is interested in looking at the Soviet leaders *as they are*. And the statement of my own views, which I mentioned a moment ago, is designed primarily to satisfy my own conscience—as something for the record—not because I think it will do any significant good.

Last year I had occasion to visit, briefly, both the new south and Chicago. In each case, I was heartened by the freshness of spirit one encounters in those parts, such a contrast to the hopelessness of the New York area. I wish the country could be split up, so that the various sections could go their own way. Some might not make it, but others might. Perhaps the whole civil war was wrong. That Lincoln was an admirable and moving character was clear; but what was his highest aim?—the preservation of the Union. And was that really a good idea? I was brought up to think so. Today, I am not sure. . . .

J.L. to G.K.

21 December 1976

Very many thanks for your detailed and generous letter. I shall not be able to hear you or see you in Washington.* From the AHA program, I learn that you will be speaking on Thursday and I shall be leaving the day before. . . . I see from the program that you will be on the program with Karl Wittfogel. I read—or tried to read—his famous work several years ago, entitled *Oriental Despotism*, a monument of weirdest nonsense.** As Wilde would have said, it shows a want of knowledge that must be the result of years of study. I understand that Wittfogel was an enthusiastic Communist of the Weimar years, after which he became

---

*Kennan's paper read at the December 1976 American Historical Association meeting was entitled "Comments on Paper by Richard Pipes, Russia Under the old Regime."

**Oriental Despotism: A Comparative Study of Total Power (Yale University Press, 1957).

an equally enthusiastic anti-Communist, with the same humorless doctrinaire ideological tendencies of mind. You and I know the type. I never met him. . . .

I shall not bore you now with speculations about anything else; except to say that what I find most disconcerting is the failure of our leaders, and of their surrounding crowds of advisers, to recognize— let alone to address themselves—what the principal problems facing this country and its people are. They keep trotting out seemingly—but only seemingly—newer and newer answers to the same old questions. They talk about further enlarging liberties when the problem is how to secure the existing liberties; they talk about extending laws when the greatest scandal is inherent in the chaotic and corrupt procedures through which laws are misadministered and whereby the vast majority of American lawyers have become nothing more than fixers. They will spend untold amounts of money on education, when another hoary scandal is that of the shameless corruption of the standards of American public education, etc., etc. . . .

Because of your speculations about Lincoln and about the preservation and creation of a large Union, I am enclosing a Xerox of something that has fascinated me for a long time. In 1931, an English man of letters produced a little book entitled *If, or History Rewritten*, in which the finest chapter—there are some good ones in it—contains Churchill's brilliant tour de force: "If Lee had Not Won The Battle of Gettysburg."* As you know, Churchill was out of office at the time, and chronically short of money; he depended on all kinds of odd incomes from journalism; but we are the richer for that, and I have often thought that this is one of his best—no mean thing to say. And you will see that it also has a deeper meaning: it reflects his attachment to the ideal of an eventual English-speaking confederation which could have been the greatest force of the world, and which he had wanted all during his lifetime, in vain.

I close by wishing you blessed Christmas and New Year. You seem to be as full of the powers of the spirit as ever. May the Lord bless your work for many more years....

---

*J. C. Squire, ed., *If, or History Rewritten* (Viking, 1931).

G.K. to J.L.

The Institute for Advanced Study
Princeton, New Jersey
February 6, 1977

Three days ago I finished my "quickie" on current U.S. foreign policy and sent it off to the publisher. It was written in the very faint hope that it might influence the new administration along lines that I consider useful—or at least (since one never can be certain about the consequences of any actions in this field) more likely to be useful than others. I am not very sanguine about its doing any good, but thought it a duty to say what I have to say before it was clearly too late. Now, I am turning to all the correspondence that has piled up while I was occupied with this task; and I want just to acknowledge your letter of Dec. 21 and the Churchill piece, which I had never heard of and which I was fascinated to see.

I am mildly encouraged by the first acts of the new president.* There is a touch of provincial naivety about him which is at least preferable to the cynical opportunism of some of his predecessors and competitors. But I fear the consequences of his moralism—with respect both to Southern Africa and to the Soviet Union. The question of pressure on behalf of the Russian "dissidents" is one of those highly complicated political questions in which one has to work with contrary forces, carefully gauging the best compromise line between them. By that I mean that *some* pressure is desirable—perhaps even necessary. Too much of it is self-defeating. It is like the ballast in a boat, or like the drugs in pills: homeopathic doses can be helpful; excessive ones—lethal. Whether Mssrs. Carter and [Secretary of State Cyrus] Vance, egged on by the American press, who like nothing more than a dramatic conflict and would happily push one to the point of world catastrophe if they could, oblivious of the fact that they would go down with the rest of us, is the question.

---

*Jimmy Carter. Three years later both Kennan and I were appalled by national security advisor Zbigniew Brzezinski's influence on Carter; he gave bad and possibly fatal advice to this president about both Afghanistan (a country the Russians then entered to their peril) and Iran.

Having completed my dutiful little work on current problems, the writing of which I much disliked, I am eager now to return to history—to the completion that is, of the work on the origins of the Franco-Russian alliance, which is now more than four-fifths completed. To this end I hope to go to Paris once more, in March: to seek access, this time, to the military and banking archives. I find this necessary to cover the period 1888–1890, when the significant developments were all behind the scenes, at the military and financial levels—not at the diplomatic one. . . .

I had been writing my Philadelphia: Patricians and Philistines, 1900–1950 *(Farrar, Strauss, Giroux, 1981), including among other chapters six biographical essays on prominent Philadelphians of that period, one of them about William Bullitt, whom Kennan knew very well, and who was his chief from 1933 to 1936 as the first American ambassador to the Soviet Union.*

G.K. to J.L.

Princeton, New Jersey
August 8, 1978
Handwritten

You are heartily welcome to send me your chapter on Bullitt—but if you send it soon, send it to me c/o The Aspen Institute for Humanistic Studies, at Aspen—not here. I groan daily over the volume of things sent to me to read, but anything from your pen falls into the category of the great exceptions to his rule.

Some days ago I delivered to the Princeton University Press a typescript of some 700 pages—a scholarly study on the origins (in the 1880's) of the Franco-Russian alliance of 1894. (It will be a full year, I fear, before it appears on the market. When it does, there are parts of it that may amuse you.) It was prepared over the space of some 5–6 years, in the face of ten thousand interruptions, distractions, and peripheral demands on my time and strength. But it had the virtue of giving me an objective, and a direction of effort. Now that it is off my shoulders, I stand in complete uncertainty about what to do with myself henceforth.

Shamefully, at the age of 74 but still in possession of most of my faculties, I find myself as helpless as ever before the question: what was I put into this world for?—what is the most useful contribution I can make? To what should I turn my hand? . . .

G.K. to J.L.

Aspen, Colorado
August 15, 1978
Handwritten

My congratulations on your chapter on Bullitt. It is without question the best thing that has ever been written about him and the first to do him even a proximate justice. Unquestionably, he deserved better of his country than he received of it; and you are the first to make entirely clear how much this was the case, and to repair some of the neglect.

There are a number of comments, most of them petty, that occurred to me as I read the piece; and I have set them forth on a separate sheet. You are not to feel obliged to take them into account. But some of them may be helpful.

Would you mind my speaking to Orville Bullitt,* at some point, about my admiration for what you have done here, and my gratification that you have done it?

I seem not to be able to adjust very well to the altitude at this place (2,500 meters), and have passed some rather miserable days of semi-confinement in this motel. But it has left me some time to read; and your paper arrived opportunely.

P.S. Lacking other reading material here, I picked up in a bookstore, and have been reading Reinhold Niebuhr's 1940 lectures on "The Children of Light and the Children of Darkness." I was moved to think of you as I read it, at many points. For while Niebuhr was a strong philosophic critic of the Catholic Church in certain respects, I suspect that he was in many other ways himself a secret Catholic. Am I wrong about this? Consider, for example, this fine sentence: ". . . no matter how wide the perspectives which the human mind may reach, how broad the loyalties which the human imagination may conceive, how universal

---

*William Bullitt's surviving brother, living in Blue Bell, Pennsylvania.

the community which human statecraft may organize, or how pure the aspirations of the saintliest idealism may be, there is no level of human moral or social achievement in which there is not some corruption of self-love." This demand for humility is the principal message he had to impart, and I find it an impressive one. . . .

G.K. Comments on Chapter entitled "Wm. Bullitt, or the Rebel Philadelphian"

1. P. 4. For an appraisal of the political usefulness & importance of Bullitt's mission to Moscow in 1919, you might wish to note, if you have not done so, the passages about it in my *Russia & the West under Lenin and Stalin.**

2. P. 5, Line 4 Although you have mentioned this later in the paper, I miss, here, some reference to Bullitt's angry resignation and departure from the Peace Conference.

3. P. 8, Line 4. The point, as I understood it, was not that support had not yet been forthcoming, but that Bullitt had an adequate assurance that it would be.

4. P. 8, Line 6 from bottom. Should there not be a reference to Bullitt's great service in persuading the Paris police to remain through the period between the flight of the population and the arrival of the Germans?

5. P. 9, last line. Is "desperate attraction to homosexuality" the right term? I gained from a talk with [Sumner] Welles' son the impression that his father was a man whose otherwise impeccable conduct was occasionally interrupted by lapses of control (always under the influence of alcohol) leading to bizarre and sordid advances to other men—lapses, that is, of a pathological nature. But perhaps your phrase, in the deeper, subconscious sense, is correct.**

6. P. 10, about F.D.R.'s reaction to Bullitt's warnings re Welles: I would have thought a more adequate description something like this: that Roosevelt, who found the matter painful and one that put him in an awkward position, viewed Bullitt's raising of it as an indecent personal vendetta and resented it accordingly.

Russia and the West Under Lenin and Stalin (Little, Brown, 1961).
**Bullitt, wrongly, went directly to the president, accusing Welles as a potential security risk.

7. P. 10. We must recognize, I fear that Bullitt, too, flattered F.D.R. egregiously.

8. P. 12 (a more serious point). Are you sure this is an adequate description of Bullitt's final years? My impression is that he lived not only, or even primarily, in Paris, but for a short time in Taiwan, and most of the time either in Washington or at his country place in Connecticut and that he became extremely bitter and violent, associating himself with the China lobby and other extreme Right Wingers and turning publicly against many of his former friends (myself included). It was a sad, but not unnatural, ending for an unusually sanguine and unjustly frustrated man.

9. P. 15, 7th line from bottom. Was it [their temperament] really "essentially cold"? Or "outwardly cold"? Or reserved and self-disciplined after the New England tradition? I know Catherine Drinker Bowen and I did not think of her as a cold person. Or was she the exception?

10. P. 18. Bullitt had the contempt for his class that could have been entertained only by someone who felt secure in his membership in it—hence devoid of feelings of inferiority or envy. He was thus immune to its snobbery and highly sensitive to its pretences. (This is only an addendum—not a disagreement with what you wrote.)

11. P. 22. Although I have a faint, faint recollection of a female form in Bullitt's household shortly after his arrival, and his occupancy of Spasso House in 1934, neither Annelise nor I can remember her specifically, and I think her stay there must have been brief.

12. P. 23. The pen-portrait of Offie deserves to be expanded.* He deserves, in fact, a monograph on his own: a Renaissance type; earthy, extroverted, enormous energy, endless joie de vivre; a born "operator."

13. P. 24. I accept the criticism of my observation about burning the candle at both ends. The phrase may have been ill-taken. I did not mean that Bullitt became prematurely exhausted. I meant that he poured his enthusiasms too fast, too abundantly, and too impatiently into vessels too narrow to accept them—he gave to life more than it was ready to accept, at that speed, and thus drained himself prematurely of his usefulness. A lovable trait, indeed. But this, too must be remem-

*Carmel Offie, for a while Bullitt's personal secretary.

bered. He loved few people, if any, as much as himself. Was, in fact, more lovable than capable of loving—a great egoist, in short.

J.L. to G.K.

10 January 1979

A most curious coincidence—to follow up my letter of a few days ago.

I am reading a very profound book about the harmonic realities of the universe—this may sound either hopelessly eccentric or hopelessly forbidding, but believe me, there is a great deal of substance in it—by the German philosopher and scientist Hans Kayser, in which I find the following: "The physiologist E. von Cyon, a contemporary of Helmholtz, referring to the ear as the organ of spatial and temporal sense, called it the 'most important of all our sense organs.'"

The reference is to E. v. Cyon, *Das Ohr als Organ fuer die math. Sinne Raum und Zeit,* Berlin, Springer, 1908. [The Ear as the Organ for the Mathematical Sense of Space and Time]. (Springer was a most reputable scientific publishing house.) This suggests that Cyon continued with serious scientific studies even at that late time. Someone ought to write his biography . . .*

J.L. to G.K.

8 May 1979

My "interview" with Mr. Harriman** will take place on 22 May, by which time you will have left the country. Not having heard from you about this I assumed that you preferred not to participate in this kind of discussion. I told this to Mr. Harriman when he called me on the phone. It seems that he had heard of the possibility of a three-way

---

*Elie de Cyon [Elias von Cyon], *Das Ohrlabyrinth als Organ der mathematischen Sinne für Raum und Zeit* (Springer, 1908). In the published first volume of his great history, *The Decline of Bismarck's European Order: Franco-Russian Relations, 1875–1890* (Princeton University Press, 1979) Kennan dealt extensively with Cyon, an extraordinarily versatile publicist, diplomatic agent, and scientist.

**Richard Snow, editor of *American Heritage,* suggested a three-way discussion about the origins of the cold war, with former Ambassador W. Averell Harriman, George Kennan, and myself, which we then let drop

conversation from the owner of *American Heritage* and he would have
liked you to participate—he insisted that no date be set until we find
out about your best convenience—but I told him that, to the best of my
knowledge, you would be abroad by the time which would be suitable
for him as well as for myself. Let me repeat that the entire idea of this
kind of discussion came from the owner of the magazine (a friend of
Mr. Harriman's, whom I do not know, though I know the editor and the
editor emeritus) and, while my first reaction was that I should prefer a
three-way discussion, I made it clear to the editors that this was entirely
dependent on your preference and convenience. . . .

I read your article—or, perhaps, the excerpt from your book—in the
reprint from the *Jahrbücher für Geschichte Osteuropas* with acute attention, impressed as I was, as so often, with the unusual compound of
precision and insight which marks so much of your historianship. Then
last week, by accident, I ran across a somewhat jumbled page or so in
an otherwise creditable biography of Maud Gonne by a woman named
Nancy Cardozo—and, even though I strongly suspect that you know
about this, I felt compelled to bring it to your attention. Maud Gonne
(the beautiful Irish revolutionary woman, and the life-long love of W. B.
Yeats) was the mistress of Millevoye (she had two children by him) and
she recalls in some detail how she took a very secret document, given
to her by Millevoye, to St. Petersburg, traveling on what must have been
the Nord-Express, weaving her way through all kind of intrigues en
route. . . .

I do not have the Cardozo book at hand (I'm writing this at home)
but there are a few more details) mostly from Maud Gonne's r. unreli-
able autobiographical writing). The trip did take place in 1887. She
said that she traveled to Russia without a passport. She was closely
connected (through Millevoye) with Juliette Adam and she also met
Boulanger (who did not imprss her).* She was told that the Secret
Document she was taking with her was the draft of a Franco-Russian
Treaty (I find this unlikely) and she repeats this, proudly, in her autobiographical writings. She was taken up by two ladies in St. Petersburg,

*Lucien Millevoye was a Bonapartist member of the French National Assembly; Juliette Adam
was an influential writer and journalist, a *revanchiste* in Paris; General Georges Boulanger was a rising political star in France in the mid-1880s. The book mentioned is Nancy Cardozo, *Maud Gonne:
Lucky Eyes and a High Heart* (Gollancz, 1978).

a Mmr. Novikoff and Princess Catherine Radziwill. She had been told
that the "document" was destined for Pobedonestsev but, again, one
cannot be sure.*

G.K. to J.L.

> The Institute for Advanced Study
> Princeton, New Jersey
> 17 May 1979

Thank you so much for the information about the Cardozo book and
about Mrs. Gonne's involvement in the Ferdinand letters. All this was
quite unknown to me; and while it is now too late to get it into the
book, I still value the information, and will try to pursue it.

About the possibility of a professorship at this Institute:** I am not
optimistic, but would not like to throw a wet blanket on it completely
before talking with those members of the faculty here who are most
concerned with modern history. Both of them, unfortunately, are now
away, and it will be August-September before I could consult them. I
will, however, gladly do it at that time, for I have, as you know, high
respect for your work, and feel that it should be much more widely
known than it is.

G.K. to J.L.

> The Institute for Advanced Study
> Princeton, New Jersey
> 30 August, 1979

I have received and read with great appreciation and admiration your
diary passages about the Churchill funeral.*** Not only are they impreg-

---

*Konstantin Pobedonostsev was a Russian leading jurist, high in the Czar's government.

**I had not planned to apply for a professorship in the Institute. In a previous letter (p. 54). I
wrote Kennan that I had mixed feelings about that).

***In January 1965 I flew from Toulouse (where I was a Fulbright Professor in 1964–1965) to
London for three days to be at Churchill's funeral. I wrote about this in the *American Spectator*,
August 7, 1975; and again, in somewhat more detail, in *Churchill: Visionary, Statesman, Historian*
(Yale University Press, 2002).

nated with that profound sense of history that is uniquely your own but they reflect so sensitive and graceful a descriptive power that I wonder you have never applied it to fiction.

I am semi-prostrate with some sort of back trouble (I read your two pieces, in fact, in the dead hours of the night when the pain was too severe for remaining in bed, much less for sleeping), so this scrawl will be decoded by my secretary and sent on to you by her. I am asking her to send you, more as a mark of respect than as one more burden on your reading time, two pieces from my own diaries of earlier years: one, the account of a visit to Leningrad, which appeared in the *New Yorker* (if you saw it there, just throw it away); the other, one which has never been published. I send them to you because both reflect, in their own way, my own sense of intimacy with the past—one that resembles (thought it is less deeply informed) your own.

J.L. to G.K.

10 September 1979

I was—as so often before—deeply touched by your generous response to my writing; by your letter and by the two reminiscences you sent me.* I read them instantly; I read them twice. The journey to Wisconsin moved me more than the journey to Leningrad—by "more" I mean that it moved me *very* much—and I am taking the liberty (which is, in its way, a kind of self-indulgence) of telling you some of the reasons why. But first in order, as well as of importance, comes my hope and wish that your back ailment may have disappeared by now.

You write about America with a unique compound of sentiment and realism; people may see in your writing the nostalgia of a sensitive and conservative thinker; but there is much more than that. Your nostalgia is inseparable from your concern—a concern not with institutions, and perhaps not even with how things have turned out, but a concern with the national character. This concern reaches back into the past, where it is no less vivid than when it is addressed to the present. Your compound is not that of nostalgia for the past *cum* concern with

*Unpublished of the two was an excerpt from his diaries, about his revisiting his native place in Milwaukee, Wisconsin.

the present. It derives from a deep felt historical sense to the effect that the past is not dead; that while death is irrevocable, the past is not; and that, while death and the past are not the same, life and the present are not the same either. . . .

I, too, possess something of the *nostalgie du Nord* for the urban, and not merely natural, scenes of its atmosphere. When you write of yourself as a sort of Nordic cosmopolitan, your home on this earth being along the whole great arc of the northern and western world, I understand it so much, even though I cannot say this about myself because of my life and provenance. . . .

There is such an extraordinary correspondence in many of your and my reactions to the world, in spite of the great differences in our respective backgrounds and temperament. Where does it all come from? It must have something to do with our mutual feeling for the *living reality* of history; but there must be—perhaps in mysterious ways—something else too. . . .

Do you know that Orville Bullitt died? Our association, through my having written the chapter about his brother, blossomed into a kind of friendship, and I miss him greatly. I saw him in May, he was full of vitality, looking twenty years younger than was his age. One day in July he telephoned me. He said that he had cancer, discovered but a few weeks before, and that he was not expected to live; that he had a full, happy life and did not regret to go; that he would call me in a few days when he felt better and wishes to see me. I was stunned and shocked. What I did not know then was that the day was his 85th birthday. Thirty-six hours later his son-in-law called me and told me that he was dead; and that on his birthday the family had taken him out to lunch, and that he then said: "It is very hot; I might as well go to a cooler place." I do not doubt his destination. . . .

Pope John Paul II visited the United States in October 1979. My article on his visit and Mass in Philadelphia ("The Light from the East") was published in National Review *on October 26, 1979.*

G.K. to J.L.

Princeton, New Jersey
October 28, 1979
Handwritten

I cannot tell you how deep an impression he (the Pope) made on me:
The spectacle of what must have been, in terms of this world, a lonely
man (for great authority always makes lonely) but a man of great
faith; and then the wonderful combination of kindliness ("caritas," I
suppose, in the real Latin sense) with courage and political stoutness—
the deliberateness, the patience, the fortitude and good humour in the
face of the fast, pressing crowds and the unforgivable over-scheduling.
I suspect that he made a deeper impression on many of us non-Cath-
olics than he did on large portions of his own laity and hierarchy. In
any case, the image of that white figure—so small against the great
stadiums and stages—moving with such dignity and open-heartedness
among these floods of human beings—will not soon leave me, or many
others. The impact he made here (multiplied of course by television)
was not the kind that makes itself felt the morning after departure—
it was deeper and slower than that. But it was profound, and greatly
needed. . . .

J.L. to G.K.

7 January 1980

Thank you very much for your kindness of having your book* sent to
me and for your inscription in it. I received it before Christmas and
read it during a number of evenings, beginning with the evening when
it arrived. I have been waiting for a time when I could write you about
it. Now it is such a quiet winter night. I am not at peace with myself but
the world around me is blessed with that winter stillness which, for me,
is mysteriously and deeply satisfying; and the best time for the kind of
causerie—for this letter will not be more than a causerie, disjointed at
worst, and here and there thoughtful, at best—that I am directing to you.

*This was the book first mentioned in my letter to Kennan on May 8, 1979.

What can I say about the book? It is, of course, the best—the most
scholarly and the most thoughtful—book about its complex subject.
I made many notes about it but I shan't burden you with them here. I
shall say, however, that what I cherish most in it are two of its features,
features of which are, fortunately occurring in most of your books
and which elevate you beyond the sphere of even the best of academic
historians: first, your narrative-descriptive passages (to wit, Cyon's
railway journey of the Nord-Express—at second thought, I'm not sure
that it *was* called the Nord-Express as early as in the Eighties); second,
your philosophical and historical passages about the deeper and the
long-range meaning of the sequence of events that you unraveled for
the reader. And this brings me to the only query—a query, not an
argument—about the main thesis of the book. I, too, share your view
of Bismarck and of the consequences of the undoing of his European
order. Only I am inclined to think that this would have happened even
without the Franco-Russian alliance and even if French nationalism had
been more moderate than it was. For the nationalism of Juliette Adam
and of [Paul] Deroulède, etc., had its counterpart in the Germanies (and
not only in Prussia)—an aggressive and venomous nationalism that
was bound to have an influence, especially with the spread of universal
education. You can *smell* it in the tone and tenor and the style of so
many German publications, surely after 1870, and even earlier. In the
1860's Bismarck was a master in managing it for his own purposes. But
after his departure or death it could have been only managed by another
giant figure comparable to Bismarck, and perhaps not even then.

I have often thought that there is but one book left to be written, by
a sensitive and knowledgeable (and necessarily multi-lingual) historian
about 1914: and such a book would study the literature and the press
of the European nations of the period, in depth. This is in line with my
conviction that Freud and Joyce established only half-truths: because
rhetoric may be the cause of sentiments, and not only the reverse—
or more simply, that habits of speech influence habits of thought as
much (if not more) than the reverse. (And the conscious mind the
unconscious one.) This, and only this, would show us something of the
popular sentiments leading up to 1914 and operating in 1914, sentiments
without which the men of the upper classes of the old European soci-

eties who made those fateful decisions could not have made them. But this has nothing to do with your book.

Another thought occurred to me while reading the book: that peculiar, and ever-recurrent, Russian tendency of being conservative at home and revolutionary abroad. It has its roots in the peculiar Russian kind of nationalism; but perhaps there is something else to it, too—a kind of time-lag. Even in the 1880's the Russians seem to have operated along principles of *raison d'état* that were typical of the European dynastic states of the eighteenth century. They took the balance of power so seriously—more seriously than even the Germans or the English or the Austrians.

And—of course in a v. different way and in v. different circumstances—this recurs again in the 1930's. I have come to the conclusion, some time ago, that the truest explanation of the Stalin purges is to be found less in his paranoia (of course there was an Ivan Grozny in him) than in his gradual creation of a *state* bureaucracy, totally reliable and subservient to him and to his then Soviet state. You know as well as I that "state" was a hateful entity for Marx (he was foolish enough not to have been able even to distinguish it from *nation*) and also to Lenin; but by 1939 "state" interests, "state" policy, etc., became a kind of sacrosanct word in the official Soviet rhetoric.

(Perhaps even now the Soviets proceed from older perceptions of statecraft than much of the rest of the world; but—especially in relation to us—this now may serve them as an advantage, not a handicap. Aren't we, in this country, the victims—and, in many ways, the willing victims—of the ultimate enfeebling consequences of the Wilsonian turn of mind?)

The Russian nationalism of the 1880's was shortsighted and destructive, with grievous consequences—your magisterial summation of it on page 416–7 has no equal—and yet it seems to me that it could not have led to the alliance with France, had it not also been for the habit of some of Russia's leaders—and perhaps of the Tsar, certainly not [foreign minister Nikolay] Giers—to think unduly in terms of older *Staatsraison* and of an older kind of balance of power, and carrying their consequent preoccupations to the point where the alliance with France seemed both beneficial and natural.

Let me know one day if I'm wrong in this. It is not much more than speculation on my part. . . .

G.K. to J.L.

Princeton, New Jersey
January 13, 1980

First of all: the expression of my deep appreciation for your letter of the 7th. There is no one in this country whose opinion about the book means more to me than yours. It is, I know, a curious book—a compromise of sorts between history and literature, between duty and inclination, history being the duty and literature the inclination. It begins badly, I fear, and places heavy demands on the patience of the reader. But I flatter myself with the impression that if one reads through all that introductory material to the narrative chapters in the middle of the book, something comes through of the real human texture of events— at least at the Russian end. The French scene, marked by the rapid passage across it of a series of uninteresting and insignificant men, did not lend itself to that development. In the second volume, on which I am now working, this will be somewhat different; for in the 1890's there were indeed three or four men on the French side whose contribution was more solid and prolonged and into whose patterns of motivation I hope to enter more deeply. Still, the French almost always present a greater problem in this respect than do the Russians, for they are so intensely private, put up at all times so formidable a defensive shield, and reveal so little of their true selves. Also, I hope that in the second volume the deep and dangerous deficiencies of the German civilization of the time, to which you rightly draw attention, can be brought out more clearly.

In connection with what you write in the third paragraph of your letter: I have been increasingly conscious, and unhappily conscious, in recent months, of the failure of my treatise to take account of the great undercurrent of tragedy which underlay all European civilization of that day and of subsequent ones—an undercurrent both beautiful and terrible, of which the artists, the composers, and some of the

most sensitive of the writers were intensely conscious. My characters
were, for the most part, not conscious of it. Some of them, notably
Bismarck, Giers, and (rather strangely) [Prince Bernhard] Bülow, saw
quite clearly the immense dangers of a general European war; but
none of them saw, as you yourself have perceived, that those popular-
emotional trends which had so much to do with making possible a war
of that nature were themselves the reflection of deeply-buried, and in
that sense subconscious, emotional states of which almost no one was
aware in the conscious-cognitive sense, and the inklings of which only
the fine antennae of the artists and poets could seize from the air. The
diplomatic and journalistic documentation of the time does not reflect
anything of this; and it is therefore difficult to bring it into a work of
diplomatic history; but I feel that it deserves to have a place there, and
propose to try to find one in the second volume.

This introduces a problem, of course, which goes beyond the
pretentions of this particular historical work but which I know interests
you, as it does me. It is *the* great problem—the ultimate problem—
of the reasons for the tragic course that our western civilization is
pursuing—the reasons, in other words, for what must be regarded as its
imminent and inevitable failure. Obviously, there is no single reason:
there is a host of them, interacting in that mysterious way that defies
the analytical and organizing capacity of even the greatest and most
many-sided of minds. But it should be possible to isolate and recognize
major elements in this web of causality. I pointed to what I suspected to
be one of these latter on p. 419 of my book: namely, the over-rapid pace
of change—of economic, technological and social change—in the 19th
century. I still hold strongly to this view: that if you *must* have change, it
must be slow, gradual, geared to real capacities of men for adjustment—
capacities that cannot be expected of a single generation alone but
must include the ones before and after—so that the problem must be
considered in terms not of the individuals alive at any given moment
but of the continuum of human life through the generations. Having
said this, however, I must confess that I am not at all sure that the main
elements of 19th-century change—industrialization, burgeoning population growth, urbanization, political democratization, egalitarianism,
etc.,—were in themselves desirable, however gradually they might have

been implemented;—whether they did not themselves rest on what Chekhov so charitably called "misunderstanding,"—misunderstandings of stupendous dimensions—about what is and what is not useful for human beings, about the true sources of their emotional and physical health. More and more, as my own life draws to its close, I distrust these intellectual idols of our time—democratization, urbanization, and the passion to insert the machine in place of the human hand in the productive processes of our life—as instruments to the achievement of a reasonably hopeful social life on this planet. But there they are, those idols, still securely installed on their thrones; and neither you nor I, I fear, will get very far in the effort to, unseat them. . . .

Thank you for your note about Cyon. I am in the process of writing a special monograph about him, not because it has anything to do (more than what I have already written) with the Alliance, but because he is such an interesting and mysterious character in himself. He is, you know, or rather, has been, suspected of some part in the authorship of the famous anti-semitic plagiarism known as the Protocols of Zion. And his life stands as a rather dramatic example of the ferocity of the late-19th-century struggle between faith and scientific positivism.

J.L. to G.K.

9 March 1980

I called on the spur of the moment, for no other reason than to tell you how deeply moved I was (and still am) by the short excerpt that *The New York Times* printed* of your statements before the Foreign Relations Committee. I agreed with everything you said. I recognized, too, that here occurred yet another instance in the drama of your life. Alone among the public and private people in this country you said not only what had to be said: but your judgment about what had happened, about what was happening, and about how the United States should act was as realistic and practical as it was singular and honorable (in every sense of the latter). What you said was not only another

---

*"George F. Kennan on Washington's Reaction to the Afghan Crisis: 'Was This Really Mature Statesmanship?'" *New York Times*, February 1, 1980. Kennan told the Foreign Relations Committee that the Soviet Union may have now entered a period of profound troubles.

evidence of George Kennan, the independent thinker (those men and women who respect you recognize that); but in this sad moment in the nation's history, you were the single voice of sanity and of reason. This is not only the mark of a strong mind; but what the French call *force d'âme*. . . .

And the purpose of this letter is to tell you that the sense of futility is not warranted—in spite of the oceanic scene of self-willed stupidity and self-seeking cowardice surrounding us all. You must take sustenance *not only* from the fact (it is a fact) that there are many people in this country, sometimes in the oddest of positions and places, like this writer, who hearken to your voice; *not only* from the condition that future generations will appreciate your wisdom more thoroughly than perhaps that of any American patriot who lived and struggled in the service of truth during the twentieth century—but, first of all, from the knowledge that God's ways are inscrutable and that, consequently the greatest services you may render to your country, and to its living generations, may still lie ahead of you, beyond the yet unseen milestones of your persistently great and persistently honorable career.

G.K. to J.L.

The Institute for Advanced Study
Princeton, New Jersey
March 13, 1980

I was deeply moved by your note of the 9th. How well you sensed, from a distance, the feelings with which I recently entered the public discussion of certain of our problems of foreign policy.

Yes, you are right. One can never know what the effects will be of one's words and actions in the field of public affairs. One can only do what seems, at the moment, to be right and needed and pray that one's not too far off the track and that what one is doing and saying will someday, by God's grace and through His ways, be useful—asking, at the same time, forgiveness for the measure of error bound, always to be involved. . . .

IV

The Evil Empire and the End of the Cold War

LETTERS, 1983–1988

J.L. to G.K.

17 March 1983

During the last three years I have been working on an interpretation of the history of this country in the last one hundred years.* It is an interpretation, on different developing levels, not a monothematic and chronological history; it will be published next January by Doubleday. All of my previous books, with one exception, were dedicated to past or present members of my immediate family. When this manuscript was finished, I chose to dedicate it to you. . . .

An hour ago I heard on the radio that the Reagan government now proposes to send, and permanently establish, more American troops in Lebanon, in order to "guarantee" the security of Israel, etc., there. I am appalled by this, especially in view of the near silence of the Russians whose southern border, after all, is merely two or three hundred miles away, while we are four or five thousand miles distant from that part of the world. And all of this talk, for the past fifteen years, of how

*This was to be *Outgrowing Democracy:* (title foisted on me by my publishers) *A History of the United States in the Twentieth Century,* published by Doubleday in 1984. I dedicated it to George Kennan, with the motto *integer vitae scelerisque purus* (my first book dedicated to someone not a member of my family).

strong the Russian navy is, and how our navy presence in the Mediterranean has eroded! I am more and more worried about this increasing and unquestioned American commitment to nearly everything that Israel seems to want; it reminds me, more and more, of the Balkans in 1914. . . .

G.K. to J.L.

The Institute for Advanced Study
Princeton, New Jersey
September 27, 1983
Handwritten

I have your letter of the 24th and am enjoying for the following reason, the luxury of being able to respond to it at leisure. On Thursday last, after three weeks of poor health, feeling only fair myself, I decided that I would no longer go on trying to lead a normal professional life, cancelled all my engagements for the coming month (only one of them), told my ladies in the office to cope with the correspondence without me, placed myself in the hands of the doctors, and have since then, except when medical tests intervened, stayed peacefully at home, reading and writing and occasionally doing a bit of work outside. The doctors will scarcely be able to help me with my chronic problems, but five days of this peaceful life, marked by a total absence of pressures, have already caused me to feel like a different person. This is not the end of the problem, for there still remains the question as to how one does contrive to live without pressures in this busy-body-country, but at least I have learned something about myself. When the medical tests are over, I still have to return to the office and confront the usual dilemma; but I shall return a wiser man and, I hope, more effective than I used to be in confronting it.

I was much distressed to learn of your son's setback.* I know how hard it must be for you, and for him, to bear it. The workings of nature are not just; they are often cruel, and seemingly senselessly so—at least from the standpoint of human understanding. Someday, I should like

---

*My son Paul had a serious illness from which he was to recover entirely.

to talk with you about the philosophic-religious problem this presents, which is one I have often thought about. . . .

I continue, as you can imagine, to be depressed—and alarmed—by the state of American-Soviet relations. I am coming to believe that it will never be possible to achieve anything resembling a sophisticated understanding of Russia in American governmental and journalistic circles. Recognizing this, to begin to think that it should be best if the relationship between the two countries were to be, over the long term (and by this conscious choice), a cold and distant one, directed solely to the maintenance of peace, but avoiding both polemics and the search for intimacy—a disillusioned relationship in other words, in which the avoidance of unnecessary misunderstandings in practical questions would be given a higher priority than the search for any real philosophical understanding or any wide ranging agreement on political values.

G.K. to J.L.

Princeton, New Jersey
January 15, 1984
Handwritten

This is just a word about your book [*Outgrowing Democracy*]. . . .

I was deeply moved by the dedication, and hope only that I can employ these final years of my life in a manner that will not cause my friends to regret the kindness and confidence they have bestowed upon me. . . .

I hope to have—at some time during these next two months—an opportunity to go away to some pleasant place and just read for a week or so. Your book will accompany me and will take first place on the reading list. I know, from the parts I have seen of it, that it is full (as is so much else that you have written), of thoughtfulness, insight, originality and wisdom. You will hear more from me about it when I have been able to give it a careful reading. . . .

G.K. to J.L.

Islamorada, Florida
February 23, 1984
Handwritten

Being down here for a few days' rest, I have finally completed the reading of your "Outgrowing Democracy." What should have taken so long to do this is no occasion for remorse on my part, or for disappointment on yours. It is a book to be read seriously and carefully or not at all.

I hesitate to use any of the commonplace adjectives—even the laudatory ones—with relation to this work. It is not really a "history" of the U.S. in the 20th century, in the narrative sense of that term. It is rather a critical illumination of the development of American society over this period—illumination under the light of a fine, discriminating, and indefatigable mind, informed by an exceptionally broad humanistic erudition, and solidly rooted in faith (without which no consistent and coherent perspective is possible). It has the merit of being at once the view of an outsider and an insider—of an immigrant and a native—not that you *are* a native, but that you possess the faculty of seeing things from the natives' view point as well as the foreigner's, just as I flatter myself into believing that I can see them from the foreigner's as well as the native's perspective.

As for my view of the book's quality, I will only say that if I had my way, it would be required reading, and a required subject of discussion in every serious course of American history at the college level; for it goes to the heart of what American society could and should mean to itself—of where it should look for its values and possibilities—of its meaning in the historical context.

Having said this, and it being only my personal reaction, I must add that I have no idea how the book will be received by the reviewers and (if there is such a thing) by the public. I am not optimistic. A number of the very phenomena you describe in the book will militate against a thoughtful and useful reception of it. (While this sort of thing is always a disappointment, you are too wise and too experienced to be unduly affected by it. Writing such a book is essentially only another form of teaching; and of teaching, as I am sure you will agree, one should never inquire too anxiously about the results, for one never knows, or could know, where the seed will fall and take root, nor are the origins of the plant that springs from it always identifiable. Teaching, as I see it is an act of faith.)

Turning from the book itself to my own personal reaction, I was particularly affected by the chapter on the effects of latter-day immigration. My own people, as you know, were of Scottish (probably Ulster-Scottish) pioneers, descendants of families whose migration to this country—to New England, to be exact—occurred in the early 18th century. The family as I knew it—or rather, the older members of the family—still bore strongly the markings of an 18th century experience and discipline. My grandfather, whom I knew well and among whose pall-bearers I figured, was born in 1828, shortly before Tocqueville came to this country. These were rough hewn people, of necessity poorly educated; but I respect them, in retrospect, for their integrity, their self-discipline, and their stubborn independence of character—their unwillingness to be a burden to others. Their men fought in the revolutionary war and the civil war: and while I must question today whether either of those wars really needed to be, or should have been fought, I can see that this country, as I knew it in my Wisconsin boyhood, was very much *their* country, in the sense that it was they, and people like them, who so extensively gave it its original character.

Well, today I see the identity of these people and their contribution to American society being submerged, almost to the point of obliteration, by new and immense waves of immigration of people of wholly different cultural and spiritual tradition—submerged to a point where I consider myself a displaced person in what was once my own country. I do not look down on these millions and millions of newcomers. Their values, so different from our own, so little compatible with our own, are like ours, the products of a given historical experience and discipline, and for all I know, they are no less admirable in the sight of God than are our own. It is only their *differentness*, not any supposed inferiority that I regret; and even here it is not the *existence* of this differentness per se, but rather the fact that it is coming in upon us in such numbers that it tends to nullify the contribution people such as my own have made to the development of a new civilization and to cause us to be lost, historically, like so many other peoples of whom history scarcely bears a record.

I do not mean to idealize this old Anglo-Saxon element of our population, to which these ancestors belonged. These people, particularly in their more prosperous 19th century personification, no doubt bore within themselves many of the seeds of the deterioration that is now overtaking American society—bore them in the form of the bourgeois pretentiousness, the materialism, the philosophic shallowness, the belief in man's perfectibility, the lack of any proper sense of tragedy in the individual human predicament. . . .

J.L. to G.K.

5 March 1984

Perhaps the most precious portion of your long handwritten letter consists in its second part in which you have honored me by telling some of your most intimate thoughts and deepest concerns relating to your ancestry and to the English-speaking (I don't write Anglo-Saxon because this must also include the Anglo-Celtic) heritage of this country. So far as my book goes I am perhaps most pleased by your statement that I possess the faculty of seeing things from the native's viewpoint as well as the foreigner's: for this has been a principal purpose of my, otherwise self-isolated, career as an English-speaking historian (which is not quite the same thing as a historian writing in English). Yet (unlike some other immigrants from Europe) I shall never suppress, obscure, or diminish my debts to my Hungarian heritage. At the same time, I am immensely pleased that you took a special interest in my immigration chapter—the chapter that is bound to be least understood, I fear.* It was Santayana who wrote that the laws and the liberties and the institutions of this country had not been abstract ones but English laws, English liberties, etc.; perhaps it takes a foreigner, such as Santayana and myself, to comprehend this. (Tocqueville

---

*The title of that chapter: "The Leap Across the Sea: The Development of an American Nation."

understood it too.) Of course, all of this is in a kind of intellectual
shorthand. . . .

G.K. to J.L.

> The Institute for Advanced Study
> Princeton, New Jersey
> April 10, 1984

Dear John:

(Since you are understandably inhibited in using just my first name,
perhaps I am not overstraining the bounds in using just yours. It should
be taken as a mark of affection and respect.) . . .

I was very glad to have the two paragraphs of comment about your
own work. It is good, I find, for anyone (but particularly for anyone so
many-sided as yourself) to examine his own labors from time to time
in this manner; and good for his friends to have the benefit of it. My
dear friend—you have no choice but to go right on, as you do, with
your extraordinary industry, making available to others, for whatever it is worth to them, your uniquely wide, wise and compassionate
view of this tragic country, in which there is so much of selfishness,
self-indulgence, and moral corruption, but also so much of freshness
and sincerity and neighborly human kindness. You are outstandingly
a teacher, in the broadest sense; and teaching (as you have no doubt
heard me say before) is an act of faith—otherwise it would have little
reason—an act, the repercussions and consequences of which you will
really never know and cannot foresee and into which you must not too
anxiously inquire. This is your fate; and I am sure you are thankful, as I
am, that you have the strength, and the faith, to bear it. . . .

The second volume of the Franco-Russian Alliance is now in the
hands of the publishers (commercial ones, this time; and possibly this
was the wrong decision). I am told to expect proofs about the first
of May; and the book should come out in late summer or early fall. I
myself think it is a somewhat better effort than the first volume, if only
because I wrote with greater self-confidence and omitted more unnecessary detail. With all that, it remains my own peculiar style of diplomatic history—micro-history, I suppose, designed less to reveal *what*

happened than *how* it happened: to give the reader, in other words, a feeling for that right mix of confusion, vanity, myopia, folly, inadvertence, momentary emotion, and occasional wisdom out of which the recorded exchanges between governments and statesmen are brewed. I, in my way, like you in yours, cannot help it. It is the way I like to present history and feel that someone should present it. And, again like yourself, I must not inquire too anxiously into the results.

My health is tolerable, although I naturally notice, at this point, the effects of age. Their obvious significance does not bother me. I fear only senility—not death. And I would like, before that moment comes, to arrange my affairs so that my sudden absence does not constitute too much of a burden for those I leave behind me. I am indeed deeply bothered by the endless bombardment of trivial demands on time to which anyone in my position in this country is subjected, and am making my best effort to reduce it. But I am afraid I am not much good at this task; I don't like to disappoint too brutally the thousands of people in this country who seem to have gained some confidence in me. . . .

Readers may now find that from now on an increasing number of our letters became addressed to spiritual (rather than to intellectual) and to theological (rather than to epistemological) matters.

G.K. to J.L.

> Randesund-Dvergsnestangen,
> Kristiansand S., Norway
> July 8, 1984

Your letter of the 15th of June, with the chapter of your "auto-history"*. . .

It gave me much gratification to be described, for once, as a patriot. One's relations to one's country, like the relations among intimates,

---

*I was writing a chapter of my eventual autohistory—entitled "Great Contemporaries," a short character sketch of people that I knew personally and admired—a chapter eventually excluded from it.

are always complicated; but I conceive myself to have loved my own, or what I knew as my own when I was younger, as much as those who drape themselves in the chauvinist robes and put bumper-stickers on their cars saying: "America—love it or leave it" (which always inclines me to do the latter). The last years, I must admit, have been very discouraging ones in this respect. I am now inclined to see my country much the way that I see Russia (in the historical sense): namely, as a politically unsuccessful and tragic country, but one capable of producing out of its midst, from time to time, a remarkable literary, artistic, and musical intelligence, politically helpless and always vulnerable to abuse and harassment at the hands of the dominant forces of the moment.

You were also kind enough to mention character. I had never thought of myself as having much of it—rather, as being in many respects a weak sort of a person. True: I don't steal. I try to be kind to people. I view loyalty as perhaps the only absolute virtue. And I should be ashamed to be found lacking in intellectual honesty. But I have done many foolish and inconsiderate things in my time. My ability to contend with the devil that lies somewhere inside the human male animal has been, I suspect, less than average. Altogether, I shall have a good deal to answer for when my time comes.

So much for my person. I realize, reading what you have written, that I have never, anywhere, tried to set forth coherently my own personal philosophy, such as it is. This cannot, of course, be adequately done in a letter. But one or two points occur to me that might be relevant to what you have written; and to whom better state them, I thought to myself, than to you? They will at least stand as evidence of my appreciation for what you wrote.

This philosophy relates, as I think you would agree that it should, primarily to the nature of man and to his relationship to God. I see the principal elements of man's tragedy as rooted, ineradicably, in his own individual nature and in the predicament in which he finds himself on this earth. (I have never had anything but contempt for the philosophic shallowness of the Marxists, who ignore this individual, subjective dimension of human tragedy and believe that everything could be put to rights by a bit of tinkering with the social relationships among bodies of men.) The tragedy lies in the unavoidable conflict between man's animalistic, instinctive, primitively emotional and partially subconscious nature, on the one hand, and his capacity, on the other, for higher, more generous, less self-serving motives and impulses: for true love and friendship and charity—for a real nobility of spirit, in short. In this—in man's endlessly torn, self-conflicting nature, which the monastic orders have tried (but rarely succeeded, I suspect) to overcome, lies the first, and probably the greatest source of the tragedy. But another lies in the abundant injustice and frustration with which man is confronted at the hands of his natural environment, of the laws of chance, and of his own physical vulnerability, helplessness, and mortality. I am thinking here for example of the fact of bereavement— the fact that we do not normally die when those we love die, so that either we are left to mourn for them or they, as we know in advance, are to be left to struggle along without whatever help and support we might, if permitted to live, have given them. There is, again, the fact of our own mortality: not only the sadness and sometimes the agony of dying, but also the recognition that life, however successful, has never been more than partially fulfilled. And finally, if one has seen much of human affairs and particularly if one has been a historian, there is the recognition of the fleetingness, the impermanence, of all human under-takings and achievements.

I am content to accept what I believe to be the teaching of the Church through the ages: that all this tragic dimension of man's nature and predicament is something that, for those who see it clearly, can be endured and sublimated only by faith—and in our case, a faith resting on the word and example of Christ. I must confess to having doubts about one very fundamental tenet of Christian doctrine, and that relates to the omnipotence of the Deity. What I have in mind is a qualification of that tenet, not a denial of it. I find it hard to believe that God is really in a position to interfere with the detailed workings of the vast system of Nature in which He has found it fit that our lives should be imbedded. This system is too personal, too senseless, and too arbitrary in its workings for me to hold God personally responsible for the obvious and abundant injustices it perpetuates on so many human lives: the sufferings of little children, for example, or the ravages of disease or accident that overcome so many of the young. I can see the inception of this natural system, but not its individual workings, as the handiwork of God. I can believe that it is with sadness that He perceives that men, his children, have to be cast into this sea of fortuitiveness and injustice. But I cannot see Him presiding personally over every detail of its workings. Perhaps He knows, as we do not, why things should be this way, and why it should be *within* the laws of this system, not above them, that his work has to be done. For I do believe that there is another plane of reality—the plane of charity and love and beauty in the lives of human beings—where God is indeed supreme, where he does indeed work His mysteries and His miracles (for of these there *are* some), and where there are indeed, as Shakespeare put it, "more things in heaven and earth than are dreamed of in man's philosophy." And all that, for me, plus the assurance of Christ's compassion, is reassurance enough.

However, it is getting late. The sea beyond our windows is being darkened by the first long shadows of the brief Nordic summer night. And the rest of philosophy can wait.

J.L. to G.K.

18 July 1984

For once—a rare occasion, this—I see a divergence between our beliefs.* You wrote about your doubt of God's omnipotence, that you "cannot see Him presiding personally over every detail of the . . . system." But isn't this close to the 18th century view of God as the clockmaker of the universe, the creator of its mechanism after which He governs it as a constitutional monarch of sorts? Somehow, I do not think that this accords with your beliefs. The fact of injustice in this world—as you write, for example, the suffering of innocent children— has pained me, too, often; but perhaps oddly, this is one of the things (there are, alas, others) that have seldom troubled my belief in God. I remember how you welcomed my statement in *The Passing of the Modern Age* to the effect that truth is more important than justice (and that, consequently, the pursuit of truth is a better thing than the pursuit

*The reference is to the letter of July 8 by G.K.

of justice). If we believe this, and if we believe that what God gave us is the capacity to pursue truth (rather than the possession of Truth itself) then the knowledge that everything has some kind of reason and purpose in this world, including the suffering of the innocent, is surely a consolation; and the Christian belief that God loves especially those who suffer in this world is perhaps even more than a consolation.

Of course, all of this must rest on faith. And faith *is*—as its opponents say—a prop to lean on. But it is a very peculiar kind of a prop. It does not correspond to any of the physical—or even psychic— conditions of this world. This prop is a staff for walking, not for standing; but even so, it is soft sometimes, hard sometimes, stiff sometimes, elastic sometimes . . . I cannot say WHY I believe in God. I can only say—and not without difficulty—HOW I believe; which also must include WHY I WANT TO believe. I know that my faith is not sufficient—perhaps because I do not really want to face some of its requirements. Here are two examples. Religion requires that I love God more than anyone or anything else in this world. Yet I know that if someone would insult God in my presence I would be less upset than if he would insult my father or mother or indeed anyone dear to me. I have often thought that if I were tortured as a political prisoner I would find it easier to deny God than to deny my parents or my wife or my children. Another example: my religion tells me that there can be no greater joy than to see God. Well, I can *imagine* no greater joy than to see my mother (or my first wife) again, sitting with her on some kind of sunny terrace, telling her everything that has happened with my family since I last saw her . . . I know that there is another world than this, but somehow I am inclined to regret that the joys of that world won't be like those of this one. But then, I also know that this is the result of a deficiency of my spirituality, of my religious imagination, perhaps. Yet I do not doubt the existence of that other world. And I have come to the important conclusion some time ago that God's greatest gift is our very existence in this world, on many levels and for many reasons, very much including His "extra" gift to us whereby justice sometimes prevails in this world, too. (Honesty is often not the best, i.e., the most propitious policy but dishonesty IS the worst policy, because it eventually fails in this world, too—and perhaps this is what historical knowledge is all about.) It is as if He knew that it would be too hard for men and women to see nothing but the triumph of untruth and injustice in this world. There are expressions and evidences of the existence of goodness; loyalty, love, sacrifice, spirituality and nobility in this world too—because God is within us, not merely outside us. This, incidentally—or perhaps not so incidentally—is the main reason for my conviction that, contrary to the arrogant dogmas of modern science, this earth IS the center of the entire universe and man IS the central organism in it. (And isn't it man himself who keeps inventing and re-inventing his schemes of the universe every few thousand years?)

I had planned to include nine "Great contemporaries" in an eventual book: the American writer and critic Dwight Macdonald; the British diplomatist and writer Harold Nicolson; the English philosopher and writer Owen Barfield; the German physicist Werner Heisenberg; the Irish traveler and writer Dervla Murphy; and the Hungarian priest Béla Varga. (About Harold Nicolson I wrote that year a long essay dealing with James Lees-Milne's two-volume biography. See New Yorker, September 2, 1985.)

G.K. to J.L.

Randesund-Dvergsnestangern,
Kristiansand S., Norway
July 27, 1984
Handwritten

I have read and re-read, and appreciated, your letter of the 14th. Your footnote observation was, I think, quite correct. There is not much difference between our respective views. My doubts about God's omnipotence apply only to one sphere of man's being, and are not, for me, a derogation from faith. They rest only on this reflection that if He is, as I like to picture Him, a loving participant in our struggle— incomparably, of course, the greatest one and utterly indispensable to our own effort, if this is true, then He too, has something to struggle against, which implies a limitation of His power. If, as you say, He is within us, so is that against which He struggles; so that we are, ourselves, most tragically, a part of the limitation. However, more about that when, someday, we meet.

I promised you a comment or two about your other "great contemporaries."* The passages about Dwight Macdonald are excellent. I have no doubts as to the justice of what you say about his literary and critical capacities. But the generosity with which you have treated his personal behavior speaks more for you than it does for him. I would not have been that tolerant. Rudeness is one of the faults I find it hard to forgive. There is little we mortals can do about the indecent instinctive-emotional turmoil that lies within us, but there is nothing to prevent us from redeeming ourselves by observing the rules of common civility and courtesy in our traffic with others. Good form is more than an empty ritual; it is often the only way we have of subduing—we cannot tame—the beast that is in us. . . .

I read with much interest the passage about Harold Nicolson. I knew him faintly when I was a student in Berlin, about 1930, and he was an officer of the British Embassy there. In later years, when I read some of his works, he became my model of the diplomatic historian— the man, above all others, who taught me how this form of history *could* be written. I knew of his homosexuality from the time I was in Berlin. I also gained the impression, from what others told me, that he strongly disliked America—or what he thought that country was, just as he was prepared, on principle, to dislike any American he encountered. But I regarded the homosexualism as his own business, and merely pitied him for the problems it must have presented for him. And I suspected that the anti-Americanism came from unfortunate personal experiences (I knew of one such incident in Berlin), and viewed it as a minor blemish on an uncommonly broad and discerning view of international life. Altogether, I saw him as a tragic personality: the epitome of what an English upper-class breeding and education were capable of producing—and greatly gifted too, as a writer, but twisted and unhappy in his emotional life, and despite the brilliance of his historical insights, strangely erratic and unsure of himself in the face of the bewilderments of his own age.

*In the July 18 letter.

About Barfield and Heisenberg—there is little I can say. You are far better read in all aspects of philosophy and science than I am. (This, I must admit, is itself no great *Kunststück* [work of art]; for I have read virtually nothing at all.) I readily recognize the truth in all that they— and you yourself—say about such things as certitude and objectivity and the relationship of observer to the observed. Some of this I learned, many years ago, from [Robert] Oppenheimer. But then too, my own efforts to write diplomatic history taught me that there is no such thing as an objective historical reality outside of the "eye of the beholder"— none, at least, that would be accessible to the human understanding— there is only the view taken of it by the individual historian, the value of which varies with the qualities—the honesty, the scrupulousness, the imagination, and the capacity for empathy—of the historian himself. This is why I view every work of narrative history as a work of the creative imagination, like the novel, but serving a somewhat different purpose and responsive to different, more confining rules.

The parts about Dervla Murphy and Father Varga are very fine. The former is indeed a great contemporary in point of general insight and understanding. She is also obviously a person of indomitable courage, toughness and endurance. Whether these two sets of qualities have anything important to do with each other, I am not sure, but both are impressive, and the latter, to me, positively intimidating.

As for Father Varga; I think (as with the Russian émigrés) that I understand better than he would believe that I could, the sadness of an exile's life: and I respect him (judging by your account) for the mild and philosophic serenity with which he seems to have endured it. . . .

Aside from the ostensibly inane effort of keeping up a charming little property which is now increasingly and hopelessly under pressure from the invading forces of urbanism, industrialization and vulgariza- tion, and I will either succumb to these forces or sink back into forest when—a year or two from now—I am no longer able to tend it—aside from this, I have done nothing very useful, for myself or for others in these last six weeks, and am paralyzed when it comes to thinking about this civilization, by my profound pessimism concerning its future. I need, I fear, the stimulus of communication with others like yourself. . . .

J.L. to G.K.

16 August 1984

It is seven in the morning of what threatens to be another desperately hot day. I am writing you what is probably the last letter I wrote in this house which has been my home for thirty years.* We have begun to move into our new house which is not yet finished but we must be translated from here in the next few days. I have all kinds of mixed feelings about this which you will understand. This house and this land has been something like my tap-root in this country—tap-root with all of its fibers and protuberances. This is where I chose to live more than thirty years ago; this is what my first wife and I built, in an odd but sometimes beautiful compound of American and European tastes and furnishings and decorations and garden; this is from where I took her to the hospital when she was about to give birth to my two children; this is from where I took her to another hospital to die; this is where my children were brought up; this is where I married my second wife. For a long time I sensed that this house, with its old walls (it was an old school house, built in 1840, the land given to the township by my first wife's tragic family) was indifferent and perhaps even suspicious of me, somewhat in the way in which an old aunt looks quizzically at a new member of a family who has just married a niece or a cousin, with a mixture of detachment and disinterest. Yet in the same way in which I had to tame what for a long time was a hostile piece of ground (it took me years to clear the jungle and mow down and carve out gradually the two to three acres around the house) the house grew not only to accommodate but to welcome me—somehow not only because [of] what it meant to me but what it *was*. There *is* something mystical about such things. About the new house which Stephanie and I planned and plotted for years my feelings can be best described as those of a man who chose to order a splendid new suit from a first-class and expensive tailor, but no matter how custom-made, he is somewhat anxious about how it will really fit. . . .

*I lived with my first wife Helen and with my second wife Stephanie in our "Old Pickering School House" for thirty years; and moved with Stephanie to "Pickering Close," on the same land, fifteen hundred feet away, in August 1984.

I am again deeply touched by your somber thoughts about the state of what remains of our civilization. But allow me to close this letter with a few random thoughts about this enormous matter, in order to lift your spirits somewhat! Life being what it is and what it still offers, there is no reason to commiserate together: we must share our premonitions but also our reasons for hope.

I Things are never as bad (or as good) as they seem.

II I think that large portions of the American people—especially those whose occupations are practical and not intellectual—still possess a great repository of goodwill and common sense, and the corruptions of publicity and of their institutions have affected them only to some extent. In sum, they may be ignorant but they are not stupid.

III I also think that neither the Russians nor the so-called Third World shows any signs of rude health—mental or physical—that would indicate their potential superiority over Europe and America. In one way or another the entire world has begun to suffer from the same kinds of disease. There is little comfort in this, I know. Yet it is because of this that our situation is quite different from the otherwise so similar situation of the Roman Empire toward its end. Where are the fresh, the tough, the virile barbarian Germanic tribes? Of course all of this may change, and sooner than we think. There may arise a new wave of barbarian spirituality, God knows where, with a new Mahomet, to whom millions would flock in our very midst. Or nuclear technology may produce a catastrophe of such global extent that all of our present patterns of international cooperation will suddenly prove outdated and new patterns will instantly arise.

Enough of this. . . .

G.K. to J.L.

The Institute for Advanced Study
Princeton, New Jersey
August 27, 1984

I enclose an article* by a Polish lady—a teacher in this country—which I thought might interest you and on which I should like to have your

*I cannot retrieve this article. ·

opinion. I find it quite brilliant; but it strikes me as a devastating criticism of the Poles themselves. Individual self-adulation is bad enough; collective self-adulation is even more dangerous. The Poles' pity for themselves leads them to the assumption that if they had the independent power they covet, they (free, of course, from the taint of original sin) would know how to avoid the temptations, and to master the contradictions, which the exercise of power always brings with it. What a dreadful illusion!

J.L. to G.K.

4 September 1984

I am compelled to say that I am not as critical of the Poles as you are (in your [previous] letter, that is). Their emotional nationalism has led them to short-sightedness and unreality often; their, no less emotional, identification of their nation with mystical and transcendental essences of faith is regrettable; yet their most admirable achievements, including self-sacrifice, patriotism, devotion to Western ideals, and courage, have been frequently nourished by the same, or at least by similar, sources of sentiment and dedication. It is, of course, true that because of the incredibly complicated alchemy of human nature the noblest ideals may be transmuted into visions and ideologies that essentially contradict and compromise the purity of their sources (and even the reverse can happen). I still think that, even at their worst, the religious nationalism of the Western and Catholic Poles is preferable to the abysmal distances that separate the professed Christianity and humanity of the Eastern and Orthodox Russians from the actual and often unreal enmities they nurture (as even in Dostoevsky . . .). . . .

British historian Paul Kennedy wrote a review of Kennan's The Fateful Alliance: France, Russia, and the Coming of the First World War *(Pantheon, 1984) in the* New York Times Book Review *on October 21, 1984.*

J.L. to G.K.

22 October 1984

I was thinking of you throughout yesterday. First, the review of the book by Paul Kennedy. (I have not seen the book yet.) This Kennedy is a bad lot. He starts with the truism of that silly Carr that we see the past with the eyes of the present & the reverse—well, of course.* He is respectful, and the *Times* gave you a prime space, which is only proper & just, but then he slides down into the pettiness of a "professional" historian (the quotation marks are not accidental). The rest of this paragraph is mere trivia but I am in the mood for a little causerie. Kennedy made his career on a single book, dealing with the rise of Anglo-German antagonism 1864–1914, which received very good reviews, and led to his appointment (he is redbrick univ.-English) to a chair at Yale. (American universities have an unbreakable penchant for second-rate Britishers.) The book is serious, and its main virtue is that Kennedy deals with the relations of two nations beyond (or, rather, beneath) standard diplomatic history: he deals with finance, trade, literature, etc. (I will say that I have done this in most of my books, without appreciation or notice by the literati professionals.) Yet a lot of this in Kennedy's book was superficial. I met him a few months ago, and he revealed that he knew nothing about Saki's *When William Came*—the most interesting & profound & telling (and, at that time, influential) novel about a fictional German invasion of England. . . .

I was thinking about you (and the nation) during that wretched debate last night. . . .** This time I was shocked—and perhaps even frightened—by the abysmal ignorance of these two men, the source of which—and this was not difficult to detect—was a view of the world which was narrow and unhistorical perhaps without precedent. This horrid compound of narrowness and extent, of utter parochialism and universality a—relatively—new thing. I doubt whether their vision of the world had any resemblance of what may have existed in the minds of even the most mediocre nineteenth-century presidents. It tells us something about the dismal quality of our education, including that

*E. H. Carr, the eminent (and Marxist) historian of early Soviet Russia.
**The third of the presidential debates between Ronald Reagan and Walter Mondale.

fraud of "International Relations," after forty years (at least) of world leadership. And this after a week of intensive coaching by their crew of attendants. Why, for example, didn't Mondale ask the basic question about why Reagan had sent the Marines into Lebanon at all? Because it did not even enter his (or his staff's) mind. Instead his argument was, in substance, that Reagan had not put enough sandbags around our "compounds" in Lebanon, etc. And I find this especially abysmal because the American people, no matter how ignorant, are not really stupid: they *would* react, and I think positively (or most of them would) to someone who would say that we had no business in Lebanon, and certainly no reason to send in the Marines, and that the "Middle East" (whatever that is), is not the prime area of American "security." I must stop now. This is a hurried letter, but I got it off my chest. . . .

G.K. to J.L.

Princeton, New Jersey
October 24, 1984
Handwritten

About the book. You are on my list to receive an inscribed copy, but I am waiting to receive a batch of the books from the publishers. I was naturally gratified by the nice things Mr. Kennedy said on the first page (nothing is more agreeable, from time to time, than underserved praise), but I did not think much of his criticisms on page 56. I would be happy enough if the book were recognized as a modest, but honest and reasonably well-written work of historical scholarship; an attempt to describe a given historical episode "wie es eigentlich gewesen ist." Your copy should be coming along soon.

As for the recent debate between the two presidential candidates, I must confess that the ground shook under my feet as I watched it—to think that it was in one or the other set of these fumbling, ignorant hands that the peace of the western world must rest for the next four years. You are right, of course. This is worse than the dreariest examples of the 19th century excuse for statesmanship. I would think: this must really be the end of something, did I not remember the lesson Joseph Stalin taught me, together with so many other people. "However bad things may be, never think that they couldn't be worse, and that you couldn't, and wouldn't bear it if they were."

J.L. to G.K.

9 December 1984

The [new] book is quite different from the previous volume, and not only because it is shorter. . . . Of course, this second volume, too, is something more than, as you say, "a mere attempt to describe one episode in diplomatic history." There are your excellent portraits of the people; the occasional (and so important) descriptive evocations of the atmospheres in the capital cities; and, of course, the philosophical conclusions that your dutiful and indefatigable mind cannot, and will not, avoid, for the purpose of reminding—reminding, rather than instructing—the readers of this day and time.

I do not agree with *everything* in the book but that is irrelevant. The book is a wonderful achievement; and—like almost everything you write—*sui generis*. (This causes a problem for me: in my new library I had to give some thought where to put the first volume. I have a section in German history, another in French history, another in Russian history and a—smaller one—in general modern European history. After some hesitation I had put it on the shelf with other books on late 19th century Russia. But now, with this book, this will not do. I am transferring the first, and putting it together with the second, to the general European history portion, where they even now catch my eye—because of their location—but also because they are truly *sui generis*, so different and, in their way, so much more valuable, than most of the other books whose company they must now keep.)

J.L. to G.K.

3 April 1985

I read your spare and dignified account of the Norway house and life in *House and Garden*. What a contrast to the picture of Mrs. Galbraith in all that savonnerie opulence,* from which her husband decamped to Bill Buckley's Swiss place to have the latter compose that dreadful letter to Flora Lewis which you, too, must have read in the *New York Times*. I am afraid that these kind of people will be in charge of our political and intellectual establishment for some time to come.

By this I mean three things. I. The liberal ideas and agenda are so exhausted that even on the mundane political level I cannot see how the Democrats can liberate themselves from what has become a handicap, not an advantage—even on the electoral plane. II. The Gadarene rush—for that is what it is—of the intellectuals (many of them Jewish) to the "conservative" side has begun. III. There is a fair possibility that much of the "media" (dreadful word but you know what I mean) will be acquired by "conservative" people, and that the contents and opinions publicized therein will be the productions of mixed managements in which young nationalists and the abovementioned (II) people will perform a division of labor.

But thanks be to God, history IS unpredictable, even now, and in this country. . . .**

There is a photo in your *House and Garden* article of a house (not yours) at the end of a small bay in the twilight. Well, I am pleased to tell you that it bears *some* (very little but, still, some) similarity to the location of our new house, in a much less beautiful setting: but we are on the water and that stillness, the ever varying light and colors and the sometimes numberless birds winging and splashing and ducking and floating up and down are a wondrous gift every morning (and afternoon and evening.)

---

*House and Garden printed a small article with photographs of the Kennans' summer house in Kristiansand, Norway. Liberal public intellectual Kenneth Galbraith was a close friend of conservative essayist William Buckley and a regular guest in Buckley's sumptuous chalet in the ski resort of Gstaad, Switzerland. The other reference is Buckley's open letter to the respected and gentle *New York Times* foreign affairs columnist Flora Lewis, proclaiming that she was a liberal fool.

**Readers may be interested that at this very time, only a few months after Gorbachev had become the new leader of the Soviet Union, Kennan said to me that this man may have begun the dismantling of it.

G.K. to J.L.

Princeton, New Jersey
May 7, 1985

I was glad to learn of your own situation and plans; and greatly envy you the walking journey in Switzerland—a splendid project, which my rheumatic legs would no longer permit me to pursue.

Our own journey to the middle Atlantic states was primarily for the purpose of respite from distressful pressures, arising mostly from marital difficulties of one of our children, which had plagued us both in recent weeks. Driving an automobile around some 1,700 miles of superhighways was not my own first preference as a way of relaxing; but my wife enjoyed most of it, as I thought she would, and for that reason I do not regret it. The most pleasant moments were those spent visiting friends. Otherwise, the experience did little more than confirm some of my gloomier views about the condition and the future of this country. The over-population; the near-total automobilization of life; the continuing environmental destruction; the overwhelming domination of communication by the advertisers;—all of these depressing phenomena seemed even worse, as observed on this journey, than I had pictured them. We came together, on the other hand, with some impressively nice people; so that I ended the trip with the thought that every visitor to this country should be given a card, by the Immigration Service, saying that "however appalling or encouraging may be the impressions you derive at any particular moment from your encounters with this country, never forget that you would never have to go far to find their precise opposite of what struck you."

Another subject that was much on my mind during this recent travel was something you have written about better than anyone else: the effects of immigration on the composition and the cultural coloration of the American population. This is, of course, today no less a foreign country for me than several European ones—which is not a way of saying that it is the "worse" or the "better" for that fact. I was moved to wonder at the total failure—now, at the end of some 150 years— of the better-born WASP element to hold the political and cultural ascendancy it once enjoyed, and at the complacency with which it has watched the dilution of its own standards and the steady growth of its own helplessness. Much of this, I suppose was the result of its own privatism—its individual independence—its aversion to mixing with those who did not share its *manières*—as Tocqueville would have called · them. Be that as it may, they—and I, who consider myself one of their members—have become an insignificant minority still defending a few local positions (primarily in northern New England) in a country which incongruously, and without understanding them, still does lip service to their once-proclaimed Federalist ideals.

Recognizing that American society is never again to be that into which I was born, I look largely to the newer immigrants to determine its future. And here, I find myself hoping (since all else is lost) that the immigration of orientals—Chinese and Japanese, especially—will continue and increase. I hope this not because I consider them all nice people or anything like ourselves but rather because they are harder, tougher, more disciplined, more ruthless, and possibly more intel-ligent, by and large, than we are, and because they will take charge of the negroes and the Latinos, perhaps even of the Jews, in a way that we have not been able to do—and to the good of all of those elements. If there is any one thing of which I am increasingly persuaded, it is that liberal democracy, as we have become accustomed to perceiving it, is simply incapable of coping with the emerging problems of this society. The orientals will know, if anyone could, how to transform this system into something more effective, perhaps even without sacrificing the basic freedoms of thought, or religious commitment, and of individual intellectual inquiry, which are the ones I myself most deeply value.

We are, departing from custom, remaining here this year up to the middle of June—primarily because it is my 60th class reunion at Princeton, and while I have never actually attended a reunion before, I thought I should do so this time. It is, after all, a bond with a past that few will now remember. Then, when I come back in the fall, I would like to turn in earnest to the third volume of my curious series on the Franco-Russian alliance. It poses certain problems of research and of presentation of material that were not present in the writing of the first two volumes: covers a longer time; treats of a period on which, in contrast to the period of Alexander III, there is an immense amount of secondary material; and confronts a scene on which diplomatic events were more closely associated with internal-political ones—particularly, in the case of Russia (the abortive revolution of 1905). . . .

J.L. to G.K.

29 July 1985

Many thanks for sending me the Cyon manuscript.* I read it twice with acute interest. Of course, I remember what you wrote about Cyon in the first volume of your magnum opus and especially that *unforgettable* passage describing Cyon's journey on the Nord-Express from the Gare du Nord though Berlin and Eydtkuhnaen-Wirballen-St. Petersburg, the writing of which reflects your artistry at its highest! Now, reading this manuscript. . . .

P.S. There is a contemporary of Cyon's, the Austrian Otto Weininger, whose view of the world and whose personal tragedy show great similarities to Cyon's. He committed suicide in 1902, after having written an extraordinary book, *Geschlecht und Charakter* [*Sex and Character*] that many people admired, including the young Hitler (!). In one of his wartime table conversations, Hitler said during the war that he knew only two decent Jews, Weininger and Dr. Bloch, the physician who had cared for Hitler's mother. Hitler surely overlooked a key sentence in Weininger's book that is startlingly apposite in retrospect. W's thesis (put roughly and crudely, in intellectual shorthand) was i.e. the Judaic and the Christian one: by the 19th century the first had degenerated into materialism, while the latter was the only hope for the world. Weininger foresaw the coming of a tremendous movement of anti-Semitism. "Between Jewry and Christianity, between commerce and culture, between woman and man, between earthbound life and a higher life, between nothingness and Godhead mankind will again have to choose. These are the two opposite kingdoms; *Es gibt kein Drittes Reich.*" [There is no Third Reich.] Well, there *was* to be a Third Reich . . . ruled not by the religion of Christianity but by that of the Volk. . . .

*About the extraordinary Elie de Cyon, see J.L. to G.K., 10 January 1979.

G.K. to J.L.

The Institute for Advanced Study
Princeton, New Jersey
September 19, 1985

I want to thank you for a number of things: for the letter you wrote me just at the time of my departure for Europe last June; for the later one in response to the Cyon manuscript on which you were kind enough to comment (and very usefully, I may say); and for the reviews from the New Yorker, both of which, I thought, were excellent. Is it not remarkable—and sad to think—that there is probably no one else in this country—or at the most one or two—who could have done justice to Nicolson: this talented, highly civilized, but emotionally handicapped man to whom I look up—as to my master and teacher in the writing of diplomatic history.

I was grateful for your comments about Cyon. I have now completed the paper and will try to have it printed somewhere— probably very modestly and only as a minor scholarly contribution. I shall try to enclose a copy of the conclusions, which I have just written (too hastily, I fear) and appended to the document you saw.

Now for news: July and August were passed in Norway, where we had a cold and rainy summer. Conditions there are not conducive to any sort of writing, and I got little done. I have been struggling very hard to detach myself from participation in the public discussion of such subjects as the nuclear arms race and Soviet-American relations, not because I don't think that there are things that ought to be said or that I lack the wit and the authority to say them, but because I know from experience that any dabbling in that particular whirlpool tends to result in one's being sucked in to it and losing all effective control over one's life and forfeiting all possibility of doing any serious historical research. But while I have, for some time now, successfully avoided all television interviews and public speaking engagements, the calendar still rapidly fills up, for months ahead, with other things—family, friends, residual organizational connections, visitors, neighbors, etc., etc. We are leaving again day after tomorrow for another three weeks in Europe—back in the middle of October. Then I would like to see what we could do about getting together once more—a pleasure that life has long denied me.

I witness the current scene—mostly through the columns of the New York Times—not only without enthusiasm but largely without hope. I have no confidence in the statesmanship of people who have failed to recognize that war among advanced industrial powers in this modern age has lost all rational purpose. I regret, mildly, the passing of the value of the martial virtues that had dominated so much of European thought and policy since the age of chivalry. I know that we shall have to find surrogates for them—because with most young men the sensation of danger is a chemical-glandular necessity of personal maturation. Perhaps in future our male youth will have to become in a limited sense emasculated. I think of Pushkin's lines:

Whoever, in the flush of youth, as the true defender of freedom,
The sight of death before him has not seen—
He has never tasted the full flavor of life
And is not worthy of the caress of woman.

But I see what I am speaking of as a cruel necessity. And I am not convinced that exposure to danger on the field of battle is the only way that women's caresses can be deserved or won. In any case, what worries me most deeply about Mssrs. Reagan and [Secretary of Defense Caspar] Weinberger is their inability to extricate themselves from the military thinking of a century ago—their figurative playing, that is, with hand-grenades as though they were fire-crackers. . . .

Kindly keep the draft article about morality and foreign policy strictly to yourself; for it awaits publication, and I would be most embarrassed if it got spoken about, or rumored about, before it appears.*

G.K. to J.L.

Undated: Early October 1985

I am, at the moment, in a state of despair over the seeming futility of my efforts to break out of the thickets of trivia that lie across my path (thickets that seem to become denser the greater my efforts to free

---

*This would appear as "Morality and Foreign Policy," *Foreign Affairs* (Winter 1985–1986).

myself from them) and to get down to some solid work. I would not feel so desperate did I not know that the shades are already beginning to close in on me and that the time in which I could hope to do anything worthwhile is narrowly limited and rapidly decreasing.

I appreciated your kind and understanding words about my sweet wife, Annelise.* My struggles and complaints have been not much easier for her to bear than for me; and although her needs are part of the problem, I am aware that without her stiffening, I would probably not have become the little that I am.

Kennan's response to my critique of his draft "Morality and Foreign Policy," which had just appeared in Foreign Affairs.

G.K. to J.L.

The Institute for Advanced Study
Princeton, New Jersey
15 October 1985

Let me first say that I am deeply appreciative of your interest in this article, and of the trouble you took to let me have your views about it. You know of the exceptional respect I have for your opinion, your insights and your reactions. Knowing this, you will need no assurance of the seriousness with which I took your comments. With some I found myself in agreement; with others not. But they all helped me to rethink the portions of the article to which they referred. You will see the reflection of them in the final product; and the latter will be the better for the trouble you took.

Now for a few detailed comments.

1. *Change of title.* I don't quite understand your suggestion. I had in mind, in writing the article, the relation of morality not to the nature of national interest but to the actual conduct of foreign policy. National interest can be, and is, one motivation for the conduct of foreign policy; moral considerations are another. But they are two different things; and

---

*Mrs. Kennan's illness passed rapidly. Sixteen years later they would celebrate their 70th wedding anniversary. She would survive her husband by three years.

I have merely tried, in this article, to suggest where each of them should properly come in.

2. *Second paragraph.* I agree that this is not needed, and am striking it out.

3. You dispute my assertion that what is at stake in this discussion is the behavior of governments and not of individuals or entire peoples. Excuse me—but our government is plainly charged, constitution- ally and by tradition, with the conduct of America's foreign relations. Private individuals are not; nor could they acquit themselves of the charge if they were. Of course government consults private opinion and is influenced by it; but that does not affect in any way the uniqueness of its responsibility for the conduct of policy.

Nor can I concede that collectivities react like, or share the same moral possibilities and responsibilities as, individuals. The attitudes and positions eventually adopted by the United States government are the product of multitudinous interactions among great bureaucratic and political establishments embracing millions of people. These people are not united by any common ideals or persuasions or (since so many of them are little concerned with history) traditions. There is, among them, no clear common understanding of what would be "moral" and what would not. What emerges, in the end, from their interac- tion represents only some sort of primitive common denominator. It is this with which the politicians and statesmen have to work when they decide on questions of foreign policy. To suggest that they, when they reach this point, are at liberty to consult individual conscience (as though they were absolute despots of some sort) and then to react, morally, as might the unhampered individual, does not seem to me to meet the realities of their situation. To see the difference one has only to reflect that the individual has the option of total self-abnegation, even to the point of heroic self-sacrifice. The governmental official, precisely because he is an agent and not a principal, does not have that option. He has to be the final judge of the best interests of his national constitu- ency, in the light of what he knows about their views and feelings (and in the light of what he knows that they do not know); but he may not act as though there were some unity of conscience among them and as though he had been authorized to represent it.

4. I have difficulty, again, with your insistence that there is a moral quality to the national interest of the United States. This country as it stands today (and no one knows this better than you do) is not the product of any moral decisions; it is the product of the infinitely complex workings of history—a process embracing what is for all intents and purposes an infinity of private and public decisions, embracing every variety of motivation human beings are capable of experiencing. Whether it is or is not a good thing that the country exists as we find it today, is an idle question. (I myself can see no very distinct moral component in the rationale of the original revolutionary war; and with all my respect for the person of Abraham Lincoln, I am not at all sure that the preservation of the unity of the nation was of such moral significance that it was worth fighting a civil war about.) The country exists; and from that very existence springs its national interest. But certainly it should not be idealized. I am not even sure that its world influence has been, on balance, a beneficial one.

5. The mention of the Helsinki Accords in the article was an afterthought. (It was not in the original draft.) You may be right that they are not the best example of what I was trying to illustrate. But they have recently been so much in the public eye that I was sure that, if I did not mention them, I would be called upon to explain. Stimulated by your observations, I have revised the introduction to the paragraph.

6. You suggest, on page 8, the replacement of the word "sensibilities" by "opinions." But surely moral convictions—concepts of right and wrong—are more than just "opinions."

7. You have a good point when you suggest that I should refine the concept of military security. I accept the force of your observation; and I have introduced some wording which I hope will meet it. . . .

This letter is a coda to our arguments about morality and foreign national policies.

J.L. to G.K.

20 October 1985

There is my affectionate respect for you. There is my view of you as America's John the Baptist, a lonely proclaimer (and, more important, a duty-inspired incarnation) of a view of the world so sorely needed. This is why it is so important that your message be properly understood by those who *want* to hear it. Your strictures of American legalism-moralism have been so often misinterpreted (a) by those who thought that you were a hard-headed and hard-hearted *Realpolitiker*, eschewing morality altogether; (b) by those—more numerous nowadays—who thought and think that you had undergone a conversion from conservative to liberal, from anti-communism to appeasement, from a tough realist to a soft moralizer. I understand and know the essential and existential consistency of your thinking through all these decades. But others must too. . . .

Perhaps my conception of morality is wider (though not necessarily deeper) than yours. I say this because of what you wrote under 1. in your letter: that "national interest" and "moral considerations" are "two different things." Yes they are, but somehow they aren't; they cannot be categorically separated, since "interest" (and purpose) in the life of a man (as in that of a nation) is to a great extent formed by what he thinks it is. And what he thinks about it may be the surest clue to his character, to his virtues and vices and eventual failings. A nation is more of an organism than it is a mechanism. It is not immortal; it does not have a soul. Only human beings have that. But there is such a thing as a national mind, and a national mentality. And that mentality inevitably affects the conduct of its government, not in the least in its relationship with foreign nations. It is that mentality which you—with such valiant principled, lonely and deeply moral efforts—have tried to correct during most of your life. . . .

The Kennans were planning a journey to Hungary, where George's knees would be bathed and treated in a thermal hotel in Budapest.

G.K. to J.L.

Princeton, New Jersey
February 17, 1986
Handwritten

Should you happen to know of a good short history of Hungary which
I could buy here? I would be obliged for the tip. Otherwise, I will try to
find a German one in Vienna.

G.K. to J.L.

Hotel Thermale Budapest,
Hungary
March 27, 1986
Handwritten

I had thought to send you a picture from here, but only towards the end
of my stay, which has now arrived. But I doubt that even the little I have
to say at this point could be crammed into a postcard; hence this note,
which will also not tell you very much.

I tried to get hold of Mr. Szegedy-Maszak.* It appears that he was in
the U.S. just when we were here. As a matter of fact, over the first two
weeks of our stay here, neither of us, for various reasons, was very well.
So we lived very quietly and hardly saw anyone. This week, our last one
in Budapest, we have seen a number of people, including some highly
intelligent and agreeable Hungarians, and have had long, though not
intimate, exchanges of opinion, in which I found them frank and uninhibited in stating their own views. In addition to which, we have made
a number of rather touristy excursions into the city and its environs
(tomorrow we are going to Eger).

You would find it, I think, only right that after two and a half weeks
of such experiences, if I were asked: what were my impressions, I could
answer only—very confused and uncoordinated yielding no firm
conclusions. I come away with a very considerable admiration for the

---

*Mihály Szegedy-Maszák, an outstanding Hungarian historian of literature, with a very fine
command of English

Hungarian people—this without any illusions that I really understand them. The women (a great many of them extraordinarily beautiful), are more comprehensible to me than the men (to extent that the individual women can ever be fully comprehensible to a mere male); and yet I remind myself that there would always be a side of them—the Hungarian family side—that no foreigner could fully share, even if he understood it. This is a people which, despite all the schmaltz of the gypsy music and the beauty of Budapest, does not wear its heart on its sleeve, and which has an inner pride, or self respect, which saves it from being either obsequious or arrogant—although in its heart, it is aware of its many unusual talents. I find the more thoughtful of the Hungarians somewhat subdued, bewildered and depressed by the many bitter blows fate has dealt them over the centuries, largely in consequence of their uniquely vulnerable geographic location and their small size. Their dreams and hopes tend to be beyond reality—their appetites beyond the size of their stomach. They are conscious of having been able to make, had circumstances permitted, a larger contribution than history has permitted them to make. Their great parliament building (which I visited this afternoon), stands as a symbol of this disparity between the dreams and what is possible.

I both respect and fear the intensity of their national feeling. I view the uniqueness of their language—its total lack of affinity to the surrounding linguistic world—as both a strength and a burden for them.

I see, in other words, many contradictions in their character and their predicament—contradictions so profound that it is perhaps presumptuous of me even to speculate about them as I have in this letter.

My knees are, I think, very slightly improved by the treatment they have been given in this highly impersonal establishment. (After nearly 3 weeks here, there is literally no one in the hotel who even knows my name or cares to know it.) During the time we have been here, the season has changed from winter to very early spring. We have walked daily in the extensive park of the Margritsziget—watched the melting of the snow, the appearance of a few song birds, the up-thrusting of the crocuses, and the beginnings of navigation on the Danube, (starting with the appearance of a number of kayak enthusiasts). At night we listen to the rumblings of what I suspect to be the movement of Soviet supply-truck convoys, on their way from the railway yards to the great military base a few miles further up the river and whenever I go out and meet people, they ask me, in a way that wrings my heart, for the answer I am unable to give them.

G.K. to J.L.

> The Institute for Advanced Study
> Princeton, New Jersey
> April 7, 1986
> *Handwritten*

One note scrawled out in Hungary, went forward to you this morning. This one follows: to tell you that I have just read your piece in the *New Yorker* about the visit to the Dresden opera house, and am full of admiration.* I think of it one of the finest things you have ever written. A commentary not just on Dresden, but on the D.D.R. [East Germany] generally. My warm congratulations. . . .

———————

The Kennans were in Budapest (my native city) for about a month for the purpose of treating George Kennan's ailing knees in a thermal-spa hotel on Margaret Island.

G.K. to J.L.

> Princeton, New Jersey
> April 16, 1986

What you wrote made me ashamed to think of what a skimpy, inadequate note it was that I wrote you from Budapest. The reason for this was, I suppose, that the individual impressions of this visit to Hungary did not congeal into any general impression, and for that reason I questioned their value.

*"A Night at the Dresden Opera," *New Yorker*, March 17, 1986.

I shall try now, however, to record a few of them. Perhaps you can put them together.

The hotel? It was all right—exceptionally good for one in a "Communist" country—very impersonal, as most hotels are—the food neither bad nor very good, only a bit monotonous. I had no appetite, strangely enough, when I was there. Aside from the baths and the mud-packs and massages, administered by people for whom I was only one more body in the course of a day's work, my strongest impressions were of the musicians in the main restaurant: a 6-piece orchestra in the evenings, all very good solo players: a highly skilled violinist; an excellent clarinetist, who was the violinist's father, others, too, at the top of their skills, but all corrupted, I thought, by the fulsome, groaning, swaying method of play which I suspect of being less real Hungarian than self-conscious false Hungarian for the tourists. I felt very sorry for them, playing for these colorless German visitors who scarcely noticed what they were doing, despite the violinist's wandering about the room and playing in the ears of individual tourists who were evidently taken for easy, sentimental victims. And then, at lunch, three lady harpists, one of them excellent, the other two mediocre, but all with a similarity of repertoire that betrayed the tastes of the music teacher.

We walked, every day, in the still quite wintery park, passing the many busts of earlier Hungarian literati, whose faces and forms contrasted so tragically with the few Communist brutal figures that had been added to their number—past the little reconstructed mediaeval church, now—incongruously, a sort of Protestant chapel, past the boarded up athletic stadiums, past the little steaming pool where there were always passersby, usually with little children, marveling at the warm water and the ducks and the gold fish. We admired the lay-out of the park, the magnificent old trees, and the obvious excellence of the gardening, and pictured to ourselves how beautiful it would all be two months hence.

The people in the American Embassy were touchingly nice to us. The ambassador, who was leaving the following day, came out to the airport, as did people from the Foreign Office and the scholarly community, to meet us. We were impressed (as is so often the case) with the qualities of these people, in contrast to those of the government they serve. The Chargé d'Affaires and the head of his political section had both taken the trouble to learn a respectable amount of Hungarian (as had the Chargé's wife). (This, they found, was appreciated by ordinary people, but was viewed somewhat askance by the government officials, to whom it appeared—or appeared to appear— as a rather suspect invasion of Hungarian privacy: the disconcerting penetration, for dubious reasons, into a secret they were not supposed to know.) There was also a young lady economic specialist who was absolutely first-rate: knowledgeable, lucid and literate, and whose summary of Hungary's economic condition and problems would have done justice to the standards of a country (Hungary) which is itself, man for man, the greatest national fountain of good economists.

(Ah, my poor country, these people caused me to reflect: so much casual and occasional excellence, all so little appreciated—so poorly used.)

Taking advantage of the car placed at our disposal by our kind friends in the Embassy, we made two excursions: one, the usual tourist trek to Szentendre and Estergom and Visegrad; the other, to Eger. The first of these jaunts was on the coldest of winter days, but always interesting and not unpleasant. The visit to Eger was on the only warm lovely spring day of our entire visit. The *Sehenswürdigkeiten* [things to see], on both these journeys, were indeed worth seeing; but we had no guide-book; the signs were mostly in Hungarian; and when, on very few occasions, the signs were translated into several foreign languages, the best, clearest and most illuminating of the translations were, incongruously, the Russian ones—don't ask me why. It was a strange experience, looking at these various architectural monuments—some still ruins, some restored, some of the newer ones extant in their original form—and trying to figure out, from this mere visual image, what their history had been. It was like watching a movie in the airplane without the ear-phones on and trying to guess at the plot. I was grateful for the little Hungarian history (three small books, actually) that I had read before coming. I was appalled at the ubiquitous evidences of great and repeated destruction: almost nothing now standing that predated the Turkish occupation, unless recently reconstructed; and I was impressed to realize how the small intense flame of Hungarian national feeling had continued to flicker and refused to be extinguished through all these vicissitudes. But I longed for a well-schooled and intelligent person at my side who could have told me a bit about what I was seeing.

On the visit to Eger, I marvelled at the excellent condition of the fields—even those that were obviously in the hands of collectives. Comparing them with what I had seen in other "Communist" countries, I was moved to recall Tocqueville's penetrating observation that it is not the institutions that are most important in a national society but rather *les manières* of the inhabitants.

I spent one afternoon and evening, at the University, with what I might call "think-tank" people, selected from all around, from the different institutes and offices, including, I should suppose, the Foreign Office. One way or another I talked with those people seven hours straight, and suffered, the next day, from the exertion. I found them highly intelligent, uninhibited by each other's presence, feeling perfectly free (so far as I could tell) to ask questions and voice opinions, more interested in my views than in my person (which I welcomed and found refreshing). I thought to detect in them a great restlessness and unhappiness—primarily over their restricted position under the shadow of the Russian tree, but also for a deeper reason, I thought: namely, brought with their recent relative prosperity, which had brought them closer to the West, they had also begun to experience something of the empty dissatisfactions of a boring materialist affluent society, and did not know what to do about it. I felt for them. We, by comparison, are steeled, after a fashion, to this emptiness, and contrive to live in spite of it. For them, it was new.

Dear John this is as far as I can go, tonight. I have already written, today, an address I must deliver a month hence (I shall send you the draft of it for your comments) and I cannot do more in a single day.

The above will not tell you much; but it will tell you how little I really saw, and why I am inclined to reserve judgment.

J.L. to G.K.

15 April 1986

I read and re-read what you write about my native people. Your letter is both beautiful and truthful about them. I do not know whom you met, but your reflections on the native national character are very precise. There has been, I think, a slight—not sufficient, but slight—diminution of that sentimental romanticism bedeviling Hungarians through the centuries. At least this is what I think. The odd thing is that with all of our great native talents—and talents which individuals have been able to employ with astonishing success in foreign countries—we are a politically rather inept nation; and not only because of our unfavorable ethnic and geographical circumstances. This has something to do with the Magyar national temperament, which is also reflected in the Magyar language. Some time I'll tell you about my speculations about this matter. . . .

It is now the morning after Reagan's Libyan "strike."* I am very disturbed. Apart from the senselessness of it, it reflects—at least to me—something fatally juvenile about a certain American attitude to the world. Just as the scruffy—and dishonest—young radicals and "revolutionaries" of the Sixties were not really revolutionaries but *playing* at revolution, this movieland President does not really want war but he likes to *play* at war! And that is not only dangerous but somehow despicable. . . .

G.K. to J.L.

Kristiansand, Norway
May 31, 1986
Handwritten

This note is just to let you know that I received your paper just before leaving the U.S. some ten days ago, & took it with me.** The first of the ensuing days were spent in Finland where I was receiving an honorary degree under such formalities as probably now exist nowhere else in the world: the protocol, in fact, of 17th century Sweden: all in tails and white tie, in the presence of the Finnish president, the honorant being presented with a most elegant, traditional hat and with a sword, the latter signifying that he, now holding the doctoral title, was now (if he

---

*President Ronald Reagan ordered the U.S. Air Force to bomb Libya on April 15, 1986.
**Refers to my article "The Soviet State at 65," *Foreign Affairs* (Fall 1986).

had not been before) a member of the nobility and entitled to wear that weapon. . . .

His very detailed comments are about my "The Soviet State at 65," in which I emphasized the primacy of state (and national) interests over ideology.

G.K. to J.L.

Kristiansand, Norway
June 1, 1986

It is a rainy Sunday morning, and I have asked our guests to excuse me while I do some writing, by which I have in mind my reactions to your paper. This will be a sloppy job of typing, for I seem not to have even a proper eraser; but that you will understand.

Your thesis—that it is not ideology but the interests of the Soviet state, as a great power occupying a certain territory and acting as the heirs to a certain history and tradition, that inspire and inform Soviet policy—is of course entirely correct, and it is important, in the light of the contrary view so assiduously peddled by the Reagan administration, that this be understood. So you will find no argument here with the basic thrust of your paper. But there are a number of the points it brings forward on which I should like to comment—in some instances critically, in others not. In addition to which, I have indicated by pencil notations on the text a number of suggestions, mostly stylistic but sometimes substantive, which you might like to take into account, but must not feel obliged to heed. In some of them I may of course be wrong; in others it may be only a matter of preference, and yours may be as good as mine. Please, therefore, do not take them as "corrections": merely as the sort of remarks I might make if we were going over it orally.

Now for the comments, some of them raising only questions of petty accuracy, others more substantive, some not even conceived as criticisms of what you have written but rather as reflections of my own inspired by it.

p. 3. The reference to Russia's "Withdrawal from Europe" in the period 1919–1939 strikes me as a bit too strong. In the mid-thirties Russia joined the League of Nations and [Ambassador Maxim] Litvinov developed a very active diplomacy, the purpose of which was to induce the western powers to fight Hitler in order that the Soviet Union might be spared the danger and effort of doing so. There were even efforts made, as you will recall, to arrive at something like a new Franco-Russian alliance. But the effort was of course a two-faced one, devoid of all real cordiality. It had, for various reasons, to go hand in hand with a bitter ideological hostility which, to be sure, no longer involved serious efforts to overthrow the western governments but had, for political reasons, to be carried forward quite vigorously at the rhetorical level.

p. 3. The modifications of the Russian borders in the West to which Lenin was obliged to accommodate himself in 1920–21 were actually the restoration the old borders of Russian national-religious orthodoxy as they had existed prior to the Petersburg era of the preceding two centuries. The fact that the territories just west of those new frontiers were lost for those two decades was actually a blessing to the Soviet leaders of that period; for it was easier to consolidate their power among a purely Russian population accustomed to despotic rule than it would have been had they been obliged to deal with the Baltic peoples and parts of Poland as well.

p. 4. The reference to [Georgi] Chicherin and Litvinov, while not fully inaccurate, strikes me as being a bit cryptic and misleading. These were, of course, very different people. Chicherin the scion of distinguished family of the old regime but a sincere Marxist of the idealistic-moderate variety—a scholarly and—in his selflessness and lack of political ambition—almost saintly sort of a person, never mind how misguided. Litvinov, as I recall it, had been, like at least nine-tenths of other Russian students of the period, a radical student when he studied in Kiev long before the Revolution, and had carried that coloration with him when he went to England to marry and to work in his father-in-law's publishing company. In the many years he spent in London (17 of them, I believe) he had served as a business agent for the Russian Social-Democratic Party generally, and had obviously retained, as did so many exiled Russian Jews, his sympathies for the Russian revolutionary movement. But neither he nor Chicherin were members of Lenin's inner circle nor could they be regarded as true Bolsheviks. The fact that they were both accepted as foreign ministers, and the even more striking fact that Litvinov survived the purges, may be attributed to two interesting factors. There was, first, the Russian tradition of employing, for the foreign-ministerial position, persons who were not at all members of the inner ruling group, and in some instances even foreigners. If I remember correctly, not one of the foreign ministers of Nicholas I was even a Russian. They were selected more as a tight wealthy family would have selected a good attorney to represent it in worldly affairs, prepared, if the attorney made good, to give him their confidence in business matters but never dreaming of taking him into the family circle. Chicherin was eventually eliminated—probably because Stalin's cynicism became too much for him and Stalin correctly sensed it. Litvinov, his successor, was kept on because he was useful in the position and was, politically, a helpless person. But the last thing Stalin dreamed of was to consider him or treat him as a member of the inner circle. He was never admitted to the Politburo. And I suspect that any Marxist illusions he may originally have had did not long survive the encounter with the Stalin regime. From 1932 on, his problem was his own personal survival; and neither in his mind nor in Stalin's did his ideological inclinations have anything to do with it.

p. 4. You speak of Koestler's scenario, in *Darkness at Noon*, as being "wholly devoid of reality." My impression is that this was true of the men who conducted the purges but not necessarily of a number of the victims. In some instances the latter were suffering, in fact, precisely for the stubborn idealism of their Marxist faith. Stalin couldn't stand people like that. They were, in his eyes, not only undependable (you never knew where their emotions might carry them) but, worse still, apt to be, in their heart of hearts, Trotskyite sympathizers more closely attached ideologically to the Communist movement outside Russia than to Stalin's own criminal-conspiratorial regime. I recall the account of Kedrov, a fiery, heartless, but dedicated old Communist bigot, going to his death in the purges screaming: "I believe, I believe, I believe."

p. 5. Are you sure about the word "grazhdanin"? I have no etymological dictionary here, and cannot recall ever looking up the origins of the word. But in the development of the Russian language the older version of two "o"'s separated by a consonant, as in "gorod" (a town) was often simplified and rendered by the consonant alone followed sometimes by an "a." The word for gold, for example—"zoloto"—sometimes became "zlato" (or the Polish "zloty"). I suspect "grazhdanin," accordingly, of being a derivative of "gorozhan"—i.e., a city-dweller. Do get some Slavist-friend to look this up for you. There are excellent Russian etymological dictionaries. I would not like to see you get caught up on this one.

p. 6. These seeming contradictions, to which you draw attention, between a more relaxed Soviet foreign policy and a tightening of the dictatorship at home had their logic. The regime, for one reason or another, wanted to reap the benefits of a greater apparent liberalism in its external relations, but feared that this would be misinterpreted within Russia and that people would try to use it as a lever to weaken the disciplinary hold of the regime over the population. The normal reaction was thus to tighten the reigns of power internally as one relaxed—or wanted to be seen as relaxing—the isolation of the country in its world environment.

p. 6. About Stalin's relationship to the apparati of Party and State. In the pre-revolutionary period Stalin, insofar as he "belonged" to anything at all, belonged to what might be called the criminal-conspiratorial, rather than to the cosmopolitan-ideological, wing of the Party. He was a "loner"—diabolically sly and calculating—wholly at home in a criminal environment—ambitious, jealous, envious, and dangerous for anyone who stood in his path. He was not above serving as an informer and using his relations with the police to get competitors out of his way. Lenin knew what sort of a man he was but thought he could be useful, particularly in the Transcaucasus, where the Party was predominantly Menshevik and where there were few Bolsheviks. The police, too, finally got fed up with him and exiled him in the final years before the Revolution. When he was released and popped up in Petersburg in 1917, he had had very little previous contact with the men around Lenin. Most of them, I suspect, never liked or trusted him, and he knew this. Most of these others were well-educated men, intellectually cosmopolitan, with western experience, knew languages, etc. He was none of this, envied them and hated them for being what he was not and could not really be. As he worked himself up into power after Lenin's death, and his qualities become increasingly apparent to the others, these latter saw more and more clearly what he was; and precisely because they realized how dangerous it was to oppose him, they would much have liked to be rid of him. He perceived all this, and seldom, if ever, trusted any of them. This had, of course, a lot to do with the purges; for he realized that his task was to get rid not just of a few individuals but of a whole generation of the older party bureaucracy; and he was not above sending hundreds of thousands to their death, confident that among them would be most of those who wished him no good.

It had been recognized early on, after the Revolution, that the Party, if it was to retain its unity, could not be made sufficiently numerous to constitute a state bureaucracy—that a state apparatus would have to be established alongside, but presumably dominated by, the apparatus of the Party. Hence the bureaucratic dualism that has always characterized the Soviet regime.

Stalin, however, realizing that the ambitious ones would always naturally be attracted into the Party and would, by their very nature, tend to become competitors for his power, and recognizing, too, that his domination of the Party rested exclusively on the terrorization of its members and not on any reliable loyalties, never felt comfortable with it—never fully trusted it. He therefore did indeed look to the state bureaucracy to serve as a counter-weight to it, and took care to see that he held the supreme positions in the state apparatus as well as those in the party apparatus. He played the two off against each other quite effectively whenever it suited his purposes. It was not, then, entirely without reason that Khrushchev, when in the late 1950's he moved against the remaining Stalinists in the Politburo (Malenkov, Molotov, etc.), dubbed them the "anti-Party group" and denounced them accordingly.

It is significant that in Stalin's time the three great and sensitive pillars of power in the Soviet Union—the ministries of war and foreign affairs and the administration of the great state-security apparatus— were all administered through the governmental, not the party, system. Party cells were not permitted in their senior bodies. At lower levels, as everywhere else, the Party controlled personnel appointments and changes; and of course it could influence policy at the supreme level through the Politburo. But the actual orders issued to these great bureaucratic empires appear to have been transmitted at the state, not the Party, level.

As the whole economic system becomes more intricate and advanced there was an increasing need for technocrats—engineers, scientists, highly-skilled technological personnel, etc.—in the process of administration. The Party apparat, staffed primarily only with people who are essentially dilettantes—agitators, propagandists, and party administrators—tends therefore to become increasingly superfluous and redundant. Yet the party *has* to continue to exist, not only because of its unique role as the supreme coordinator of all public life but, even more importantly, because it is (as you correctly point out later in the paper) theoretically the sole source of legitimacy for the regime, replacing in this sense the monarchical principle that had always previously prevailed.

Incidentally, please check your statement about Stalin's being the first head of the Party to be prime minister. I seem to recall that Lenin held the position of Chairman of the Council (Soviet) of People's Commissars—essentially the premiership.

p. 7. (Last sentence, running over onto p. 8.) I was troubled by this sentence and tried, in vain, to find a wording that would better satisfy me. Phrase it as you will. But I would leave out the example of Finland. Great injustice has been done to the Finns by the way the term "Finlandization" has recently been used; and I think you might be misunderstood. Much damage was done, particularly in the first years after the war, by the fact that the representation of Soviet interests in Eastern Europe was given over to the Soviet secret police rather than to the Foreign Office. This, as you correctly indicate, was what Tito could not stand.

p. 8. Are you sure about the abandonment of the "Internationale" as the Soviet hymn during the war? Do check on this. I seem to recall its being played incessantly over the loud-speakers in Moscow at that time. But ask a specialist.

p. 8. Stalin and the Jews. His attitude towards them, initially, seems to have been that of most of his Georgian compatriots: i.e., he did not fear them as many westerners have done, regarding them as tricky, wily, pushy and threatening to others. The Georgians themselves could be all those things in equal measure, and were much fiercer and more warlike in the bargain. Stalin recognized in the Jews an extremely high level of intelligence, and had no aversion to using them where he advantageously could. They were smart; often, like Litvinov, they knew the outside world as the Russians didn't, and hence could be made good use of. In these instances he would brook no interference. When someone opposed his appointment of Karl Radek as editor of the Izvestiya, his angry response is said to have been: "That's my little yid [zhidok was the word]; where I want him, there I will send him." This, of course, without racial feelings one way or the other. Later, of course, after the establishment of the state of Israel he came to see in the Russian Jewish population a dangerous cosmopolitanism, threatening the isolation in which he thought it necessary to hold the Soviet peoples, and particularly dangerous now, because it had a pole of attraction in another governmental establishment. This was a different thing.

p. 9. You are absolutely right about Stalin's espousing the war aims, or the political aims, of the earlier Tsarist statesmen. The reason, I think, was that he didn't trust his own ministers and helpers to be capable of any useful judgment as to what Russian national interest, in the permanent sense, really were. "Those dopes," he thought to himself, "what would they *know* about it? the Tsarist ones were much better educated and much smarter." He turned, therefore, automatically, to the Tsarist precedents. When his turn came to triumph over the Japanese, what he demanded, in the peace settlement, was precisely what the Japanese had taken away from Russia in the war of 1904–1905—nothing more, nothing less, whether it now made any sense or not.

p. 9 (final passages). It is true that what Stalin tried to obtain for Russia in Eastern and Central Europe and the Balkans checked very closely with the aims of the Russian military leaders of the Tsarist time. But it must be borne in mind that for the peoples who were the real or intended victims of those designs, the Soviet hegemony was far, far worse than the Tsarist one, especially as executed in Stalin's time by the police authorities.

p. 11. The reason given for Khrushchev's fall—"mostly because of his unpopular errors in foreign policy"—seems to me to be somewhat inadequate. I am no expert on the Russian politics of that time, but I have the impression that there were, in addition to the normal resentments and intrigues of politics in a dictatorial regime, three main reasons for his fall: (1) the U-2 episode, where the U.S. government, in its insatiable thirst for military intelligence, embarrassed him acutely; (2) his efforts to reduce the armed forces; and (3) the impression, wide spread in the bureaucracy, that he was impulsive, erratic, and headstrong in administrative questions and had weakened the whole economic system by abrupt and hair-brained efforts at reform.

p. 11—5th line from bottom. This may be debatable, but it is my impression that the word "convince," used as a verb, cannot be properly followed by an infinitive after the direct object—by which I mean that you may indeed convince someone else *of* something, say of the necessity of doing this or that, but you cannot convince him *to do* something. You may *persuade* him, but not *convince* him, to do it.

I may, of course, be wrong in this. The usage you gave to the word is, I believe, now common; but I am not "convinced" that it is correct.

p. 12. Gorbachev, if my recollection is correct, was indeed involved in the police "apparat" in the early stages of his career; but most of his active professional life seems to have been in the Party.

p. 12. I am not aware that there has been any announcement of Dobrynin's admission to Politburo status. he may be on the verge of it; I would think it likely that he is. But if there has been any announcement, it has escaped my notice.

p. 12, re Andropov. It was observable in Tsarist times as well as in Soviet ones, that the political police, precisely because of their relative immunity to criticism and interference from elsewhere in the regime but also because of their greater intimacy with the very opposition and foreign elements they were charged with observing and controlling, had a much more intelligent and sophisticated understanding of the outside world and of the faults of the regime itself than did the rest of the bureaucracy. Their ingrained cynicism may also have played a part.

p. 12. Yes, you are right. The Russian masses would like, of course, a benign and understanding ruling hand, but they have no patience with a weak or vacillating one—and, incidentally, no desire to replace it with a popular democracy, for which they have neither the example nor the understanding.

p. 13. I find it hard to accept the thesis (assiduously put forward by the Carter and Reagan administrations) that there has been a serious increase of Soviet "expansionist tendencies" in these past 25 years. Soviet relations with Third World countries have undergone changes, to be sure. The emphasis is now more on military factors, less on ideological considerations. Certainly, there has been a great increase in arms sales and the despatch of military advisors; but this, aside from being largely an imitation of American practises, reflects primarily the emergence of new capabilities—not of new policies—on the Soviet part. Like every other great power, Moscow would like "to win friends and influence people"— but to do this with the minimum of responsibility or risk of unwise involvement. Aside from Afghanistan and possibly Cuba, I think of no instances in which they have sent regular Soviet armed forces beyond their own borders. They did not do this even in the Korean War. And regardless of what their motives may have been, their successes have been so meagre that the professed anxieties of the Carter and Reagan people are bound someday to appear rather ridiculous.

In conclusion let me just observe that the extreme tensions that have marked Soviet-American relations in the postwar period have their origin primarily, in my view, in two factors: (1) the continued division of the European continent into competing military alliances; and, closely connected with the above, the emergence of the nuclear weapon and the resulting competition in its cultivation, with all the great doubts and anxieties this engenders. Neither of these factors (and I say this in support of your thesis) has to do in any way with the difference in the idiological foundations of the two societies. . . .

One of the principal themes of our correspondence: the relationship of history (of historical knowledge and historical description) to literature.

J.L. to G.K.

1 July 1986

I just read the text of your Academy address about history and litera-ture, reprinted in the *N.Y. Times Book Review* of yesterday, and I am compelled to write you about one centrally important matter.*

It is a beautiful essay, involving your rare mixture of self-examina-tion and moral exhortation. *Ces choses*, between us, *vont sans dire*. I will say that it reminds me of another essay you had written perhaps more than twenty years earlier, about this problem of the relationship of history and literature, a problem that has preoccupied me, too through my life. If I remember correctly, you wrote at that time about the atmo-sphere of the last Russian rail station at the Finnish border, including a tethered goat. Your "confession" (if that is the word, but surely not a mot juste) or having used a bit of memory-laden color in the descrip-tive invention was similar to the Giers funeral "confession" (except that in this case you were driven to look up the meteorological information of that day, which impresses me deeply, since I know how few dry as dust academic historians would have bothered with that). . . .

What concerns me is your distinction between what is "objective" and "subjective." I have devoted to this problem many years (and wrote about it in *Historical Consciousness*). Allow me, then, to tell you where I (and a few other men, scattered throughout the West, in different situations and in different disciplines) have come to stand. I have to be convinced that all human knowledge (and especially historical consciousness which is an inevitable element in all human under-standing) is *personal* and *participant*—which means: neither "objec-tive" nor "subjective." Indeed, that Cartesian division of the universe into "object" and "subject," or the separation of the observer from the observed, can no longer stand—and not only is this true of human relationships where, after all, observer & observed belong to the same

*"History; Literature and the Road to Peterhof," *New York Times Book Review*, June 29, 1986.

species; but it is true in the very world of matter. (This is what the great physicist Heisenberg began to realize, and what Einstein could not accept.)

What is wrong with "subjective" is that it is merely the other side of the coin of "objective"—and, therefore, captive of the same overall category of determinism. "Subjective" means: "This is, after all, how I see things; this is what I see, the world may as well accept it, because I cannot do otherwise." But I (and everyone else) *can*. The human mind (and only the human mind) breaks through the determinism of the cosmos. Indeed, our very perception (and interpretation) of the cosmos is circumscribed by the limitations of the human mind; and, paradoxically, it is through our recognition of these limitations that the power and the quality of our vision becomes enriched.

At the same time, what this means for the historian-novelist relationship is very much in accord with what you wrote. The historian's task is more difficult because there are certain things—people, motives, etc.—that he is not allowed to invent. That is why it is more difficult to write a great history than a great novel; conversely, it is easier to write a mediocre history than a mediocre novel. But the essential mode of their thinking is the same—personal *and* participant. And their main instruments are the same, too: words. Unlike other so-called "social sciences" history has no language of its own. It must be written, because it is spoken and thought and imagined in words; and, moreover, in words of our everyday languages. Not "facts," not "numbers," etc. (Kierkegaard said that numbers are the negation of truth.) History and literature: the self-knowledge of mankind.

Self knowledge, indeed! In his Glassboro speech, our President, who offered a strange olive branch (wrapped in a bundle of thorns) to the Russians said that in the U.S., unlike in the U.S.S.R., anyone could walk into his office—the White House—bang the table, and say "Mr. President! You are doing this or that wrong!" Now does he *believe that*? He also said, at the end of the speech, that the students ought not follow the history of the past but follow the "dreams of the future." And he is categorized as a conservative! . . .

G.K. to J.L.

Kristiansand, Norway
August 8, 1986

As for my writings: you are much too kind. I could, with greater justice, return a number of these compliments; for I owe to you a considerable proportion of my insights. But if half of what you write is true, then it has the virtue of reminding me that the time I have left for any sort of writing is narrowly, and uncertainly, limited; and that I owe it to myself, and to friends such as yourself, to write more seriously, and on more important subjects, than I have done to date. I have tried, as you know, to avoid theory (which to me, as to Goethe, is "grey") and to let what was important in what I had to say shine through the descriptions of how one kind of life—the diplomatic one—really proceeded—"wie es eigentlich gewesen . . .". That seems to me to be the most honest way one can express one's self, when it comes to personal and political philosophy. But it is a slow way. It gets through to a very limited number of readers, and then only dimly. But there are many people, especially in Europe and above all among the French, who can be induced to read anything only if they are led to believe that it presents some sort of a theoretical structure. (Strange that they should fall for this sort of pomposity!) To get their attention I suppose that one must at last appear to fall in with their expectations.

In any case, I have, thanks to your letter, all this much in mind; and shall try, when I return, to do more to justify the sort of confidence you have shown in me.

J.L. to G.K.

22 August 1986

What you write about the French—I think that their problem is not obsession with theory and theoretical frameworks (this *is* true of many of them; but then they produced some of the greatest anti-theoretical thinkers and writers: Pascal, Stendhal, Flaubert, Bernanos, etc.) Their great shortcoming may be egocentricity, coupled with the quickness of their minds. They will not pay attention to matters and people that should deserve their attention and from which they may even profit. In the alas, too rare, cases that they *do* devote their attention to something in which they espy an interest going beyond their selfish preoccupations their mental activity becomes easy, masterly and, at times, unsurpassable. (Whether they are merely formal or pompous, they do have their wit; but alas, only rarely a sense of humor.) . . .

I think I wrote you that I am beginning to work on a book "Budapest 1900." Well—I would not have thought that this will create an emotional involvement, perhaps more than in any other book I have written. I was a history student when I left my country, at the age of 23, and I thought that I knew something about its relatively recent history; and now I see things that I *had* seen before, and perhaps even thought about them, but *not* in this way. . . .

G.K. to J.L.

Princeton, New Jersey
September 23, 1986

I hope you realize that I am deeply grateful for the interest you have taken in my work. Even if you are too indulgent in your judgement of it, you do me a rare service in thinking about it and giving me your impressions. Interesting that you should single out the diaries, letters, and other miscellaneous writings as a category on which I should concentrate when it comes to publication.* I had myself thought to do just this: taking the accumulation of such papers from the year 1963 (with which year my memoirs ended) and publishing from the ensuing period of—say—twenty years, in place of memoirs, a volume of diary notes interspersed with letters and possibly also excerpts from a few other unpublished papers. Since the letters are quite different from the diary notes, the first tending to be more political and intellectual, the others more personal, it seems to me that there might be a certain useful tension between them, breaking the monotony that would ensue if either series were to be published alone.

I would already have tried to get down to that task had I not, foolishly, no doubt, allowed myself to become inveigled into trying to

*I hoped to urge him to consider an eventual publication or excerpts from his diaries.

write a review of a book of essays by Arthur Schlesinger, now about to appear.* Since there are fifteen essays, all on different subjects, a number of them in depth and importance little books in themselves, this proved to be a difficult task technically, and has pre-empted a lot of my time. I think, incidentally, that you might be interested to see some of those essays, particularly the ones in the first part of the book, dealing with what is essentially the view, or views, that Americans take of themselves as a nation among nations. Schlesinger is of course, by political affiliation and in some respects by persuasion, a Kennedy liberal, which neither of us are; but he is also a historian and (within his field of American history) an excellent one; and here he is much more conservative. You will be interested, perhaps, in his polemic against what he terms the "ideological" (Reagan-Moral-Majority) school of thought on these matters, singling out, as it does, the ahistorical quality of their outlooks, the born-yesterday character of them, and the dreadful poverty of understanding for human nature. . . .

Aside from this, and other secondary involvements, these last weeks since the return from Europe have been difficult ones for me. I seem to be experiencing some sort of a crisis connected with the advance of old age.**

This is, in a sense, a certain change of life, like others—one connected with the advance of old age: with the loss of nervous and psychic vigor, with the recognition that there is much of the bad that will never be corrected, and much of the good that will never be done, and with the awareness that one is no longer at one's best, is no longer wholly up to the strains one has borne in the past, that one is, in a sense, a species of scarecrow which has outlived its time and ought not to be exhibited in public. My only hope is that this is not something final—that it, too, is a passing crisis—and that it can be followed by a process of adjustment after which, frail as may be the body, some sort of joie de vivre and personal balance can be recovered.

---

*"In the American Mirror," *New York Review of Books*, November 6, 1986.
**In spite of his extraordinary physical discipline, Kennan had a tendency to exaggerate his symptoms of old age.

J.L. to G.K.

26 September 1986

I start with what you write about your problems with your children. I must proceed on speculation. But I shall draw on my experiences. You will agree with me, I think, that in these times of the dissolution of an entire epoch in the history of a civilization, the most intimate and personal relationships are affected: those between men and women, husbands and wives, parents and children. That is no source of comfort for you and me. But there is another side to this. The children who break away from us nowadays—not only in the normal and expectable way at a certain stage of their lives: by breaking away I mean their abandonment of those standards of behavior and ways of life that we think are naturally good and proper for them—do not do this with that happy, thoughtless and often arrogant optimism which is a natural mark of the young leaving the old. Our children in these times, are not really happy, not thoughtless, and seldom arrogant. They do not *think* that their parents' old fashioned standards are not good for them. To the contrary: they *feel* that they themselves are not up to those standards. These are of little use for them because of their own, strangely wanting, self-confidence. This is surely sad; but there are three consoling elements, I think. The first is that things are never as bad (or as good) as they seem to *us*; and *they* will outgrow their problems— perhaps, alas, very late—but in ways and with sadly beautiful results that are not given to us to know now. The second is that, unlike other generations in the past, they love and respect their parents deeply— precisely when these parents possess old-fashioned standards and virtues. *Of this I am convinced.* I have seen umpteen examples of this among young people during the last twenty or more years, including "rebels" and "radicals" during the silly "youth rebellion" of the Sixties. Completely contrary to the then accepted opinions and superficial appearances they were (and are) thirsty for authority—for authentic authority. It is therefore that we must continue to impress them with our own convictions, together with our concern and love for them. (Note that I write "together with," not "tempered by.") This combination may be difficult for some parents, but far from impossible for others.

This is why you must not worry about your "certain special vulnerability and lack of elasticity in (your) reactions to them." That may be
indeed an asset for them—not because it is identical with the older
traditions of discipline but because it will furnish them with the inner
sense of a constant reminder. This is the third consoling element: that
they will be (and probably already are) profoundly grateful for your
concern about them (your "vulnerability") *and* for your own exempli-
fication or incarnation, of your convictions (your "lack of elasticity.")
And this gratitude of theirs serves purposes beyond being a liniment
to the bruised spirit of a father. Their gratitude will be a good thing
for them. It will guide them—in strange ways that only God knows—
in their lives; at the most unexpected moments and in unexpected
ways. . . .

G.K. to J.L.

Princeton, New Jersey
January 13, 1987
Handwritten

The arrival of the letter found me, curiously enough, in a state of comparable despair. This state of mind came in part from personal reasons,
notably the realization of the failure of my efforts of so many years to
bring about a better public and official understanding for the problems
of nuclear weaponry and Soviet-American relations; but beyond that,
I, too, sense the imminent arrival of great calamities, and recognize the
general inability of our society and our official establishment either to
recognize this danger or to do anything effective to avert it.

However, depression, at least in my case, has much to do with my
physical and psychic state of the moment; and, being essentially a
healthy person, I recover from it by indulgence in the little satisfactions
of the moment: small tasks accomplished—small words of encouragement from others—sometimes the sense of having given small
comfort to others. "Freut Euch mit mir, dass morgen ein Tag uns tagt"
(Hermann Hesse).*

*"Rejoice with me that there is a tomorrow."

I also agree very strongly with your feelings about what you call Constantinism:* the attempt, as I read it, to associate religious faith with the purposes and doings of governmental power. I think you know my views. Government, in my view, is a sorry, regrettable necessity of man's fallen state: a form of tribute, it you will, to his imperfections, his beholdenness to the flesh and to animalistic instinct, his inability to free himself from the myopia caused by self-love and the cultivation of the own ego. These are the things that necessitate the constraints of government; and the acceptance of those constraints is the price we pay for them.

Since government *is* a necessity, however humiliating, no one should be reproached, on principle, for taking part in it; but the true Christian should never accept any governmental responsibility, however minor, otherwise than with a prayer on his lips for forgiveness—forgiveness for the injustices he will not be able to help committing, for the limitations of his vision, for the promptings of self-love that can seldom fail to be indulged by even the smallest sense of power over other people. If this sense of humility is there (which it seldom is), then participation in government is permissible.

But what one may *not* do is to confuse the purposes and activities of the governmental power with the advancement of divine purpose. To attempt to associate these things is to misconstrue and abuse the real nature of government and to blaspheme that of God. Particularly is this true when we attempt to picture ourselves in the form of a national community rather than as morally responsible individuals. Real love of country, implying as it does the sense of a people's tragedy as well as of its virtues and accomplishments, is one thing; romantic nationalism and illusions of superiority are another. The Christian God, in contradistinction, I suppose, to the Jewish one, recognizes no nations—only the human soul. And the summons addressed by millions of aroused people in the Almighty to bless their cause in the two horrible wars of this century, was of course in itself a form of blasphemy. . . .

---

*"Constantinism" is the temptation of the Church and its hierarchies to react to emperors' or dictators' toleration and support of them by subordinating themselves to the state, indeed, to make obedience to the ruler of the state a dogmatic article of faith.

P.S. I wrote the above hastily, before seeing the collection as it was finally put together. On seeing it in this form, I realize more strongly than before that it simply will not do. Too scrappy. Too disjointed. Too much of the irrelevant.

If you agree, I should like to re-do it: shortening it, omitting a number of the smaller diary excerpts as well as some of those of the letters, returning only some of the longer diary pieces such as the trip to Ripon, and putting in more of the public statements such as the Pacem in Terris speech and the testimony on Vietnam before the Senate For. Rel. Committee.

G.K. to J.L.

The Institute for Advanced Study
Princeton, New Jersey
February 7, 1987
· *Handwritten*

I have, as you see, mixed together, although in chronological order, personal letters, diary entries, and bits and pieces of public statements. They are not designed, in this jumbled form, to give a coherent running account of my goings and comings or even an organized comprehensive picture of my thoughts—rather to suggest the variety of interests, responsibilities and undertakings that characterized such a life, and the tension between emotion and reason, between the aesthetic and the mundane, by which that life was racked.

I am very uncertain about the result, and quite prepare to hear you tell me that it is not, in balance, successful. I think it possible that the diary entries and travelogues for later years may be richer and more abundant. But even then, I am not convinced that this is a very successful way to express myself, or rather, to express what I once was. But this you will be better able to judge than I am; and you will be doing me a favor to give me your frank opinion—even if it is an unfavorable one.

Please bear in mind that these various passages have not been edited for final publication. Were they to be published, not only would that editing be done but a number of them might be omitted—as too trivial or tedious for publication. If there are any you would care to designate for that fate, that, too, would be useful.

One impression that is borne in on me in glancing over these snippets, is that the things I was saying publicly were by and large, because more *reflechis* and more balanced better than what I was saying to myself in the privacy of my momentary moods and reactions. In any case, thank you—in advance—for your trouble to look at it all. . . .

J.L. to G.K.

10 February 1987

I do *not* think that you should make a book out of *this* combination of materials. . . .

There are two volumes of the Memoirs. And there are your diaries, letters, papers. I consider all of them—and the third *not less than the others*—as an invaluable corpus, unique in the history of this country, finer than anything—and I mean anything—Henry Adams had done: a rich corpus of capital treasure and worth from which future generations will draw and learn. Yes, there might be the Collected Edition at some future time. But the Diaries and Letters book should not be left with such a potential edition. I repeat what I told you, that I should be honored and pleased to serve as the Editor of George Kennan's Diaries and Letters some time. Perhaps sooner than you think, perhaps later. That is for you to decide. (I shall be always ready for that.) But that is not the point now. The point is that the present kind of compilation would reduce the interest and the meaning of such a Diaries and Letters volume (whether one or two volumes) when that will appear, for appear it must, probably after your serious and extensive biography is published. And now—at least I think—I *am* at the heart of the matter, which is this: In my opinion you should put together a book selected from your *descriptive* diaries *and* such letters (which comprise about one-half of the present manuscript). And from the beginning—not only from the post-1963 years.

Such a book should be published soon, independent of the publication of your biography or of a more detailed volume of Diaries & Letters. It would whet the appetite of intelligent men and women for what is yet to come. These are reflections of your mind at its best. They are vivid, esthetic, often very beautiful. The consistency of your mind and character are there: they are soaked with your humaneness, suffused with an historical sense that is rare and precious and that instantly evokes the delight and interest of the reader. (I doubt that the title of such a book should be "*Places*" but it should consist essentially of your description of places: which, in your case, invariably would include not only places and sights but the people and their times and the presence of their history.) . . .

Finally—would it not be *pleasurable* to collect those descriptions? "There is no duty we so much underrate as the duty of being happy" wrote R. L. Stevenson. . . .

In July 1987 hearings of the so-called Iran-Contra scandal were televised; publicizing the illegal and secret transfer of armaments and monies from one theater of the world to American intervention in Nicaragua, with the knowledge of President Reagan—spectacularly defended by Colonel Oliver North, who defended that transfer, before Congress.

J.L. to G.K.

1 July 1987

I suffered an accident five weeks ago—I fell from a truck (on which my son and I were moving something). For awhile I could hardly move; but during the last ten days improvement came fast; I am typing this from a wheelchair but in a day or two, I won't need it any more. I was in a hospital, and for some time immobile at home: so I watched the now famous hearings. *In a way*, they gave me some sense of reassurance: no matter what is wrong with the way Congress operates, the system of checks and balances still works; and one *does* find congressmen and senators representing now rather old-fashioned American standards of decency. What is worrisome is that none of them asked a few essential questions. They did not ask Col. North why he described Nicaragua as a *Soviet* base. They did not ask why the National Security Council must have an office *within the White House*. They did not ask why this

President—who keeps talking against Big Government—has a national security staff that is three or four times larger than previous ones. They did not question North's and [national security adviser John] Poindexter's and even [secretary of defense Caspar] Weinberger's assumption that we are involved in a relentless global struggle with the Soviet Union—which is how and why North justified the entire intrigue with Iran. They did not ask (or say) that the entire harebrained idea had come from the Israelis, etc., etc.

The proceedings—especially the North performance—reminded me not of Watergate but of the Joseph McCarthy days. The equation of anti-Communism with patriotism is, alas, still widespread among the American people, and among those who should know better. I have come to the conclusion some time ago (and I think that this applies very much to Ronald Reagan) that there is a very evident psychological impulse for certain Americans to attribute everything that is wrong to the USSR or Soviet Machinations, etc. The source of this impulse is not really, at least to me, an unwillingness, rather than an inability, of mind to depart from what is, after all, a fairly comfortable assumption: that America represents what is good in the world, and that everything that goes wrong has an *outside* evil power responsible for it. So, in essence, the problem with this psychic syndrome may not so much the ignorance of *others* but a peculiarly wanting American willingness to self-knowledge. . . .

G.K. to J.L.

Kristiansand, Norway
August 7, 1987

Today (just a week before our returning to the U.S.) we have been enduring the second of the two greatest gales we have witnessed on this coast in many years, and this time—directly in upon us from the open sea, so that the great waves have been slamming in against the rocks just below the cottage, and the the rain has been slashing, in great bursts, against the windows. In early evening, Annelise and I, tired of being prisoners all day in the cottage, donned complete sets of foul weather gear—the sort we use in bad weather at sea—and went for a walk, in the course of which we suddenly realized that we had not even opened the mail box, out at the end of the lane, assuming, no doubt, that even the postman would never get there in such weather. But open it we did; and there we found your recent letter, which I stuffed, as well as I could, into the oil-skin pocket. And I have just opened it—damp and limp, but fully legible, at home.

First of all, let me add my own packet of sympathy and affection for the accident that recently overtook you.

And I could not agree more strongly with what you wrote about listening to the congressional hearings. I could even have added to the list of questions which, as you have said, ought to have been asked by the legislators of those they were questioning. What most depresses me is the utter failure of the press and the other media of communication to see to it that these questions were asked. We have almost totally lost the beneficial influence that responsible journalism was once capable of bringing to bear on people in power. And what most deeply appalls me is the realization that if these journalists and television "anchor men" were incapable of perceiving, and drawing attention to, the incredible weaknesses of the Reagan foreign policy—if, in other words, they did not know a bad policy when they saw it, they would be equally unable to recognize a good one if they should see it. Even if one had the governmental power, and even if one used it wisely, judiciously, and effectively, the press and media would be incapable of perceiving that one had done so. . . .

J.L. to G.K.

4 October 1987

Enclosed you will find my copy of the Russell Baker book* that I think is an American classic, and I know that you will enjoy it. I am less sure of Tatiana Metternich's autobiography that I promised to send Mrs. Kennan.** (I borrowed it from a friend.) I read it now, and it has its interesting parts, but it does not compare even remotely to those diaries

---

* Russell Baker, *Growing Up* (New American Library, 1987).
** Tatiana Metternich was the sister of Marie Vassiltchikov, who wrote a very authentic and interesting book about her life in Berlin during World War II.

of that blithe spirit, her sister and not only because of style; Tatiana V. seems to have been much more of a calculating woman. . . .

One thing occurred to me—again, at the risk of presumptuousness. If that compelling desire to sum up your opinions—no, convictions, resting on a lifetime of experiences—about essential themes persists: you may wish to consider a volume (not a large one) about *persons*, after the *Places* book; and perhaps use your portraiture of persons as a vehicle with which to illustrate the themes. Your insight and ability to describe certain people (an ability tempered by your natural charitableness) is at par with your fine descriptive abilities of places; they would balance your more serious and somber ruminations about human problems and institutions. Thus, for instance, a page or two of your thoughts about government (a more long-range and essentially philosophical discussion) would be followed, (perhaps separated by asterisks) by your illustration of the philosophical disquisition. (In that order, not the reverse: because for the reader the softer, and humane delineation of the portrait would both ease and enrich his mind after having read the sterner part). . . .

G.K. to J.L.

The Institute for Advanced Study
Princeton, New Jersey
November 6, 1987

First of all, I must thank you for letting us see the two books: the one by Princess Metternich and the autobiography by Russell Baker. Annelise read the first, and with much interest, since this was a time when we, too, were in Berlin, and we knew several of the people whom she wrote about. She did not think it as good a book as the one by her sister—but still worth reading.

As for the second: I share your admiration for it and hope, some day, to have an opportunity to tell Mr. Baker so. Although my family did not experience the dire poverty he describes from the time of his youth, we were almost of an age, and there was a great deal in the book with which I could identify. Thank you for letting me see it. . . .

I know that this should not be allowed to take up too much time or to postpone the remaining scholarly work to a point where I am too old to accomplish it. And whatever I might produce probably should not appear publicly, if it is to appear at all, until after my death. . . .

J.L. to G.K.

12 November 1987

For some time you and I seem to have agreed that the fundamental shortcoming of our so called "conservatives" is that of their juvenile and single-minded ideology of foreign policy—while there are many things in their domestic advocacies with which you (and I) agree. But now many things prove that this is no longer so. With few exceptions, our—so-called—"conservatives" are irresponsible and self-serving, *tout court*. Here are two examples. Just a week or so before the stock market crash [William] Buckley proclaimed in a column that the criticism according to which the personal savings of Americans are at an all-time low is no reason to criticize the Reagan administration's economical and financial policies: in a society where we have social security, pension plans, etc., the idea that saving is meritorious is *passé*. Last week an article in *National Review*, entitled "What to DO?" proposed that the Federal reserve "should quickly cut the margin requirement on stocks from 50 to 20 per cent." The word *conservative* evidently has lost all of its meaning—except for those for whom it is a convenient label to assert their radical ideological nationalism and profit-seeking.

Thank you for returning the two books. I knew that you would like Russell Baker's memoirs. Tatiana Metternich does not come close to her sister—either in her writing or, I fear, in her character—but I thought that Mrs. Kennan would find it interesting. . . .

G.K. to J.L.

Princeton, New Jersey
December 12, 1987

I spent some days of this last week in Washington and attended two of the functions for [Soviet president] Mikhail Gorbachev. He received me personally with great kindness and tact, embracing me (to my astonishment) at first sight, then proceeding to say, before the assembled journalists, photographers, and others: "Mr. Kennan, we consider that a man may be the true friend of another country without ceasing to be a loyal and devoted citizen of his own; and that is the way we view you."* He is indeed a remarkable man in many respects. Whether he is destined for further success (it can, at best, remain limited) or for some sort of early political martyrdom, I am sure that he will go down in Russian history as one of the great, and probably tragic, liberal figures of the post-Petrine age. I have just completed a review of his book—or rather, a review article—a piece with which I am not wholly pleased, myself (I think I could have done better in the literary sense) for the N. Y. Review of Books, to appear, I suppose, in early January.

J.L. to G.K.

20 December 1987

You may or may not remember one of my theses, which I developed in a chapter in my book about American history.** This is that the *visible* (and, therefore *in the short run*, decisive) movements of history and politics and ideas in this country are no longer the results of popularity but of publicity. The deterioration of the republican political structure of this country to a popularity contest began, of course, in the 1820's; and this was what Tocqueville described as the dangers of the tyranny of the majority. But I think that we are a step further (or lower) than that. Our elections—indeed, the very commerce of ideas and goods

---

* This was, I wrote twelve years later in *George Kennan: A Study of Character,* "Kennan's apotheosis."

** *Outgoing Democracy: A History of the United States in the Twentieth Century* (Doubleday 1984).

in the so-called "free market" (ha! Ha!)—have moved from popularity contests to publicity contests. (I have written about this in that chapter, out of a simple recognition which, if inflated into a book, would establish the career of a well-situated historian in this country for life, but that is not the point—though I am sometimes, but only sometimes, disconcerted that no one has noticed that obvious argument.) My point is that the quantitative discrimination will no longer do. What we face is no longer the danger of subjecting ourselves to the sentiments of a rude and uninstructed majority. What we face is the existence of *hard* minorities and soft majorities—wherefore the first may exercise an influence well beyond their actual numbers; and in ways that are often not visible except for very discerning observers. In sum, the danger to the democratic process—and to its eventually authentic reconstruction—may no longer be the occasional tyranny of public opinion but, rather, the frequent and inauthentic *simulation* of public opinion— through the influence of "hard" and determined minorities upon "soft" and sometimes undetermined majorities. . . .

––––––––––––

About Reagan's 1988 visit to Moscow, heralding the end of the cold war. Both Kennan and I saw (indeed years before this event) the retreat of the Soviet empire from Eastern Europe, and even from East Germany. (This and the end of the Berlin Wall were denied by the then head of the CIA, Robert Gates, as late as 1988.)

J.L. to G.K.

3 June 1988

I have mixed feelings about the Moscow meeting. The behavior and the expressions of our President—at least to me—reflect a split-mindedness: about Russia, about Communism, about our relations with Russia and, you, about America's relation to itself. That split mindedness has not much weakened. It exists among many people (even though I sense that the sentiments of the American people about our relation to Russia may be more reasonable than those of many people in the government.) I wonder whether there are people in Washington who have begun to see not only that the United States and the Soviet Union have fewer conflicting interests than in the past but that there are important—perhaps the most important—portions of the world where their interests actually coincide, threatened as both are by some of the races of the so-called Third World.

I am afraid that I cannot discount the influence of the many vested interests—and of their newfangled intellectual allies—who will continue insisting on a policy of suspicion and interference aimed at the Soviet Union. Yet there is hope in the condition that there are vast developments in the world over which Washington (or New York) have no control.

How odd the world has become. We live in a post-Communist, *and also* in a post-Liberal vacuum. Something new will emerge: but very, very slowly. In Eastern Europe, for example, I am inclined to think that a multi-party system should not be an ideal alternative even if and when the political monopoly of the Communist parties will disappear. In any event, when a new political structure will arise, its intellectual proposition and explanation will follow, not precede, its birth. How I would like to know what you think of this. . . .

V

The End of an Age: American Hegemony

LETTERS, 1988–2004

G.K. to J.L.

Kristiansand, Norway
June 15, 1988
Handwritten

After apologizing for this extraordinary paper,* let me thank you for
your letter of the 3rd. Yes indeed. What you call a "split-mindedness"
runs through the entire fabric of American policies & attitudes towards
the Soviet Union. One great part of the U.S. government professes to
be seeking peace with Moscow; another great part of it—C.I.A. & the
Pentagon—appears to live and act on the assumption that we are either
at war with Russia or are about to be. Both of these attitudes have their
domestic cliques and constituencies; and our good president, anxious
to return the support of both of them, wages peace, demonstratively,
out of one pocket, and war, clandestinely, out of the other. Hence—his
split mind.

   I am now (not for the first time), going to presume on your
friendship—first to tell you something of my concerns & projects in

---

* Kennan was referring to the stationery on which the letter was written.

my own writing; and later, if things go well, to ask you to look at some specimens of what I am trying to do.

I left the U.S., three weeks ago, dominated by the thought that, since the time left to me is now limited and rapidly shrinking, I should not bother to write anything more that is closely related to the passing scene—rather only such material as might be expected to return its value long into the future. With this in mind, but also because I have sometimes been charged with being cryptic about my political philosophy, allowing glimpses of it to be revealed here and there. In views I have expressed on specific subjects but never trying to state it in more rounded and comprehensive form, I am now trying, if only in the somewhat disjointed way forced upon me by the circumstances of life in this cottage, to commit to paper a more comprehensive and logical exposition of that philosophy than I have ever offered for publication. I have tried on two or three past occasions to do something of this sort, but it was never successful.

It goes against the grain of my own conviction that truth can be usefully approached only obliquely—indirectly—never head on. I must quote to you, in this connection, another striking passage from John Donne (Satyre III) in which he states the same view:
"On a huge hill
Cragged and steep, Truth stands, and he that will
Reach her, about must, and about must goe;
And what the hill's suddenness resists, winne so;
Yet strive so, that before age, death's twilight,
Thy Soule rest, for none can worke in that night."
This, as you see, touches me in two ways. And it could, of course, stand as a warning against precisely what I am proposing, and with difficulty attempting to do. But I shall persist in my efforts. And I will, before the summer is out, try to complete at least a chapter or two and ask you to look at these and tell me whether you think the effort has merit and should be continued. You will know that should the answer be negative, I would only be grateful to you for letting me have it; for you would be doing me no favor in encouraging me to go forward with a clearly unpromising undertaking.

My health has not been good in these past three weeks: nothing serious in itself, but one component of the troubles obviously being simply old age. All of which gives, or should give a certain urgency to what I am trying to do; for as Donne so correctly says, "none can worke in that night." . . .

P.S. I was greatly struck with the final paragraph of your letter, profoundly observed. Yes—something new must and will emerge, and very, very slowly. And you will see, if I ever complete and send to you what I am now writing, how deeply I agree that "a multi-party system should not be an ideal alternative."

J.L. to G.K.

30 June 1988

Those striking lines from John Donne correspond exactly with something that I read by Kierkegaard some time ago: a passage in which he says that Truth is given to God alone: but what is given to us is the pursuit of truth. (Thucydides, too, says something similar in his introduction to the history of the Peloponnesian War: his purpose, he suggests is the reduction of untruth.) . . .

My Budapest 1900: A Historical Portrait of a City and Its Culture *was published by Weidenfeld and Nicolson in August 1988.*

G.K. to J.L.

Kristiansand, Norway
July 5, 1988

I have received your *Budapest 1900* and have read it from end to end. At the risk of crossing communications with you, and with apologies for the paper and the typing, I am hastening to give you my reaction, because tomorrow other members of the family begin to arrive, and this cottage will rapidly become no place for peaceful writing.

Yours is truly a remarkable book. Even allowing for my own ignorance of the other literature with which it might be compared, I am
confident that it is the greatest work anyone has written on modern
Budapest and in a general way, although not so intended, on modern
Hungary, by which I mean, of course, the Hungary of the past 120
years—since the Compromise. It is not just a book on Budapest and
Hungary. It is also a book on Central Europe. (For much of what you
wrote I found interesting parallels in my own memories of Prague
and Vienna.) And beyond that, it is in many respects a book about the
culture, the underlying weaknesses, and the inevitable tragic disinte-
gration of bourgeois Europe of the time in question. A great portion
of Budapest's experience was of course unique in a way that few other
European capitals could have rivalled, containing elements not shared
with any other city anywhere. But another portion was generic—almost
strangely so, as though in their striking aptitude for taking on the outer
aspects of all the Western-European civilization of the time, the inhabitants of Budapest had brought out many features of that civilization
with a special vividness and pathos.

About the reception and fate of the book in the United States and
elsewhere in the West I simply can make no predictions. As concerns
America in particular, I am not optimistic. The general book-review
editors will find the work hard to classify, and that will confuse them.
History? Yes, but more than history. Sociology in historical perspective?
Yes, but more than sociology. They will have a hard time finding the
qualified reviewer. Indeed, that person probably does not exist, because
there is no one who has looked at the subject as broadly, sensitively,
and deeply as you have, nor with anything like the same background
and experience. You suffer here, as you have on other occasions, from
the very catholicity (I use the term here in its philosophical, not in the
narrowly religious, sense) of your interests and your way of thinking.
This is what gives all your works their long-term value; but it renders
them only in limited degree intelligible to a contemporary reading
public (including most of the reviewers) accustomed neither by habit
nor by educational preparation to viewing things in broad philosophical and historical perspective.

But how the book is received in the United States is not, as I see it, what is important. Its greatest significance surely lies in its effect on the Hungarians. It must of course appear in Hungary—and not (God forbid) in someone else's pedantic translation, but in your own Hungarian prose. Nothing else would give it its flavor and effectiveness. I see no reason why the government in Budapest, in present circumstances, should object to its publication in Hungary; but even if it did, the objection would not be important. Were a good Hungarian version of the book to be available in bookshops in Vienna, London and New York, no one would be able to prevent its reaching a great number of avidly-interested Hungarian readers.* And this, I think, is of great importance. For it seems to me that you will then have done the greatest service to Hungary of anyone of this generation, teaching your former compatriots to see themselves soberly and realistically, in historical perspective, as reflected in the view of someone who has full knowledge (how many others could have?) of their own virtues as well as of their faults, and with feeling and sympathy for the beauty, the tragedy, and yet the capacity for seeing things through that has marked so much of their history.

Things have gone, on balance, reasonably well here. Health has had its ups and downs, as has the weather. My interest in Norway has greatly declined. How many people, and peoples, there are who can stand hardship and poverty better than they can stand prosperity!

Sincerely,
George K.

P.S. I regretted having to press you to accept another burden of writing—i.e., to get, one way or another, a good Hungarian version of your book; but am I not right in my feeling that you, having written this book, can do more for Hungary and for Budapest in making it available there than anything you could do, with the same amount of time and effort, for our poor unsuccessful but thick-skinned country.

---

* It was translated and published in Hungary in 1991 (after the change of regime) with enduring interest by many readers.

J.L. to G.K.

24 July 1988

I did not write this book for Hungarians. (Of course it is written for them, too; so many of them, in exile or in Hungary, know English; and I think that a Hungarian translation—which I shall want to go over very carefully—is possible. A German translation has been arranged.) I wrote this book for English-speaking readers, for many reasons—the principal one being the absence of such a book about Budapest *circa* 1900, when such a plethora of books about Vienna *circa* 1900 exists. But there is another element. Because of the relative intellectual freedom in Hungary, developing for at least the last twenty years, detailed monographs and studies and works dealing with my subjects about, and often of a very good quality indeed. If my book has any meaning to Hungarians—besides the fact that it may contribute to the knowledge and estimation of Hungary abroad—this consists in the quality of its synthesis, of my having brought and connected many things together that belong together, and perhaps with a perspective to which my former and present compatriots may not be accustomed. There is one last consideration. I could not merely translate this book into Magyar. I would have to write it anew—with a different rhythm of language, and often with different expressions, from beginning to end.

I am now coming to another matter in your letter. You wrote about my book: "History? Yes, but more than history. Sociology in historical perspective? Yes, but more than sociology." My addendum to this veritable praise is that this book, as also are my other books, *is* history—nothing more, nothing less. Not necessarily history of a radically new kind, but the kind of history that ought to be written now. You know how, until relatively lately, history was considered and written as the history of politics (national and diplomatic). Of course cultural history, art history, social history, economic history all began to appear about one hundred years ago: but they were not brought together for some time. The French made a conscious and methodical attempt at such a new kind of social-scientific history in their "Annales" school, beginning around 1910. Since the last war, this has burgeoned into something bigger, of which the principal representative has been Fernand Braudel, attempting to write "total history." Despite his reputation and despite the evidences of his research of many oddities, I think that his achievements do not measure up to his pretensions: but this is not the place to detail what is wrong with the Braudel school. . . .

J.L. to G.K.

20 November 1988

I am not so sure that Luce would be today to the right of Bush.* Yes, I know the shortcomings of his American Century propaganda (but wasn't it, and is it still not—though not for long—"The American Century"?) and I, too, was vexed and saddened by the opportunism of the TIME-Life magazines at the height of the cold war (I remember one *Life* editorial, circa 1953, that "McCarthyism" was merely a "venial sin," while Communism was a cardinal sin—some of the same people who praised Lenin and Stalin to high heavens in 1942). At the same time I regret the passing of that Eastern-Republican elite to whom, after all, Luce belonged, who had by and large, a not altogether deleterious influence in helping to set and affirm the course of the American ship of state both immediately before and after the last great war. That they had many shortcomings, and that their vision was, alas, ideological rather than realistic, remains true. But, after all is said, the Stimsons and the Knoxes and the Marshalls and even the Luces were preferable to Taft and Wheeler and Hearst and Patrick Hurley. These liberal Republicans are, all, gone now; and it is the second group's descendants and direct inheritors who rule the Republican party and influence the nation's destinies now. . . .

* Refers to Henry Luce (founder and head of Time-Life-Fortune) and to president-elect George H. W. Bush.

G.K. to J.L.

Princeton, New Jersey
November 25, 1988
Handwritten

I have just completed, by way of meeting a commitment backed into some months ago, an article on the problems of Germany arising from the extraordinary events now taking place in Russia and in the Russian-dominated parts of Eastern and Central Europe. . . .*

Then, if God continues to be kind to me, back to history—which would be a great relief. . . .

G.K. to J.L.

Institute for Advanced Study
Princeton, New Jersey
December 23, 1988

I have, in particular, taken the liberty of suggesting the omission of several parenthetical clauses (what I think of as "asides") that seemed to me to detract from the force of the principal assertions in which they were imbedded.** These clauses are, I know, the reflection of a high degree of conscientiousness and of what the Germans would call the "nuanciert" quality of all your prose. But they involve the danger of an excessive denseness of exposition through which it becomes more difficult than it should be for the average reader to make his way. All of these modifying insertions are in themselves well justified. But one has to make concessions to the limitations of the reader's attention span. He has to be easily carried along, without finding himself obliged to pause, at the end of a sentence, to say: "How's that again?" and to this necessity one has to make concessions.

I was much struck with the final sentences of the review, and pleased to see them appear. I have tried, occasionally, to make the point, in what I have said and written, that the establishment of the

---

* This may be the article, published almost a year later, "This Is No Time for Talk of German Reunification," *Washington Post*, November 12, 1989.

** I cannot find my article (or review) to which Kennan's letter refers.

Soviet hegemony over eastern, and parts of central, Europe in the period 1945–1947 was essentially the penalty the western powers had to pay for their inability to defeat Hitler without massive Russian help. The fault, in other words, goes back less to the Roosevelt of 1945 than to the western statesmen of the period 1936–1939, who failed to read the abundantly clear writing on the wall and to take the logical consequences. . . .

J.L. to G.K.

30 December 1988

You put a thin and elegant question-mark on the margin of my statement that Hitler "hated" Roosevelt. This goes back to January 1939 where Hitler recognizes that Roosevelt was standing towards intervention, and supporting the hard-line politicians in Paris and London. Later Hitler thought that behind Churchill stood Roosevelt, and behind Roosevelt, the Jews. In his *Tischgespräche* [table conversations] he rants and raves against Roosevelt more often and more feverishly than against Churchill.

J.L. to G.K.

11 February 1989

I read the German article with great care. . . .* One thing I missed in the article, I think that the erection of the Berlin Wall in 1961 marked a drastic change in the inclinations of the Germans—though probably not immediately of their thinking. Their entire Ostpolitik** (not a good word), which began to crystallize only many years later, was a consequence of 1961 when they were forced to recognize that the Adenauer policy—the hope that a close and strong association with the U.S. would sooner or later lead to the weakening of East Germany and potential reunification on Western terms—did not work. (Before

---

* I cannot find the article to which I refer in this letter.

** Ostpolitik refers to the gradual tendency of the West German government to increase, rather than freeze, contacts with East Germany.

that—without studying the events in detail—I was also intrigued by the condition that during the negotiations of the 2nd Berlin crisis that Khrushchev had opened in 1958 the Western Powers had never, to the best of my knowledge, brought up the question of East Berlin as a potential negotiating asset; they seem to have restricted their agenda to the West Berlin situation.) I remember another article of yours in 1959, I think, when you so cogently argued that sooner or later our rearming of (and perhaps also our military presence in) West Germany would cease to be a potential negotiating card with the Russians, like the virginity of a woman which after a while becomes much less of an asset than before—. . . .

I was instrumental in convincing Kennan (and, indirectly, his literary agent and his publisher) to publish a selection from his relatively recent travel diaries. I had read many of them he had sent me, and I was struck by the fine quality of his style and of his insights. He then chose a somewhat dull title, Sketches from a Life *(Pantheon, 1989), for this volume, which nevertheless turned out to be a modest publishing success.*

J.L. to G.K.

7 May 1989

So many thanks for your book, and for your magnanimous inscription that I shall always cherish and that I, at best, only partly deserve. . . .*

I shall only tell you how the book affects me. I was not in the least surprised by its quality, since I had had the privilege of reading some of your diaries earlier. I had not read Alfons Paquet** but somehow I do not doubt that your writing—and I am not speaking of the scope and the depth of your thinking—is of a higher quality than his must have been. Your book (as many other writings of yours) is in a genre of its own. One of its assets is its artistry, springing not only from the

---

* "For John Lukacs—to whose inspiration this volume owes much of its origin and to whom it will come as a token of the Author's gratitude for this and for much more—"

** Paquet was an excellent writer of *feuilletons* (often descriptions of places) in some of the serious German newspapers in the late 1920s.

sensitivity of your observations but of your capacity to render that fine-
ness in a special kind of prose. (That asset was often evident in the first
volume of the *Memoirs*.) Two matters occurred to me throughout my
reading. First: the long gaps between certain years. I wished (and not
because of some kind of intellectual or historical curiosity but rather
because of the very pleasure of reading) that there were more of it,
more excerpts, more scenes. Second: the extraordinary coherence of the
tone from the very beginning. An exceptional maturity suffuses your
observations and your writing: astonishing in the case of an American
as early as in the third decade of his life. But I am not only thinking of a
maturity of Judgment. I am thinking of a sensibility of heart (which, in
this case, is an American and not English quality.) To be fine-spun and
strong-minded, idealist and realist: what an attractive combination! . . .

G.K. to J.L.

Kristiansand, Norway
June 11, 1989
Handwritten

I have two things from you to acknowledge: First, the letter you wrote
me about my book. . . .
   I have also seen a formidable quantity of fan mail, and found it of
interest, and to me somewhat reassuring, that some of the most sensitive and perceptive reactions came from simple, modest people in my
own Middle West. . . .

G.K. to J.L.

Kristiansand, Norway
June 19, 1989

It is a mark of your prose, when you write about ideas rather then about
individuals, that the reader sometimes has to resort to a second look.
   Whether this is good or bad, I shall not attempt to judge. When,
many years ago, I delivered the annual Reith radio lectures, in London,
the excellent B.B.C. editor charged with helping me with the task

warned me never, in such lectures, to say anything that would cause my listener to say: "How's that again?" I would, she assured me, lose his attention at once. . . .

As befits a work that is intended as a history of the author's "thoughts and beliefs," this book* is pure Lukacs: a quintessential summary of all that has been meaningful to him and all that he has represented: the respect for a 19th-century patrician way of life the values of which—continuity, tradition, family cohesion, privacy, self-respect, quiet comfort and restrained elegance—have been so cavalierly treated by the intellectuals of the last 150 years; sweeping philosophic rejection of a purely secular and materialist liberalism; insistence that the human individual is an active participant in the creation of what appears to him as external reality; the conviction that a proper consciousness of the individual's place in history provides a better access to the understanding of his predicament than do all those pseudo-sciences—statistical, economic, sociological, or what you will—that treat man's environment as something existing outside the limits of his own perception; and, finally, acceptance of a faith that takes account of man's flawed nature—original sin, in effect—and recognizes that it is only through faith, as defined and exemplified by Christ, that he can hope to come to terms with the predicament into which that nature has placed him. But, associated with this historical-philosophical foundation, is the account of a most unusual life that is partly the source and partly the product of it. And, similarly associated with that foundation, there are the critical passages that seem to me to be the strongest features of the book. I think particularly, here, of the treatments, respectively, of the distortions of anti-communism, and of the efforts to fuse nationalism with religious faith (a temptation, incidentally, to which both the nationalist and the priest are vulnerable). So strong are the critical-biographical essays in other books and articles (the book on the various Philadelphians, and the *New Yorker* pieces, for example) that I find myself wondering whether this—the critical appraisal of interesting individuals—is not the field in which you have the best prospects for a successful and useful inter-action with your readers. This is not to depreciate the value of your historical-

---

* Refers to my autohistory, *Confessions of an Original Sinner* (Ticknor and Fields, 1990).

philosophical contributions; for it is out of this foundation, of course, that the critical efforts are drawn; without it they would lose their quality. And, like all superior literary-critical efforts, they are more than just what they purport to be. For truth, as I believe you noted in the book, can sometimes be most usefully approached only through the talented stripping-away of the crusts of half-truth that so readily attach themselves to it and obscure it. You may recall the passage from Donne where he said that truth sits at the pinnacle of a very high hill, and that he who would approach her "about and about must go"—that he cannot hope to go the direct route. Perceptive, understanding and constructive criticism is therefore, as I see it, in itself a form of creative philosophical thought. And it is sometimes (because so many are incapable of looking the bright light in the face) the best way of communicating that thought to others. . . .

Written before the end of Communist governments in Poland, Hungary, Czecho-slovakia, Bulgaria, Rumania, East Germany (including the fall of the Berlin Wall)—all in the last months of 1989.

J.L. to G.K.

18 July 1989

I am looking at the evolving kaleidoscope of the world with a mixture of hope and dread. I think I need not detail the elements of hope; they do not only include the events in Eastern Europe, and my respect for this extraordinary—and how extraordinary—Russian leader, but also some of the inclinations I begin to detect in our government, in spite of their often puerile and graceless expressions. The dread rises from a larger vision—which, I know, may be exaggerated or wrong. I think that all over the world, and perhaps especially in this country and in eastern Europe, the collapse of Communism opens up a very great vacuum. That vacuum is not only large but worrisome, by its nature, since it also involves the bankruptcy of most of the—so-called—liberal views of the world and of its society. That vacuum is bound to be filled. But with what substance? A kind of credulity that, of course, is very different from faith; and the cementing bond of which may be the kind of nationalism that is (though its adherents will neither see nor admit it) a substitute for faith. But I do not, for a moment, believe that such a development is inevitable, or that other elements may not be already at work the very existence of which soften and eschew such harsh alternatives. What is already evident is the slow but deep spreading of a realization in which you and I believe, that we must rethink the entire meaning of "Progress". . . .

G.K. to J.L.

The Institute for Advanced Study
Princeton, New Jersey
August 24, 1989

Most of what you wrote about we can discuss when we next meet, which I hope will not be too far in the future. There was, however, one point you made that not only represented, as I saw it, a remarkable insight, but struck me with great force by virtue of the profundity of its implications. It concerned what you correctly called the vacuum that is being opened up by the collapse of Communism in Russia and eastern Europe. For it seemed to me that in considering that question one finds oneself confronting the great problems of forms and purposes of government to which the thinkers of all ages, from Plato to Burke and Tocqueville have addressed themselves, but which now present themselves in a somewhat altered light in the face of the challenges arising from modern science and technology.

There are, and will continue to be, a great many people here in the West, and particularly in this country, who would say that the answer to this question was a simple one. All those peoples have to do, they would say, is to appropriate to themselves the true principles of democracy as we know them here in the West, turn power over to the voters and wait for the correct solutions to be revealed through the workings of the innate wisdom of popular majorities. This view rests, of course, on the assumption that western democracy as we now know it, is an essentially and reliably successful form of government, and represents in effect a final solution to the classic problems of the government to which I just referred.

Well, this, as I scarcely need tell you, is not my view. I see the institutions and concepts under which these western peoples are now living as essentially inadequate to the mastering of the challenges they face. This judgement applies even to what many people would regard as the most successful form of modern democracy: the Scandinavian welfare state. These political systems are not coping with a number of serious problems which are developing in these final years of the present century. And if they are not coping with them here, where they are supported by centuries of political experience, habit, and tradition, how much less adequate will they be for countries where none of all that exists at all, where things had not come to any acceptable political equilibrium even in the decades prior to the Russian revolution, and where what little understanding there is for the responsibilities of citizenship in a democracy has been weakened and corrupted by several decades of communist abuse!

But if I say, as I have just been doing, that the "capitalist" democratic state of the West cannot serve as an entirely satisfactory model of any of these people, then I am obliged to ask myself: what could? What would I recommend in its place? And here I find myself face to face with all the fundamental dilemmas of political theory; order vs. justice; authority vs. license; hierarchical structure vs. egalitarian mediocrity. And this leads me to one or two thoughts which I would just like to expose to you in answer to the question you have raised.

I can concede, rather reluctantly and in a way perhaps not too different than that of Tocqueville, that a system of government based on consultation of majority sentiment, while not ideal, is probably in the long run not only the most stable form of government but also the one that offers over the long term the greatest possibilities for personal development and for what our forefathers called "the pursuit of happiness." I can even concede that the *vox populi* should be the final arbiter of the great decisions of state wherever they cannot be suitably delegated to executive authority. But I have come more and more to believe that the voice of the people, while it should be given this ultimate respect and power, should not be the only voice to be heard in the affairs of the state. Alone, it is not adequate. If there is to be a successful modern society, that voice has to be supplemented by another one of quite a different nature. That voice would have to flow not from people whose positions are the product of the electoral process and who are caught up in the toils of immediate political responsibility, but from people who are precisely not subject to these limitations, but who would be qualified by integrity, breadth of experience, maturity of judgement, as well as by the general respect in which they are held in their respective communities, to look at national problems in the long term (as scarcely any active politician is able to do) and to direct attention to those general directions in which public policy will have to move if the greatest problems of the given society were to be adequately met.

There were efforts in earlier days to achieve something of just this nature. The English House of Lords, I suspect, was originally thought of in much that way, as was indeed, originally the Senate of the United States, which was not conceived by the founding fathers as being a directly elected body. There have also no doubt been many informal efforts to achieve some-thing of this sort, as in the excellent use made by the Japanese, in earlier decades, of what they consider to be their "senior statesmen." But it becomes clearer and clearer to me that in modern conditions these two functions—those of legislation and of ultimate decision, and those of advisory guidance by persons suitably qualified to give it—cannot be combined and should not be confused, and that the one, in a democratic society, is not adequate without the other.

These reflections underlie, as you will readily see, my own conviction that we in the United States cannot move forward successfully, in the face of the problems now bearing upon us, without something in the nature of a Council of State, as an entity not designed to replace any of the elected authorities in their constitutional powers but rather to look at problems in a way which the political establishment simply cannot do and to give to that establishment its advice and guidance, for whatever use may be made of them. This may not seem, at first sight, to be a very serious modification of American institutions, but if properly instituted, its importance could be greater than many would suppose, and without it I see no favorable way into the future at all. The voice of the people, in other words, ought of course to be heard in public affairs; but it ought not to be the only voice that is so heard. And it ought really, as Burke so clearly showed in his letter to the Electors of Bristol, to limit itself, as far as in any way possible, to the choice of political representatives, eschewing any effort to solve by plebiscitary means questions which should be the duty of those representatives themselves to decide on their own responsibility.

As you will see, these reflections run counter to assumptions and practices that are becoming common not only in this country but elsewhere in Europe. I am appalled at the extent of the tendency in Norway to submit great problems to plebiscitory decision by popular majorities which are far from qualified to pass any mature and thoughtful judgement upon them.

The reason I expose these reflections to you is that they present a personal problem for me to which I have found no answer. They lie at the heart of my own reactions to the failures of the American political system which have become so obvious. On the other hand, any attempt to put them forward publicly in a manner commensurate with their momentousness would have to be the product of a great deal more in the way of study of the whole situation than I have been able to give it. It would have to be, in short, work for a younger man.

What should I do? Should I keep such thoughts to myself? Or should I, at the cost of my work as a scholar, attempt to plunge into this whole tremendous problem of political institutions and to say something that would have some useful effect? I could easily waste, on a task beyond the time and energies available to me, what little I could do in a more modest way—i.e., as a student and writer of diplomatic history—in the limited time still remaining to me.

Don't feel that you have to come up with an answer to this problem. I wanted merely to expose it to you as a way of informing you of the questions with which I have to wrestle at this point in my life.

Otherwise, all is well. I am no worse off, physically, than I have had any right to expect; and I am grateful for all the blessings by which I am surrounded.

J.L. to G.K.

29 August 1989

All in all, I believe that a summation of your political philosophy—even in view of the new global and national conditions in the midst of which we now find ourselves—would be an unnecessarily burdensome effort on your part, out of proportion to its eventual benefices both for your-self and for its recipients, that is, the nation. . . .

I am now returning to the sentence or two in my last letter that had stimulated your thoughts and your profound response, about the fact (and it is a fact) that with the dissolution of Communism, a great vacuum, is opening in the world (and not only in Eastern Europe.) That vacuum, I believe, may be as dangerous as the dissolution of land empires which, as you and I know, have so often led to greater wars, and more suffering than had their earlier formation. On one level—of course all of this may be washed away by some man-made physical catastrophe—the present ephemeral combination of socialistic "capitalism" is going to prevail in vast portions of the world. (I write "socialistic capitalism," since we, in this country, have moved very far from old-fashioned "capitalism." In reality, our economic and financial practices consist of an increasingly abstract materialism, resting not on contract between individuals, but on the credit and the status they acquire from all kinds of institutions.) Anyhow—"free" enterprise, particularly in Eastern Europe, is the expectable and natural reaction to Communist mismanagement. With it comes—in my opinion, again ephemeral—appearance of multi-party democracy, about the merits of which you and I have our doubts. But there is, in my opinion, a more profound development. The three main forces of the twentieth century have been Western capitalistic democracy, Communism, and National Socialism (often wrongly and falsely labeled "Fascism.") Of the latter, the German variant was so powerful that it took the strange alliance of the other two to defeat it. What I see is the rise of nationalism almost everywhere in the world, and I am not only referring to its worrisome portents within the Russian empire. This nationalism is different from old-fashioned patriotism; that is, of course, regrettable. Yet a return to its Hitlerite variants is unlikely, too—even though a recurrence of some of the latter's tendencies and even a partial rehabilitation of it are already palpable. Oddly enough, one of the guarantees against that kind of intolerance and extremism resides in the petty materialism of the masses, in the gradual but overwhelming development of vast middle-classes (that word is outdated too: what I mean are societies that are non-proletarian as well as non-aristocratic). But for how long that condition will last, I cannot tell. . . .

I participated in a historians' conference in Paris, dealing with the 50th anniversary of the start of the Second World War.

J.L. to G.K.

4 October 1989

Paris was very beautiful, its buttery facades washed by the sun. On the western edge of Paris, an inhuman complex of fantastically high office buildings: not visible from the city, except for a frightening arch more than 400 feet high. Hardly anyone lives there: but it gives one a fore-taste of the 21st century. Not very promising, I'll say. The traditional Paris, however, is a living repository of a great civilization that still breathes here and there beyond its well-preserved monuments.

At the historian's conference, the British historians were best, the Germans quite good, the French either very good or very bad, the Soviet ones (including one dissident) very disappointing, the Japanese wretchedly impossible, unable (or unwilling) to answer any questions. . . .

G.K. to J.L.

Captiva Island, Florida
February 15, 1990
Handwritten

Thank you for sending me the book by Bernanos.* It arrived just as I was leaving. I took it along and I read it right through.

A curious book. In certain respects, it is of course dated. One of these respects is in the rather 19th century preoccupation with wealth and poverty—not wholly unrelated to Marxism. The modern welfare state has taught us that, not only is physical poverty, in the context of modern technology, unnecessary, but that, once overcome, it can easily lead to other forms of poverty, psychic and spiritual, that are even more insidious and dangerous. Our country is full of this. And then, too (getting back to the book): there is a certain amount of romanticism in the figure of the young priest—romanticism in the sense of the intense preoccupation with self, the lack of a tension-relieving humor, the insistence on carrying everything to emotional, intellectual, even religious extremes. (And, I might add, physical extremes as well. I found myself wondering why his wiser friends did not take him to task for abusing so fatuously his own physical frame, itself a gift of God, and a most wonderful one at that.)

But there were incidental imperfections. Some of the monologues (although one senses clearly that they were all really spoken by the same person—of course, the author) are magnificent—the Catholic Church, as I see it, at its best: full of wisdom, insight, irony, and of a lovely, trusting sense of intimacy with the Holy Spirit in all its forms— the Trinity, the Holy Family, and even the saints. I was not born, or bred, to just this sort of faith; but I recognize its strength and its beauty; and I have nothing but respect for it. . . .

---

* I had sent him Georges Bernanos's *Diary of a Country Priest*.

J.L. to G.K.

18 February 1990

The other day something occurred to me that I never told you, which is that *your* portrait of Gen. Boisdeffre* is at least as good, if not better, than Proust's in *Jean Santeuil* (how many professional historians are there who would so modestly, so elegantly, and so knowledgeably include a portrait by a novelist at the outset of their book? Hardly any).

I am appalled by the shallow superficiality with which our government (and, to some extent, the British and the French) approach the German question. They are (with the possible exception of Mrs. Thatcher) hardly aware that "vient l'appetit en mangeant" [appetite arises in eating] which (like self pity) is a peculiar German inclination, and Herr Kohl seems to be much affected by that. He acts and speaks like a Kleinbuerger who suddenly won the lottery or, better, who suddenly came into an unexpected inheritance which he now considers his natural due, though he had nothing to do with it. I am worried about the German-Polish frontier (I am more of a Polonophile than you are). In a larger sense, I am affected by the unwillingness of so many people in this country (and not only by this Administration) to rethink what national defense and national security means, or should mean. A crude sentimental nationalism (as distinct from old-fashioned patriotism) is the dominant force all over the world now. It is a dismal substitute for religion and tradition. Perhaps it is an inevitable consequence of democracy that, on the surface, homogenizes national societies. It fills many of the intellectual and spiritual needs of hollow men. . . .

J.L. to G.K.

19 March 1990

Nationalism has become the only cement that holds popular political sentiment together—in Germany, Austria and also in Hungary and

* General Raoul de Boisdeffre, chief of the French General Staff and the main French architect of the Franco-Russian military alliance signed in 1894.

Rumania too, where I think that the nationalist and not the more cosmopolitan party will win an impressive victory next Sunday.* (These terms are very imprecise: I am only using them for the sake of some kind of intellectual shorthand.) That business of an economically "united" Europe is of tertiary importance now—and, I believe, for the foreseeable future. In the long run Europe may grow together—but not at all like the United States; if everything goes well, "Europe" may become for the rest of the globe what Switzerland became in Europe 150 years ago—and that, for Switzerland, had taken 600 years, I mean, its political unity. . . .

I received a book from Princeton University Press, about Dulles and the cold war, edited by someone by the name of Immerman.** I merely leafed through it and found your magnanimous words about Dulles. ("Die Hoeflichkeit des Herzens" [the courtesies of the heart], as Goethe said, is one of the highest of human qualities.) But what I read in those essays I find shallow and insubstantial. There are essential issues here that they do not address at all. And the writers' very understanding of human nature is sadly wanting. Alas, this is true of [John Lewis] Gaddis too. That Dulles' character was complex should be obvious (so were the characters of Hitler or Stalin or Genghis Khan or Groucho Marx). But complexity of thought processes and single-mindedness are not necessarily mutually exclusive; and the very fact that some of his private opinions were different from his public ones makes men like Dulles more responsible, not less. I was convinced then, and I am convinced now, that Dulles and Eisenhower were deeply, and I mean deeply responsible for the missed opportunities and the monstrous develop-ment of certain structures that they had permitted and promoted in the 1950's, the decade which (and not the imbecile 1960's) was the turning-point of American destinies, with the consequences of which we're condemned to live even now, and for years to come, alas.

---

* It did. In Hungary, while not principally "nationalist," the moderate rightist Hungarian Dem-ocratic Forum (MDF) won over the unabashedly liberal Alliance of Free Democrats–Hungarian Liberal Party (SZDSZ).

** Richard H. Immerman, ed., *John Foster Dulles and the Diplomacy of the Cold War* (1990).

G.K. to J.L.

The Institute for Advanced Study
Princeton, New Jersey
March 28, 1990
Handwritten

With respect to the Russian retreat from Eastern Europe: I am afraid I
cannot agree with you. Except in the field of military security—i.e., the
question of the military alignments and involvements of the respective countries, where the Russians have a clear defensive interest—I
cannot see them attempting—for many, many years to come, if ever—to
restore anything resembling the political control over that region which
they established in the years after W.W. II. Their traditional empire
is dissolving—the last of the great multi-national and multi-lingual
empires to do so—under the pressures of modern nationalism. They
will be lucky if they are able to preserve any substantial part of it, and
even this would probably be at the cost of much confused and bloody
conflict. No one knows what will be left when this process of disintegra-
tion has been halted—possibly only the Russian heartland; but whatever it is, it will be decades before it could enter into a serious military-
political competition for control of the eastern-European region.

But beyond that: the Russian people, as such, have no aggressive
impulses. The Russian expansion of earlier decades and centuries has
been the doing of governments, not of the people—of governments
rendered over-anxious and jittery by the very backwardness and
fragility of their own rule at home, and fearful of any weakness or lack
of order in neighboring regions that might lend itself to penetration
by other great powers. Onerous and unjust as this often was for the
peoples who fell victim to these anxieties (and this tended to be the
case with the western border peoples rather than the Asian ones), the
basic motivation was defensive. One has to remember (as many people,
these days, forget) that it was initially Hitler, not Stalin, who destroyed
most of whatever stability existed in eastern Europe in the period
between the two wars. Stalin simply took advantage of what he saw as
an existing vacuum—a disaster, to be sure, for the affected peoples, but

one arising from a profound sense of internal necessity on the part of Stalin and those around him.

Enough of that. I see serious dangers in what is now going on in that region. . . .

G.K. to J.L.

The Institute for Advanced Study
Princeton, New Jersey
April 2, 1990

First of all, let me say that if the earlier chapters have the quality of your Chapter VI and of most of what I regard (and what should, in my opinion, have been so designated) as the epilogue (beginning in the middle of p. 340), then I think I would agree with what I believe was your wife's opinion: that this is your best book*—best, not just in the profundity of some of the insights, but also in the effectiveness of its impact on the public.

Also, I find myself questioning, in the other excellent paragraph at the top of p. 342, the concept of Hitler's "hatred" of the Jews. "Hatred" is a personal, individual, relationship. When one is talking about an attitude towards great masses of people, something more complicated is involved. I doubt that Hitler, although himself, I believe, not without an admixture of Jewish blood, knew many Jews, as individuals. He resented, of course, what he considered to be their collective negative contributions to German society. But there was something deeper, as well. Being himself largely devoid of humor, he couldn't stand the highly developed and penetrating critical faculty that is the hallmark, and often the glory, of Jewish culture. Erik Erikson (then Hamburger) whom I met on a ship, coming to the U.S., in 1933, said to me, as I recall it: "Der Deutsche fürchtet den Juden in sich selbst" [The German fears the Jew within himself].

To that, too, there was no doubt a measure of truth. But none of what occurred would have taken the nightmarish forms that it did without the combination of Hitler's heartlessness, which you yourself

---

* Refers to my The Duel, 10 May–31 July 1940: The Eighty-Day Struggle Between Churchill and Hitler (Ticknor and Fields, 1991). The pages Kennan refers to are actually 240 and 241.

note, with something which Helmut Moltke, in his farewell letter to
his sons, called "the absolutely merciless consistency which is deeply
ingrained in the Germans and has found expression in the National
Socialist state."* What a marvelous insight—that word "consistency"!—
the failure to recognize the limits of all things—to recognize that the
environment of human life is not something static but something
always in motion—that we live in a world of never-ending change—
that no concept, as a phenomenon of the moment, must ever be carried
to its ultimate conclusions—that we can never know the ends, only the
means.

How a word could be found, in place of "hatred," to express all that,
I cannot say. I have to leave you with my impression.

J.L. to G.K.

5 April 1990

In your letter,** as in your past letters and even in some of our talks
before, you regard over-population as a main curse (if that is the word)
or the world today.

I am not sure about this; and, believe me, not only because of my
still strong belief in the Catholic teaching about human life. I can only
produce two arguments that are surely very different in nature and, I
fear, in their cogency. One is the relationship of populations to their
movements, to space, and to their quality in general. It is not only that
countries such as Japan or West Germany are among the most prosperous today, with a ratio of people per square mile that is 10 or 18
times greater than that of the U.S. There is the fact that in many western
European countries and cities the sense of crowdedness is less than in
other countries and cities with a much lesser density of population,
including the United States, where people tend to be improvidently
wasteful of space and land where they also have the strange inclination
of going to the same places at the same time—besides, changing their
residences, too, with astonishing and, to me, lamentable frequency.
In sum, I believe that vast—and habitable—portions of this planet

* Helmut von Moltke, prominent member of the opposition to Hitler, executed 1945.
** Not included in this book.

(consider, for example, much of the American West) are still greatly under populated, by which I do not mean that I am looking forward to their peopling. What I mean is that the crowdedness of places on this planet is largely the result of thoughtless, and often barbarous, methods of living, rather than of overpopulation per se.

My second (and perhaps unduly apocalyptic) argument against the argument of overpopulation is the sense that God must have some design in this: to plant enough human beings on this earth so that many of them would survive whatever tremendous catastrophes— now more and more potentially man-made, and not only "natural" catastrophes—might happen. But this sense is not really an argument, only a feeling: though not, I think, a feeling *entirely* resulting from mere sentiment. . . .

Something has been occurring to me that I wonder why it has not occurred to Gorbachev. Would not a solution of the Baltic problem be a Russian statement that the 1940 incorporations were illegal and now null and void, but *not* their October 1939 treaties with these states? Those were, after all, still made with the legal governments of the letter. Those treaties did not abrogate the sovereignty of the three republics, save in the sense that they had to accord their foreign policy—tacitly— with the requirements of the Russians who then could station military and naval garrisons there. Yet these limitations did not mean the expunging of all Lithuanian or Latvian or Estonian freedoms, or even sovereignties, until June–July 1940. (The Lithuanians ought to also be grateful to Moscow: had it not been for the latter, Wilno in 1939 would have remained within Poland. But that is not my point.) Stalin's brutal annexation in the summer of 1940 was a unilateral move, spurred by the then German conquest of Western Europe, and not a direct result of the August 1939 Pact or of the Secret protocol, in which the term "sphere of interest" was geographically laid out but its conditions were never defined precisely enough (as involving Finland, for example). I think Gorbachev could do worse than to offer to the three republics their October 1939 status; but, of course, that would still involve the diminution of the territory of the Soviet Union proper.

(And the *hubris* and the arrogance with which American columnists and politicians demand that Gorbachev now do our bidding in

regard to Lithuania, about which they knew—and still know—hardly
anything . . .). . . .

---

*Written in the morning after my return from Hungary where I was a witness to
and a participant in a historical milestone.*

J.L. to G.K.

5 May 1990

I hope you will not mind the length of this letter. During the last eight
days I kept thinking that there is *one* man in this entire world to whom
I *am* compelled to tell some of these things: you.

The newly and freely elected Hungarian parliament met for the first
time three days ago. I was invited to be present, because of three men I
know. I must explain this in some detail.

The first man (Monsignor Varga) is someone I may or may not
have mentioned to you in the past. (I dedicated my *Budapest 1900* book
to him; those few words on the dedication page might give you some
impression of him.) A summary of his biography is on the top of the
English translation of his speech which I enclose. I have known him for
47 years. (I have been a member of his party, the Small Holders, in my
youth.) He is now in the 89th year of his life, afflicted with Parkinson's
disease. He was chairman of a Hungarian National Committee in New
York, an exile grouping, from the time of his escape from Hungary in
1947 until about 1960. (This was not something like that silly "Captive
Nations" stuff, though it was surely financed by the CIA.) He has been
living in a tiny room in a convent in New York. We have become very
close during the last 25 years. Since he was the last Chairman of the last
freely elected Hungarian National Assembly, the present interim President of Hungary and the coming Prime Minister invited him to return
to the opening of the new Parliament. He hesitated for a long time,
and not only because of his health. We had innumerable conversations
about this between New York and Phoenixville, over the telephone.
He said that he would only go if they were to ask him to say something, and perhaps not even then. *But*: both he and I knew that some

things *had* to be said. He asked me to write his speech. He was not sure whether he would go and deliver it in person. In the end—nine days before our departure—he decided to go. He insisted that I go with him. We left a week ago today.

The second man (G. [Géza] Jeszenszky) is a Hungarian historian, now 48 or 50. I met him during my first or second return trip to Hungary, about 18 years ago. I helped him with his first serious book in diplomatic history. We are friends; he visited this country often since. He will be the new Foreign Minister.

The third man (J. [József] Antall) I have known for many years too. He is the uncle of Jeszenszky's wife. His father, then an Undersecretary of the Interior, was a close associate of Msgr. Varga during the war. Antall will be the new Prime Minister.

Apart from these people very few know that I have had anything to do with Msgr. Varga's speech.

We left New York in 90-degree heat. The old priest bore the burdens of the trip fairly well. We paid the plane fare ourselves, not wishing to rely on the hospitality of the government in Budapest. But when we landed, on a bright and windy morning, the government—old and new, including Antall and Msgr. Varga's sister, in her eighties, were there on the airport asphalt, with flowers. I kept back, fighting my tears. Then we were driven to a kind of Government House (in the Buda hills, not far from where my grandparents' summer villa had been.) There we were lodged very comfortably. Msgr. Varga returns eight days from now. I could only stay for five days.

Now I come to the gist of this long-winded letter. The newly elected Parliament assembled in the morning of 2 May. I had expected to be inspired; but not moved in the way I was. Even now my mind is full with my thoughts and memories of that day. You will know that my native country has a long (though often compromised) parliamentary tradition, older and more deeply rooted than that of any other Central-Eastern European country, including Czechoslovakia. I know the Parliament building in Budapest well. (For a few months I even worked there, in 1945.) 45 years later I was in charge of the preparations for my old friend's arrival, the difficulties of getting him to the rostrum, the length of his speech, &c. About the latter he and I were subjected to many pressures, some political, some personal. I shan't detail them. Until our cortège of cars pulled up at Gate VI of Parliament Building, all of my thoughts and anxieties concerned those practical details. I was partly oblivious to the superb weather that early morning, with a radiant young sun bathing the streets and the trees in green and gold. (Many people remarked later the symbolism of that beautiful day, full of promises, atmospherically and historically.) Then we entered the great building. The day before, when I had gone through the interior routing and sitting arrangements, I was impressed with the excellent quality of its refurbishment. I was moved by the sight of those corridors, historically known to me, with such things as the intaglioed panels and the heavy brass cigarette- and cigar-ashtrays set into the windowsills for the Hon. Members, 1900-style. And now, on Wednesday morning, 2 May 1990, it was 1900 again, with that crowd of new elected Members and officials milling around in those corridors. Or, to be more precise: there was a faint but, for me, deeply inhaleable aroma of historical continuity. That aroma evoked more than nostalgia; it carried a small, but vital, sense of promise.

I think you know how aware I am of the great weaknesses of Hungarian political rhetoric, and of the many trespasses against both decorum and reason in that parliament at the high noon of Budapest's fortunes, circa 1900. Yes: plus ça change, plus c'est la même chose. Almost. But not quite. The solemn session began with the national anthem, the somberest national anthem of any country I know. Then an actor ascended the lower rostrum and read the poem of the romantic and tragic national poet [Sándor] Petőfi, written in 1848, "To the National Assembly." It is a bad poem, and the actor declaimed it in the traditional (and, to me, quite irritating) Hungarian declamatory manner, his voice rising and falling to excessive extremes of proclamatory and sentimental emphases. Then my friend the old priest, leaning on his cane, with his hands trembling, moved up the eight steps of the rostrum, assisted by a Hungarian-American friend of ours, who did his best (as well as his worst) to emphasize his association and *his* close friendship with Monsignor Varga; but that did not matter.

I was not an important guest. I had expected (and hoped) to get a seat in one of the galleries. But I was pleased to find that I had a reserved seat in one of the ceremonial boxes on the Parliament floor (next to Walburga Habsburg, Otto's daughter, who was there, too, in his capacity as member of the European Parliament). And now I was a witness, as well as a participant, of a great historical occasion.

I now had an experience that I do not remember having ever had before. I was listening to my words, to my sentences, to my phrases, thoughts, ideas—pronounced by someone else, a very dear old friend. This was something very different from hearing oneself on a tape or on the radio, or even hearing oneself quoted. I am always uneasy about those things. They seem artificial; they are secondary. But now this meant something that was both important and true—in the sense that some things were being said that had to be said. It was not the historic setting that made it important. It was the opportunity, at this particular time and in this particular place, to have done so. And now it was done. My old friend cut it somewhat short. His voice was strong and clear; but he did hurry through the end of a few sentences, having been told that his speech must be short. (Wrongly so.) But, all in all, it went very well. He ended it less than 8 minutes after he had begun. There was a hush; and then a standing ovation.

This was followed by two other speeches. One (following tradition) by the oldest elected Member, a former general (aged 89), and then by another Member of the Small Holders' Party who too had been in the 1945–47 Parliament as its official secretary then. Both speeches were too long and somewhat self-indulgent. Then there was a 60-minute inter-mission, and a reception in the sunlit large presidential chambers above the Danube. I met a few of my friends. Monsignor Varga was tired. We left together, driving back to the Government House.

The Parliament went on with its sessions till mid-afternoon. We had been invited to a midday luncheon and to another reception by the Parliament but we both declined. It was a sunny, an incredibly clear and beautiful day.

I was very pleased to read the Hungarian papers next morning. Every one of them emphasized Msgr. Varga's speech, reporting it in greater detail than the speeches of the others, even though the length of his speech was a fraction of the latter. They also cited what I thought were the more important portions. The "Frankfurter Allgemeine" (which I think is now the best daily paper in the world) ran two very good articles on the opening of the Parliament, one of which was largely devoted to Msgr. Varga. I am enclosing a xerox of it (it is brief.) The "New York Times" did not send a reporter. Miss Bohlen was not in Budapest. Another Times correspondent wrote a brief and indifferent report about the day. (I think I know why. The "Times" editors seem to have concluded that the new Hungary shows anti-Semitic tendencies. The latter do exist; but the "Times" and their crowd see the whole matter wrongly.) I think (and not because of my participation) that the occasion, and the speech, deserved much more attention in the United States than what it got. (It hardly got any.) But I am not complaining about this. It does not matter much. I am mentioning this to you only because it is a symptom.

I am not a public relations person or a press agent. Before I left home I ran off a few copies on the xerox machine in my stepson's office in Phoenixville. I also made a hasty and unpolished English translation, a mere first draft. But I am enclosing it for you. You will see what Msgr. Varga (and I) meant to achieve by it. I am very desirous to hear your opinion.

(Some of the sentences, including the one about Gorbachev, evoked especial interest & were cited in every one of the newspapers. That was good, I think.)

The Cardinal Primate of Hungary invited Msgr. Varga and myself but I could not go to see him, even though it would have meant much to me. I flew home yesterday morning. Msgr. Varga went to visit the village of his birth, and his parents' graves yesterday. On Monday he visits his former parish in the country where he is now their honorary citizen. He comes back to New York in a week's time. I pray and hope that his health withstand all this strain. He has hardly left his room in that convent during the last years, and he walks with difficulty.

*****

Now I wish to tell you (1) two important matters that continue to impress me deeply; (2) a sort of shorthand summary of my views of the prospects & situation in Hungary.

I see this time as bright and promising for my native country, full of difficulties but also when, despite insufficient signs of political maturity, a fair amount optimism seems to be warranted. *At the same time* I am deeply—very deeply—worried that this sunshine may be transitory. I do not mean the internal Hungarian situation but the enormous storm gathering over the Russian empire. It is not that the Russians would reenter Hungary. It is that the chaos during the collapse of a great empire brings consequences that are incalculable. In sum: beyond the Hungarian sunshine I see the blackest of clouds gathering on the eastern horizon. How will they affect my native country—and the world? I cannot tell.

And now about my adopted country. I landed at Kennedy airport in New York. (Before that, on the plane, I read the column of that unspeakable [William] Safire, comparing the Lithuanian business with 1776: an impertinence without equal.) And once I landed I found myself struggling through one horrible scene after another. A stench of evil was weighing me down. The stench was not physical; it was spiritual, even as its components were visual and audible. The greed, the jostling, the inhuman indifference, the crude hostility of people in New York is not new. But all of this has now brought results that in the past in this country did not exist: the breakdown of functioning institutions and processes, a widespread incompetence, and the helplessness of anyone who does not have enough money to secure the most expensive arrangements for his private comforts and transportation. (I had enough money, if needed.) I had to get a taxi and drove into Manhattan with a sinking—no, a sunken—heart. A Calcutta of the North is no longer an apposite phrase to describe those myriads of lights falsely masking an urban presence of omnipresent sin, peopled by men and women (and, alas, children) whose better impulses hardly exist now, as they are ruled by the barbarian impulses of their manners and of their minds—a new kind of barbarism without precedent.

In sum, I returned from my native country and city where I had not expected to live to see a democracy, with some of its real promises, during my lifetime—to a city and, I fear, a country where democracy may have entered its most dangerous and degenerate phase. I was proud—unusually proud—about my native country; I was sad— unusually sad—about my adopted one. All of this may be, and probably is, exaggerated. I do not even know why I am foisting these sentiments on you now. But I also think of Tocqueville who wrote that from now on the choice is only between two kinds of democracies: a more or less orderly, though perhaps enduringly mediocre one, and another one increasingly ruled by greed, chaos, and decay. (Still, *pace* La Rochefoucauld: things are never as good—or bad—as they seem.)

Now back to Hungary for a last time.

Positives: A very strong (though often uninstructed) respect for tradition which, for the first time, involves even the lower (?) classes, amounting to something that is considerably more than nostalgia.

An impressive portion of intelligent, irreverent, and realistic youth.

A general and widespread wish to be part of "Europe," which is more than a reaction to the last 40-odd years, even though few people really know what "Europe" now means or could mean.

Many honest impulses, reaching beyond selfish ambitions—in politics. A general absence of emotional hatred of Russians.

The reemergence of a sharp and sardonic sense of humor, including that inevitable element of self-knowledge. These things in the past were restricted to the urbane bourgeoisie and aristocracy, and to the Jewish intelligentsia; but now they have spread to segments of the population formerly untouched, indifferent, or insensitive to it.

A very widespread respect for all kinds of cultural and artistic manifestations.

The national (and especially Budapestian) ability of skating rather ably on thin economic ice.

The persistence of an unusually deep inclination to pessimism *together* with instantly recurring thrusts of a personal joie de vivre.

Negatives: The old, bad compound of thickskinnedness and thinskinnedness on the part of many politicians, carried forward by their personal animosities.

Not much interest in the Church (including indifference to the person of the excellent Cardinal-Primate)—at the same time a burgeoning of pornography, etc.

The strong persistence of nationalist and populist rhetoric, including populist anti-Semitism and the suspicious ignorance of non-Hungarian cultures. Most of this is motivated by envy. (Also, much of the anti-Semitism is now unwarranted.)

The nationalist and ideological rhetorical habit: on the second day of the Parliament, a long and fairly quarrelsome debate about the text of a declaration supporting Lithuania. (When I said, even to intelligent people, that with all of our sympathy for Lithuania, is this really our business, *now*? I was met with amazement—though not with hostility.)

Much of this very much evident in the last elections and in the bitter quarrels between the now two leading political parties. (At the same time they did make a good compromise about the future President of the Republic and the Chairman of the Parliament.)

The wanting education and intelligence among members of the new ruling party (43% of the votes, able to construct a majority through a coalition with two, similar and populist parties). The only exceptions seem to be its two, well-educated leaders: the Prime Minister, whom I know, not devoid of abilities, but still a politician and not a statesman; the putative Foreign Minister, a v. close friend, a history professor, but entirely devoid of *any* kind of administrative ability.

His choices of the future ambassadors are very mixed, including some of his friends who are not suited to such posts.

The overwhelming unwillingness of their party to avail themselves of the demonstrated talents and capacities of officials of the former regime, the merits of which include their having guided the country through this transition without much trouble, let alone bloodshed.

Their unawareness of the long-range prospects of rapidly increasing German economic and political influences, in sum: the prevalence of many of the Hungarian non-political and non-diplomatic mistaken inclinations of the past—and yet together with the prevalence of the, at times astonishing, non-political talents of this small nation.

Will you ever forgive me for this long effusion of a letter?

This is Kennan's early warning against the disastrous policy of later American governments—of Bill Clinton as well as of George Bush—to extend the American alliance system, including NATO, into Eastern Europe, up to the very borders of a diminished Russia.

G.K. to J.L.

The Institute for Advanced Study
Princeton, New Jersey
Remarks for Milwaukee Forum
May 12, 1990

I would like to say that it never pays, in my opinion, for one great power to take advantage of the momentary weakness or distraction of another great power in order to force upon it concessions it would never have accepted in normal circumstances. In the short term this may seem to have advantages. Over the long run it almost always revenges itself. The Russians are justly proud of their great war effort; and they will expect to see due recognition given to it in the dispositions that are under discussion today.

G.K. to J.L.

The Institute for Advanced Study
Princeton, New Jersey
May 18, 1990

I was deeply moved by your letter of the 5th (which only yesterday did I have opportunity to see) and by Msgr. Varga's great and moving address to the new Hungarian parliament—an address with which you had so much to do and in which your spirit and thoughts were so intimately reflected. I can well imagine (for, whatever my other faults, I am not lacking in sensitivity or imagination) what this occasion must have meant to you: surely one of the greatest, perhaps the greatest, of the days of your life to this point. And a day, it seems to me, in which, as though by the workings of some unseen hand, all that you had experienced, and learned, and suffered, during your youth in Hungary and the decades of exile that followed, found a form of expression, justification and purpose they could have found in no other way. Who else but you, after all, could have rendered this service at the time you did and in the manner you did—a service all the finer for the reticence with which it was offered: without ostentation, for the sake not of effect but of what was really at stake? Few have such an opportunity in life.

I could also imagine that this great experience might be unsettling for you as you face your further life here. You life here as a teacher and an untiring but inadequately appreciated writer and historian, has offered, I am afraid, no comparable satisfactions and excitements. And it would not surprise me if the question were to arise in your mind: if I, albeit in a quiet way, could be so much to my native country in one of its great historic moments, could I not be more to it in other times? And does my usefulness not lie in that direction, rather than in Phoenixville?

I would strongly urge against any such an effort to out-guess Providence. Two years ago you could not have anticipated the momentous day we are talking about. The forces that led you to it were not of your conscious shaping. Has not Providence earned a certain margin of respect? Take your time. Do your duty, for the moment, as you find it. If Providence wants you to do a further service of real value, I am sure it will lead you to it, as it did to this one.

Your letter, both as an account of this historic occasion and as an analysis of the strengths and weaknesses of the Hungarian people as they confront this new challenge in their national life, is a remarkable document. I can understand that it was hastily written, and you might want to polish it up. But I hope it will at some time, and in some way, find its way into the Hungarian state archives; for there was no more sensitive, more informed, or more qualified witness to that occasion than yourself, and none whose reaction to it rested on a deeper and broader foundation of historical understanding.

I could not help bur reflect, as I read what you wrote, that while those who remained at home in Hungary over all these difficult years no doubt learned certain things and gained certain forms of strength from the experience, there were also ways in which their situation retarded their understanding of themselves, of their history, and of the modern age. In the case of those of you who were in the emigration, the situation was just the opposite. Life was less harrowing, of course, and physically easier; but in other ways it was, perhaps, psychically even harder; and in any case you could swim in the currents of free expression and discussion of world problems—currents that had certain useful things, if not always pleasant ones, to teach. This being the case, you now come to them knowing certain things, and understanding certain things, they know and understand, if at all, only imperfectly. Thus you (and by this I mean: you, the exiles) have a certain gap to fill in their development—certain aspects of strength, the products of your own experience, to impart to them. Let none of them, consumed as so many of them are with what I think of as the "snobbishness of the oppressed" (the assumption that no one who was not with them could understand how they suffered or what it meant to suffer at all), try to tell you differently. It is not their fault if they are, after this long experience of foreign rule, in some respects deprived. But they should recognize it, and learn where they can.

As for the rest: I think I understand all that you say about Hungary. It all speaks to me. I admire the balance and discernment it reflects. Yes, of course: your Hungarians are in every way a talented people—talented, unfortunately, beyond their geographic and material resources. For this reason they will be not be able to find within themselves and within their own boundaries the outlets they need for their talents and their creativity, not to mention their economic prosperity. For all this they will need a wider field of activity; and for this reason I was glad to read what you said about the widespread wish to be part of Europe. There will have to be, for them, a certain diaspora, and one that can be lived in, let us hope, as it has for you, without loss of affection or identification with the homeland in the wider cultural sense. But they will have to guard against the tendency, to which others have fallen prey who had exotic languages, formidable talents, and extensive diasporas, to become a sort of conspiracy—a secret society—to themselves. Talent, in other words, demands of those who possess it a certain *noblesse oblige*, to which the Hungarians, so long locked up by themselves, will now perhaps be unaccustomed. And, if they are to express themselves fully in their new role as "something outside themselves," they will have to overcome the nationalistic and populist rhetoric, the refusal to compromise, and the quarrelsome exhibitionism that have (or so I understand) so often marred their own parliamentary life, and find a more relaxed and good-humored acceptance of the imperfections and absurdities that have been a characteristic of politics everywhere and it all times in human history.

And if, as is alleged (and I fear with some truth), a goodly number of Hungarians are inclined to a species of self-serving anti-Semitism (a silly and unworthy inclination, involving as it does sweeping generalizations about entire peoples—always a mistake), then let them eradicate these feelings by overcoming in themselves those qualities by which they fancy the Jews to be disfavored. They will find, I think, that helps.

So much, then, about Hungary. I was also struck, of course, by the shock you received from your taxi-ride from Kennedy Airport into Manhattan, upon your return. I have little quarrel with your observations. What you saw there, of course, a shameful and dreadful spectacle. I must tell you, though, that I have just spent four days in Milwaukee, the place of my birth and boyhood, being honored (and exploited) as one of its native sons. And I came away with the impression that there are still values—elements of strength and even of propriety—cultivated in that part of the country, the existence of which the traveller arriving in New York would never suspect.

J.L. to G.K.

20 August 1990

About Eastern Europe; good God: your caveats *re* Timothy Garton Ash's sympathetic and intelligent but so often Pollyannaish estimates are coming true, here and there.* Hungary is better off than the others; but I will (when I see him) tell my close friend, the new Foreign Minister (a historian) that he should be very careful *not* to commit Hungarian sympathies on the side of Slovak and Croat nationalism. . . .**

---

*Ash's optimistic but also illusory portrait of an Eastern Europe entering something like a golden age of liberal freedoms. Ash was one of the most visible commentators on postcommunist Europe.

** Of course I failed.

G.K. to J.L.

North Haven, Maine
September 5, 1990
Handwritten

The piece in the Harper's* is superb (all except perhaps the title
and subtitle, but titles are normally an evil), and not just because it
expresses a number of insights I thought were mine alone. Bravo—for
the recognition that the Russian retreat from Eastern Europe began
soon after 1945, and there are others.

Only a quibble. Stalin, you say, preferred communists in Eastern
Europe. He preferred a certain type of person, the morally corrupted,
politically compromised police official, ostensibly a communist—but
in whom corruption and abject dependence, not communism, were
for Stalin the most important qualifications. [Boleslaw] Bierut, the
first Stalinist head of Poland, was quite unknown in Poland but had, I
believe, been for eight years chief of the Polish section of the N.K.V.D.
[Soviet secret police] in Moscow. He was a helpless stooge—a tool in
Stalin's cynical hands. His ideological commitments (if indeed he had
any), were decidedly secondary in his value to Stalin. . . .

G.K. to J.L.

Institute for Advanced Study
Princeton, New Jersey
November 1990

I have now completed the reading of *The Duel*. It is, as you can imagine,
history after my own heart. The epilogue is magnificent—a document
of major importance in itself. But the book as a whole gives the sort of
insight that no one else has given to what was going on in the minds of
the two greatest participants in the determining crisis of the Second
World War.

---

* Refers to my article "The Stirrings of History: A New World Rises from the Ruins of Empire,"
Harper's (August 1990).

I see the book as of particular historical importance in two respects. The first: in making it clear to an Anglo-American readership that Hitler was everything else but the silly mountebank many western writers and others (Charlie Chaplin among them) have made him out to be. Of course, one part of his emotional makeup was psychotic (the same, though of course in a different way, was true of Stalin); but beyond that Hitler was no inconsiderable personality. He had resolution, and the courage of his convictions. He never shrank from bold action where the possibility presented itself. He had insights and instincts. There was much that was justified in his contempt for the weary indecisive liberalism of the democracies in the inter-war period. He was not entirely lacking in the qualities of statesmanship. And in some ways (perhaps because he had no liberal inhibitions) he had a sense for the needs and the weaknesses of the times that few others had. (Witness: how much, even if most of it is what I personally dislike, we owe to his innovation: the superhighways, the cruise-ships, the Gesell-schaftsreisen [group travel], the techniques of mass-manipulation, etc.)

But the second point that stood out for me from the book was the revelation of the fragility of mass opinion, even in England, in the face of the challenges of the initial war period: how close many people were to opting for what appeared to be the easier road of collabora-tion: how dependent they were on resolute leadership—how helpless they would have been without it. One gets the impression from much of the existing literature on that period that the British public by which Churchill was confronted when he took over the government was one already committed to the sort of heroic defiance of Hitler's challenge that marked his own attitude. You have, as I see it, shown how little that was true—how essential was Churchill's role in arousing that spirit of resistance by his own words and example. That says something to me—something about the need for strong moral and political leader-ship even in the democracy—which the American enthusiasts for the supposed great wisdom of the electorate would do well to ponder.

First mention of the book summing up his political philosophy—eventually published as Around the Cragged Hill: A Personal and Political Philosophy *(Norton, 1993)—which I had counseled him not to write.*

G.K. to J.L.

Institute for Advanced Study
Princeton, New Jersey
March 15, 1991

I, here, have persisted in the painful and, very possibly, misconceived effort to set forth something in the nature of a personal and political philosophy. I know you did not take kindly to the suggestion of such an effort. I will not deny the possibility that you were right in your skepticism about it. The effort is hard for me. I do not enjoy it. I don't know what will really come out of it (and will not know, it occurs to me, until I get your judgement of it). I do not know whether it will even be publishable. Perhaps it will have to repose in my papers, for the edification of the biographer. But I feel that the very effort, if not pleasant, is good for me. And there begins to emerge from it something in the way of an understanding on my own part of the deeper sources of my differences with the conventional thinking of our time. You touched on them, in your letter, with the reference to what you called the "populist democracy"; and I am grateful to you for the phrase. The task of the populace is to select, through proper electoral procedures, its own rulers; God forbid that it should ever itself attempt to rule.

J.L. to G.K.

Budapest
30 March 1991

In medias res. I am heartened and more than pleased, with what you write about the writing progress of your personal/political philosophy. I was (and, to a lesser extent, I perhaps still am skeptical). Not about its value (and I mean the personal validity of the effort itself as well as its *ultimate* value) but about its reception by people who, due to the insufficiency of their culture and character, might misunderstand you. It now occurs to me—and I have been thinking about it ever since your letter came—that you may give some thought in writing this "Summa" in a *terse*, and perhaps not only necessarily brief but consciously unconnected (if that is the right word) manner. By this I mean that the rich plethora of your thoughts and ideas—always resting on a lifetime of serious thinking, that is philosophical in a tangible and historical but not at all abstract manner—*might* have its greatest impact in the form of crystallized and perhaps short (though not always) paragraphs. These, unlike a philosophical narrative, might appeal not only to such people whose attention-span is nowadays, only too limited; but the sharp and clear summary of your thoughts may be more liable to produce the sparks of recognition that would be of greatest value for them and the most lasting result of your endeavor. Added to this is the condition of your mind which is not only clear but—Deo gratias—at your present age, too, unusually rapid; the practical consequence of this might be that you would draft these various seminal paragraphs or short pages as they occur to you, and when most or all of them are written, you may then with relative ease arrange them and separate them under various headings. . . .

G.K. to J.L.

Kristiansand, Norway
May 22, 1991
Handwritten

As of today, in any case, I am not ashamed of what I have done. And if it gets published as it is, so be it. But the Russians have, for this sort of thing, one of their terse and telling phrases: "Nye to," meaning: "Not quite what it was meant to be, or should have been," "Nicht vollkommen geglückt" [not entirely successful] in German. I should, in other words, have done better. But it was a first attempt. And there we are. . . .

J.L. to G.K.

Budapest
28 May 1991

What you write (and what you think) about this unexpected little
chapter of my life here is exactly on the mark.* I could tell you very
many things about it—and without being unduly self-indulgent, I
must say that so much of it involves my own "Selbstbewusstsein" [self-
consciousness]. After 45+ years in the U.S., I belong here as much as I
belong to Pennsylvania (and this is perhaps a new discovery)—while at
the same time my *home* is in Pennsylvania; and that "home" is not transitory, for two very different reasons. One is my family—my greatest
blessing, my wife and my children, with whom I have succeeded in
establishing a now fairly old-fashioned kind of existence. The other
reason is that I am an *English* writing and speaking writer. This has
nothing to do with my academic career, and it is not vitiated by the
condition that my usage of my native language is, I believe, flawless. But
I *must* live in an English-speaking country, at least for the major part of
my life. . . .

G.K. to J.L.

Kristiansand, Norway
June 16, 1991
Handwritten

This letter will find you, I trust, at home again in Pennsylvania and I
hope that even the heat of the east-coast summer does not deprive you
of the pleasures of returning after a long absence, to the principal home
(which is as one of my daughters once told me, "the place where, if you
come there, they've got to let you in") . . .

   I have interspersed that work with a careful reading of the *second*
part of Tocqueville's *De la démocratie en Amérique* [*Democracy in
America*]. This part, as I am sure you know, was written and appeared

* I was a visiting professor in two universities in Budapest from January to June 1991, having
rented an apartment there for those months.

five years after the first part, and has generally, I believe, been much less widely read than the first. (I myself had not read it before.) It was not nearly, in my opinion, as valuable a work as was the first part; and this, precisely because (and this is why it has interested me at this time) Tocqueville endeavored to set forth here numbers of theoretical considerations drawn largely from his observations in America, but not entirely from that source; and so intended to bring out conclusions of universal validity on the subject that so greatly interested and absorbed him. . .

The subject that interested Tocqueville so intensely—the effects of the egalitarian spirit on all aspects of the life of a society—will not, of course, go unnoticed in what I am writing. I feel no less strongly about its danger than did he. But I think I am more aware than was he (after all, I have another 150 years of historical evidence on which to base my judgments!) of the many other causal factors that have entered into the development of American society, and it would be shameful if I did not take a wider view of the subject. So I go on scratching out a paragraph now and then, as the spirit moves and as the business of life in a cottage on the Norwegian coast permits, and will try to put it altogether when I get home.

As for the Norway I see all around me: I view it in some ways with respect and affection, but in other ways with misgivings and head-shaking which would be shared, I fear, by very few others. As perhaps the most wildly egalitarian of all advanced societies, Norway seems to me (perhaps because it is a smaller society and one with a shallow national experience and in an earlier stage of modern development) to bear a greater resemblance to what Tocqueville saw and feared in the United States of the 1830's than does the United States of today. The Norwegians are a relatively unspoiled people with many positive poten-tialities, but the combination of modern technology with an almost frantic egalitarianism (and incidentally secularism), is not, I fear, one that will do them much good. . . .

This letter is an answer to Kennan's ideas about two kinds of nationalism.

J.L. to G.K.

29 August 1991

This is a major point that I think deserves your serious consideration.

Your distinction between the two kinds of nationalism is very important. Your description of the "normal nationalist" is splendid (because, *après tout*, you are writing about *yourself* here . . .). But: "normal" and "not normal" nationalism are not clear or good distinctions. (I am leaving aside the argument that the human propensity for evil is not abnormal—cf. my treatment of Hitler, etc.) There is nothing wrong with the succinct elaboration of your argument. What is at stake here is nothing else but the proper phraseology. You yourself grapple with this when on ms. p. 21 (or 25) you revert to the word *chauvinist*— a hobbling and outdated term (as you see it, too: line 2, p. 21). I am unhappy, too, with your term of "romantic nationalist"—even though *I* know what you mean; but consider, too, how romanticism is individualist whereas the kind of wrong nationalism you describe is not.

The splendid and moving description of the proper kind of nationalism (pp. 19–20) describes a *patriot*. Please consider that there is more to this than my inclination to prefer *my* phraseology. The proper distinction is between *patriotism* and *nationalism*. These two terms have become, regrettably, confused—when Americans speak of a super-patriot they really mean a super nationalist—and this is exactly why you should separate them. I am loath to refer to, or to repeat what I have written about this subject before; but you will find an important—important only for the purpose of these comments—summation of them in a footnote of my last book that I enclose. (I have many other passages relating to this distinction; I shall not burden you with them. There is an excellent essay by Orwell on Patriotism vs. Nationalism in his *Collected Essays*, easy to retrieve, written some time around 1943, I think.)

To this I must add another important element (rarely, if ever, noticed by writers about nationalism). "Let us call it, simply, love of country"—as you put it. Bravo! (I almost wrote: "Hurrah!") That is exactly what it is. *But*: that patriotic love (which, after all, does have a romantic element) is quite different from nationalism which means a love of that mythical entity thought of as "the people." Hitler himself said on one occasion: "Im Anfang was das *Volk*. Nur dann kam *der Staat*" ["In the beginning was the *Volk*. Only then came the *State*"]. He (in this respect differing from Mussolini) subordinated *Staat* to *Volk*— or, as you write, love of country to "people"—which continues to be the mark of nationalists, especially in Eastern Europe; exclusionary, too, as that is. Among other things, populist nationalism is *suspicious* of all other people within the same country who do not seem to agree with some of their populist and nationalist ideology. Hence they assign them to the status of minorities—suggesting, and at times emphasizing—that such minorities do not and cannot belong to the authentic body of the national people. You may consider whether to include this factor in any of your paragraphs on pp. 20–24, or add another paragraph about it to the existing ones. . . .

G.K. to J.L.

Institute for Advanced Study
September 13, 1991

I naturally appreciated particularly what you had to say about the X article.* Had I known the enormous attention it was destined to receive, there were things in it that I would have worded differently than I did, and some things then not in it that I would have included. It was of course a statement evoked by the agony of confrontation with the Stalinist regime of the preceding twelve years (i.e., before 1946) in all its dark sly evil and hideousness. And it was meant as a warning to those who thought that the Stalin Regime had to be confronted either by political indulgence or by war. I still look back without remorse on some of the key passages of it. Particularly the statement that "if anything were ever to occur to disrupt the unity and efficacy of the Party as a political instrument, Soviet Russia might be changed over-night from one of the strongest to one of the weakest and most piti-able of national societies." But I do think that the second article of this nature, entitled "America and the Russian Future" and published in *Foreign Affairs*, in April 1951, while it met with much less understanding

---

* In a letter about the circumstances of 1947 and "containment."

on the part of the press and the public, was the deeper and better of the
two articles.

I agree strongly with all your concerns about the peoples now
separating themselves from the traditional Tsarist-Soviet center—the
Ukrainians, the Georgians, and Armenians and even the Baltic nationalists. Having lived for three years in those Baltic countries (of which
Estonia was by far the best), I am not moved to idealize any of them.
Their one-time German-Baltic masters of the Tsarist period, whom
they treated so badly in their years of independence, were more than a
cut above them culturally, and were the teachers for a great deal of what
they learned. Between ourselves, there were days during our residence
in Latvia in 1932 and 1933, when I could long back for the earlier, and
relatively moderate Tsarist presence, and for the contribution it made to
their economic life and their education. Well, now they must try again
to make it on their own; and that, in the circumstances, is undoubtedly
all for the best.

As for your criticisms of the pages I sent you, you have revenged
yourself in a worthy way for those that I sent you in connection with
your recent article. I have gone over them carefully and have, I think,
taken most of them into account. The most important of them was
the question of the use of the terms patriotism and nationalism. I have
thought much about this and have consulted various dictionaries. The
question is not a simple one, for most of the dictionaries seem to give
both meanings to both of the terms—nationalism and patriotism. They
see each of them as having been variously used, at different times and
by different people, to convey what you meant by patriotism or what
I meant by normal nationalism. But I think you were more right than
I was; and I am introducing the word patriotism to describe what I
regard as moderate and proper national feeling, and I have referred to
the other extreme as the "pathological" form of nationalism. I am still
struggling over this, and hope that with your help I shall get it right in
the end. As for the rest of your comments, you will see when the book
finally appears, what use has been made of them. In short, I am very
grateful for the help. . .

I entered on this task, some months ago, light-heartedly and rather
casually. The farther I go with it the more sobered and impressed with

what I have taken upon myself. You may recall that in the first passages of my memoirs I assessed my own intellect as a reasonably lucid and open one, "lazy and passive when left to itself but capable of vigorous reaction when challenged." I find that in undertaking this book I created a far greater challenge for myself than I realized at the time. And I am now taking it much more seriously, and letting it take much more out of me. But I have the feeling that, if it is done as it should be done, it could and would constitute my most important and lasting contribution to the thinking of the people of my time (and I would hope, of not my time alone) on some of the weightier problems of what you have properly recognized as the Twenty-First Century into which we are now moving. Let me thank you for the contribution you have made, in your works, your friendship, and your criticism, to the accomplishment of this task. If I do not complete it properly, the fault will not be yours.

J.L. to G.K.

19 September 1991

I was sent a review copy of Robert Conquest's new biography of Stalin.* I am appalled by its shoddy nature. I respect Conquest, and I think that his book on the great purges was an important and valuable undertaking. But this book is not only full of mistakes; his understanding of diplomatic history (if that is the term) of those times is badly missing; yes, he understands something about Stalin's Georgian-bandit background and that side of his character; but he attributes most of his acts, and crimes, to the notion that Stalin was an extreme revolutionary dogmatist, that Marxism "was obviously well-tailored to Stalin's own personality." And this stupid nonsense from one of the better "experts."

Buckley gloats in the last number of his magazine: "We won!" "We won!" He repeats that all over again, etc. etc.

The kind of people [the so-called neocons] such as the Rosenberg couple (the atomic secret people) in 1945 are today avid followers of Rosenthal and Safire in the *N.Y. Times*, and readers of *Commentary* (and of *National Review* perhaps). Deceiving themselves, as did the

---

Stalin: Breaker of Nations (Viking, 1991)

Rosenbergs in 1945 and thereabouts, with evil consequences that may befall them. . . .

J.L. to G.K.

13 April 1992

Thank you for the volume of the Johnson Letters . . .*

Differences from the Johnson letters. (1) Yours must not necessarily be a posthumous publication—though one cannot altogether disregard the prospect of such a melancholy eventuality. (2) One day this edition of Samuel Johnson's Letters will be entirely complete. Yours cannot be. (3) The annotations of the Johnson volume refer mostly to manuscripts and varia. The annotations and the references of the Kennan L& D must refer to places, events and people. Please take a look at the first volume of Harold Nicolson's *Diaries and Letters,* because of their referential and annotative formula—not because of their contents which are very different from your D&L, since the Nicolson D&L are almost exclusively political and social. (4) While the Johnson Letters have only a brief and referential Introduction, I would prefer the Kennan D&L to have a substantial introduction, dealing not only with the origin of those papers but an introduction in which—I at least—should like to point out and emphasize *the consistency* of your philosophical and moral principles throughout your life—an argument which, in my opinion, has not been adequately made by your commentators and previous biographers, no matter how sympathetic, mostly because of their concentration on your political positions and advocacies. (5) The Index of your D&L must be compiled by an exceptionally able indexer, since even more important than the entries of names and places must be the *thematic* entries in the index. (Example: GK: on evil in human nature, pp.......; on extremism, pp........&c. & c...)

---

* Kennan gave me a copy of *The Letters of Samuel Johnson* (Hyde edition, Princeton University Press, 1992) vol. 1, *1731–1772,* with many of Kennan's markings. I was coming back again to my plan of collecting, collating, editing an eventual selection of Kennan's diaries and letters.

I had been invited, amid an array of impressive political figures and scholars, to a festive conference in Bonn, given by the German government on the 25th anniversary of Chancellor Konrad Adenauer's death. I had prepared and read a short paper, praising Adenauer but also referring to Soviet (particularly Stalin's 1952) propositions for an eventually unified Germany, suggesting a potential withdrawal of occupying armies. I sent Kennan the text of my paper (which was later printed in a German summary of the conference) that I could not find in his personal library much later. This is a rare example of a missing item of my nearly 100 percent complete bibliography of all my published books, articles, reviews, etc. in Remembered Past: John Lukacs on History, Historians, and Historical Knowledge: A Reader *(ISI Books, 2004).*

G.K. to J.L.

Institute for Advanced Study
Princeton, New Jersey
May 6, 1992

I lie here, momentarily (but not seriously) prostrated by my heart problems. And I have whiled away some of these moments by reading your German lecture. Let me say at once that I found it very impressive. Properly edited and given greater fluency of style (again, dear John, as I have said to you before: less density; remember that your readers need to be led along gently), the paper deserves prominent publication both here and in Germany, but particularly in Germany. Many Germans, as you know, have a hard time with the questions you have discussed. I doubt that any of them could have perceived or written what you did. Thus they need your help.

What you wrote has caused me to glance back critically at the positions I took in those early postwar years, but particularly in the Reith Lectures of 1957. These latter aroused, as you know, Adenauer's deepest and most indignant rejection. Yet I share your high respect for him, and do not question the correctness of what you say about him. I can see the values of the firm and uncompromising quality of leadership he gave them. Patriot as he was and as you describe him, he had a lower opinion of his fellow-Germans than I did. He tended to place

less confidence in them. And who is to say he was wrong? In some way
he knew them far better than I ever could. (My justification for holding
any views about them at all rested only on the values of an outsider's
perspective.) And his concern, clearly, was to hold most of them, at all
costs, to their ties with the West, particularly with the United States.

You will note the words: "most of them." I used the term advisedly.
Patriot as he was, Adenauer was not the patriot of all the Germans—
only of those who lived west of the Elbe. For his view of the others
one could perhaps use a phrase that appeared somewhere in one of
Freud's writings, where the ostelbian [east of the Elbe] Germans were
referred to (I do not know whether this was his own view or whether
he was describing the view of others) as being "spät und sehr schlecht
getauft" [late and very poorly baptized]. I doubt, in any case, that
Adenauer cared greatly about them. In rejecting with such violence
my own urgings for an exploration, in negotiations with the Russians,
of the prospects for a mutual withdrawal of western and Soviet occupying forces from most of Germany and the emergence of a unified
but demilitarized and neutral Germany between them—in rejecting
even the consideration of any such step, Adenauer was by implication
consigning not only the East Germans but all of Eastern Europe to
Communist control for an indefinite period into the future.

Many would say: what of it? The unification did eventually come
about. And the West was not required to pay the Russians anything to
achieve it. Was Adenauer, then, not right?

Yes, if you ignore all the side effects of the retention of the division
of Germany and Europe for another three or four decades—for the
emergence of an entirely new generation of people on the eastern side
of it—a generation profoundly colored and changed by the experience
of having grown up under Communist rule. While the two situations
are not fully comparable, and while the effects in question were surely
not as serious in Hungary as in Germany, I am sure that you will understand from your knowledge of the Hungarian experience, what I am
talking about. It was not that masses of people became enthusiastically
converted to communism; almost nothing of that sort happened. But
this generation I am speaking about grew up accustomed to viewing
themselves as the wards of the state, wholly unaccustomed to the idea

that they would themselves, individually, have to develop certain forms of initiative and of personal autonomy if their societies were to flourish. And beyond that, they were reared to regard a far-reaching social egalitarianism as the natural and most desirable state of society, and to be less concerned about the improvement of their own lives than about the possibility that someone else might have more than they did. (A striking confirmation of Tocqueville's view that people would eventually come to value more greatly poverty and dependence in equality than freedom in a more varied or hierarchically arranged society.) A highly intelligent, conservative (in the truest sense), and influential German observed to me, the other day, that in his opinion the East Germans had been more seriously damaged by their four decades of Communist power that had been the Russians by their seven decades of the same thing; and I am not sure that he was not right. . . .

Nor were these subtle but profound societal effects the only price we all paid for extending the division of Germany and Europe three to four decades beyond what *might* have been necessary.* You had the effects on the city of Berlin: the crisis of the early 1960's, the erection of the Wall, and the reduction of the city to a sorry shadow of its earlier self. You had the grotesque militarization of the Cold War, with all blind spots and *Irrwege* [wrong turns] of understanding that implied. You had the dreadful and now almost irreparable proliferation of nuclear weaponry. All this on top of the wholly unexpected difficulty of integrating the East Germany region into the remainder of Germany—a difficulty about which more is being recognized and discussed in the Germany of today than was the case three or four years ago when the great change occurred. It is not too much to say that as a superficial political fact Germany has of course been united and the division of the continent overcome, but that the task of making that political change a meaningful societal one is now far more difficult than it would have

---

* Kennan went so far as to think (mostly in our conversations throughout the cold war) that Stalin did not really want an entirely Communist Germany—because then the center of the Communist sphere might move from Moscow to Berlin. He also knew (as did I) that Stalin had a great respect, indeed, even admiration for Germans. (I wrote about this in *June 1941: Hitler and Stalin* (Yale University Press, 2006). It was after completion of this book that I ran across a, to me, meaningful snippet of a conversation between Stalin and Anthony Eden in December 1941. Stalin about Hitler: "His trouble: he does not know when to stop." Eden: "Does anyone?" Stalin: "I do."

been had unification come about three to four decades earlier. And this profoundly significant difference is the price we are all now paying for the triumph of Adenauer's ideas so long ago.

No one can say, of course, what would have been the result, had the decision gone in my direction rather than in Adenauer's. All that one can say, perhaps, is that I tried at that time to make people look at the problem in its wider dimensions rather than in the more narrow framework in which Adenauer's views rested. This, as I saw it at the time, was my duty; and I do not regret that I made the attempt.

G.K. to J.L.

Institute for Advanced Study
Princeton, New Jersey
June 1, 1992

First of all: the question of a publication of my letters and diary entries. And let me preface what I have to say about it by assuring you that there is no one to whom I would rather see this task entrusted than yourself.

This being said, let me reiterate, what I believe I have already told you. I think you exaggerate in your imagination the volume of letters of the sort you have in mind. Thinking back on all this, I realize that I have never had the sort of confidant to which letters of that sort might be written. There are indeed a number of letters treating of questions of foreign policy, Russia, recent history, etc., that might be of interest to the contemporary reader; but there are very few of a more personal nature. If, some day, you would care to drop by here and peruse two or three of the volumes of copies of outgoing letters from the office, it might give you an idea of what to expect. (The *Sketches*, of course, did contain one letter to my sister; but I cannot recall any other letters like it—none, at least, from my mature years.)

The forthcoming book will contain, I suspect, more of the sort of thing you are looking for than all the letters together. I have just received the first copy of *uncorrected* proof of the book. (Why "uncorrected" I cannot understand. I had sent them my corrections one or two months ago.) Mrs. Stenard expects to receive several more copies of this bound proof; and I am asking her to send you one as soon as she conveniently can. You will, I am sure, find in it much to disagree with, and much you will wish I hadn't said. I know that your comments would have improved it greatly; but there were reasons why I thought it better to let it go as it came out from my own pen. It may be helpful to you when you think about the letters.

There are two or three subjects I had thought to write about in the book, but decided not to. I had thought to write something about them in my diary; but I may, if time permits, put my thoughts in letters to you while I am in Norway. The letters would make at least a starter on what you have in mind.

About the under-estimation of self which you mentioned in the addendum to your letter [of April 13]: there is more about this in the book. I mentioned it primarily as one example of the difficulty a person has in forming anything like a realistic evaluation of himself. How hard it is to recognize, and to hold steadily in mind, all one's past inadequacies—the inexcusable mistakes, the gaucheries, the failures, the injustices toward others, the sins, in short—and to stack these up against what one also knows to have been one's positive contributions. The sins seem so immeasurable, the achievements so impermanent, so questionable, so difficult of assessment in one's own judgement!

J.L. to G.K.

27 July 1992

The proof copy of "Around the Cragged Hill" arrived due to Liz S's good offices just before I left for California. I read it there before reading anything else, making copious notes during the reading. . . .

One thing struck me as I was reading, and it is something of which you may not be quite aware. This is your abiding concern with the present and the future of the *state*. It is not only that you were an important servant of the state and that you try (as you have tried in past writings of yours) to insist on the necessary principles and require-ments of such service. But throughout this book I had the feeling that in your view civilization as we know it, depends on the existence of the state. I think that is very true, though it goes contrary to almost all of

modern 20th century political thought. Your view is not Hobbesian—
rather the contrary. You regret the corruption of the state, together with
the weakening of its authority—because somehow you are aware that
both the modern state and the very notion of civilization are *not* peren-
nial phenomena: they are (as, among other things, any good dictionary
based on historical principles will suggest) products of the last five
hundred years, of the Modern Age now passing. All of this is implicit in
your pages, and perhaps it ought to have been more explicit: because,
apart of the weakness of modern political philosophy, it is rather
evident that we now live in a time where the authority of the state has
begun to weaken, while the power of nationalism not yet. . . .

G.K. to J.L.

Kristiansand, Norway
August 4, 1992

Thank you for reading the book and for your letter of the 27th of July.
I have read the letter several times. My first impression, upon reading
it, was that despite all the kind things you said in the letter, you were
disappointed with the book, and with me for not writing a better one.
But this did not surprise me or offend me; and perhaps the impression
was overdrawn anyway. I, too, was in part disappointed with what I had
done. On the other hand, it was about the best I could do in the face of
the pressures that bore upon me; and had I not pushed it through and
completed it when I did, it might never have been completed at all. . . .

My The End of the Twentieth Century and the End of the Modern Age *(Ticknor
& Fields) was published in January 1993.*

G.K. to J.L.

Institute for Advanced Study
Princeton, New Jersey
November 11, 1992

Housebound by a couple of days of ill-health, I have completed the reading of your *End of the Twentieth Century*.

What am I to say? Neither of us, I think, is the best person to comment on the other's books, particularly not the more philosophical of them. I certainly could not undertake to review it as I might the book of someone I had not known at all. I can only offer a few disjointed observations.

That the book brings forward a number of observations and insights into the nature of our own time and of its place in history that equal in profundity (if they do not surpass) anything else of this sort that has been written, to my knowledge, anywhere in recent years, is my first reaction. Whether this will be widely recognized, is another matter. That sort of recognition, as you know, has little or nothing to do with the "success" of the book in the sense of the size of the readership.

The book reflects two qualities of your writing—two sides, I dare say (though intimately mutually associated) in your nature. There is the sharpness and the penetrating quality of visual observations— something that came out most strikingly in your work on Budapest at the turn of the century, and is reflected in the diary excerpts included in the present book. It is through these observations that you achieve your most direct and effective contact with the general run of your readership. But then there is, also, the capacity for what I might call historical-philosophical perception. Here, there is, God knows, nothing lacking in the perception, but the transmission of it to the reader is more difficult. It would be difficult for anyone else who had this sort of thought to transmit partly because of the extreme complexity of the material, partly because of the lack of adequate historical background in most of the readership. Part of your difficulty comes, of course, from your own meticulous honesty in sparing the reader none of the intellectual agony out of which the thought emerged. While no one can fault your prose, you do not get carried away, as some of us occasionally do, with the aesthetical possibilities—with the effort to make the thought prettier than life.

I am struck with your sensitivity to the meaning of words for the people who use them. It occurred to me that much of what you write could be called "history, seen through its vocabulary." This would fall in with your view that men do not just experience history, but that they create it in their own understanding of it, of which words are the expression.

I was pleased to note the many instances in which we had had similar thoughts, and these—long before we had met. I was, for example, alone among my governmental contemporaries of the immediate postwar (1947–1957) period in holding, as I think both Churchill and de Gaulle did, the view that European union (in the sense of the centripetal tendencies) should be encouraged only in the western and central part of the continent, east of the English Channel, excluding Britain and ourselves and leaving us to shape our future in our own Atlantic world. This was, of course, anathema to Adenauer, Acheson, and all the others.

Finally, I see that you concluded your book as I did mine, with a disclaimer of despair. We were both, I am sure, right; for if despair is something a man may entertain, or fancy that he entertains, in his own mind and soul, it is also something that he has no right to communicate, or pass, to anyone else. Why? Because, while despair, kept to one's self, may be implicitly suicidal, the transmission of it to anyone else may, if it is unjustified (and who can ever be sure that his is not?), be murderous.

A silly review of Around the Cragged Hill, *written by George Will, was printed in the* New York Times Book Review *on January 3, 1993.*

J.L. to G.K.

4 January 1993

I have a mind to write a letter to the N.Y. Times Book Review. . . .

6 January 1993

To the Editor, The New York Times Book Review.

To misinterpret a book may be regrettable; but to be mistaken about an author is worse. In his review of *Around the Cragged Hill*, George Will cites George Kennan who "cannot, somehow, picture Tocqueville combining his serene meditations with the washing of the pots and pans and the removal of trash from the kitchen premises." To this Will adds a one-sentence paragraph: "Neither can one so picture Mr. Kennan."

Knowing something about Mr. and Mrs. Kennan's domestic life, I can assure Mr. Will that incidences of Mr. Kennan's washing up in the kitchen and of his attending to the garbage may be too numerous to mention.

Sincerely,

John Lukacs

Kennan had contributed an introduction on the Balkan Wars of 1912–1913 and those of the early 1990s to a report by the Carnegie Foundation, The Other Balkan Wars: A 1913 Carnegie Endowment Inquiry in Retrospect *(Carnegie Endowment, 1993).*

J.L. to G.K.

5 April 1993

I am enclosing a few interesting pages from Nicolson's *Lord Carnock* about the Ambassadors' Conference in London of 1912–1913. It is at the end of his chapter on the Balkan Wars—there is also another, earlier chapter on the Bosnian crisis of 1908–9—but those pages may be of lesser interest to you, since Nicolson subordinates the Balkan events to his larger story, the relations of the Great European Powers. I have been thinking of the Ambassadors' Conference often, ever since the recent Balkan troubles erupted. In 1913 there was no "Europe," no "European Community," no "European" authority. Instead, the states of Europe were contemplating the potentialities of war among themselves. Yet the prestige of the Great Powers was enough to help put an end to a Balkan war, by the instrument of the Conference of their Ambassadors in London. Compare this with the conditions of today. . . .

G.K. to J.L.

Institute for Advanced Study
Princeton, New Jersey
April 14, 1993

As for my recent book: I am as bewildered as was everyone else, including publisher and literary agent, by its commercial success. But this at last encourages me to hope that the book may have, as I had hoped it would have, a more lasting value for educational purposes: as in a small way a help to the teacher in the field of the ideas of Americans about their own country, its past and its future—comparable in this respect, but in a smaller way, to Henry Adams' *Education*. Had I had any idea that it would achieve such notoriety, I would—or so I like to think—have taken greater pains with it. . . .

These days are difficult ones for me. I continue to be depressed about the American political establishment, even as represented by the Clinton administration; and I am more and more convinced that the country is truly in a bad way. But beyond that I continue to be helplessly held prisoner between the demands that friends put upon me (because, as they all say, I "look all right"), on the one hand, and the real limitations of physical and nervous strength, on the other. (You, I may assure you, are not among the guilty in this respect.) The desk remains piled and cluttered with the mail produced by the success of the book. Social invitations never cease. And from the standpoint of everything of true and lasting value, I feel that I am simply wasting valuable and severely limited time. Yet I know that it is always wrong to complain; and I apologize for doing so. Complaint is, I am sure, no more than evidence that the complainer is the author of his own miseries. (This last observation, I perceive, is a reflection of my puritan upbringing. Please disregard it.)

I am including this letter from Kennan to Anders Stephanson, a young Swedish historian who had written a thoughtful study of Kennan, Kennan and the Art of Foreign Policy *(Harvard University Press, 1989) in order to suggest Kennan's evolving interest and respect for the Roman Catholic Church.*

G.K. to Anders Stephanson

Letter to Mr. Stephanson

December 13, 1993

I have your letter of November 22 and appreciate your interest in my views about the Catholic Church.

For a general response to this question, I can only refer you to pp. 49–50 of my recent book [*Around the Cragged Hill*]. What was said there understates, if anything, my respect for the great institution you mention. I have been impressed (without always sharing the various points of departure) with such evidences of European-Catholic thinking as have from time to time come to my attention. And I must confess that I owe a significant debt, in this respect, intellectually and otherwise, to my deeply respected friend, John Lukacs, historian and philosopher, who is of Central-European origin, and a Catholic.

You might like to bear in mind, in this connection, the fact that I hold honorary degrees from Notre Dame and from Catholic University, and once had the honor to delivering at Notre Dame the inaugural address on the occasion of the dedicating of their new cultural center. These events may stand as evidence, I think, that my attitude towards the Catholic Church was recognized and understood in Catholic circles; and I like to think that the respect was mutual.

You might also care to note that one of the best books written largely about my person, coming several years after your own, was the book on the State Department's Policy Planning Staff, the author of which, Father Miscamble, is now a faculty member at Notre Dame.*

In short, I feel that my life has been enriched by what I have known of the Catholic Church and by my various contacts with it. On the

---

* Wilson D. Miscamble, *George F. Kennan and the Making of American Foreign Policy, 1947–1950* (Princeton University Press, 1993).

other hand, I am not myself a Catholic and have never been moved to accept the commitment that membership in that Church would have implied. While not associating myself with all the traditional tenets of Calvinist theology, my life and character are stamped by my Presbyterian origins; and respect for my forebears would, if nothing else did, make it hard for me to think of myself in any other way.

I read with interest your discussion with Mr. West about Chekhov. Passivity? Outwardly, yes. He saw his mission in illuminating for others the deeper tragedy and irony of their lives; and this he did through hundreds of literary efforts over the two decades of his active work as a writer, describing things as he saw them, treating all his characters with charitable insight and understanding, and leaving it to his readers to come to terms, as best they might, with what he showed them. But I do seem to recall that he entered actively into the effort to see that justice was done to Dreyfus; and his life was replete with small acts of kindness to others. . . .

On February 16, 1994, Kennan was ninety years old. On that day the Council on Foreign Relations gave a festive reception in his honor in New York, which I also attended. He then sent me the following verse that twenty years earlier he had written for his children on the occasion of his 70th birthday.

Verses by Kennan on the Occasion of His Seventieth Birthday

By G. F. Kennan
February 16, 1974

When the step becomes slow, and the wit becomes slower,
    And memory fails, and the hearing declines;
When the skies become clouded, and clouds become lower,
    And you find yourself talking poetical lines;
When the path that you tread becomes steeper and darker;
    And the question is no longer whether but when—
Then, my friend, you should look for the biblical marker,
    The sign by the road that reads: Three Score and Ten.

At this point you'll observe, if you care to look closely,
    You're no longer alone on the highway of life;
For there trudges behind you, and glowers morosely,
    A bearded old man with a curious knife.
At first you defy this absurd apparition
    (For it's old Father time, with his glass and his scythe);
You swear you were never in better condition—
    The body more jaunty, the spirit more blithe.
And you laugh in his face, and you tell the old joker:
    "You must be mistaken; I'm feeling just fine."
But the wretched old scarecrow just picks up his poker
    And gives you a jab, and says: "Get back in line."
So you swallow your pride, and you march with your brothers.
    You do all the things you're instructed to do.
But you're sure this compulsion, just right for the others,
    Could not have been really intended for you.
And you turn to the thought of your erstwhile successes—
    How brilliant, how charming, how worthy of fame;
'Til a small voice protests, and the conscience confesses
    What an ass you once were, and how empty the claim.
The ghosts of the past find your deepest recesses,
    And they gather about, and poke fingers of shame:
Stupidities spawned when you thought them successes;
    Injustices done in the grasping for fame.
And you grieve with remorse for the sins you committed—
    The fingers that roamed, and the tongue that betrayed;
Yet you grieve, on occasion, for those you omitted:
    The nectar untasted, the record unplayed.
So you swallow your pride, and you scurry for cover
    In the solaces characteristic of age.
You tell the same anecdotes over and over,
    forget the same names, and re-read the same page.
And at length you concede, with morose introspection,
    That it's not on your prowess that pride now depends,
That for this you must look in a different direction:
    To the weary indulgence of family and friends.

And if given the chance to re-tread, as you've known it,
　The highway of life—to begin at the spot
Where the story began, and before you had blown it—
Would you take, it, dear friend? I suspect you would not!
So let us take heart. We are none of us friendless.
　Take up our glasses, and drain them again.
In the hope that some interval, fair if not endless,
　Will ensue
　　Before you
　　　Become Three Score and Ten.
　　　　(George Kennan)

Referring to Kennan's speech at the Council on Foreign Relations the day before.

J.L.to G.K.

17 February 1994

There were moments during your address when I thought: this may
be as important as the "X" article itself, if not more. It must not be lost
to posterity, or deposited only within your personal papers. Perhaps
not more than a minority in that room agreed with you. Never mind.
Again, and again, the *consistency* of your thought and of your principles
appeared clear and strong. The fact—and it is a fact—that there was no
difference—surely no *essential* difference—between your view of the
world and of the desiderata of an American foreign policy of 1947 and
1950 and after. Not everyone will understand this. *Tant pis.* Never mind.
　Now come my two, ancillary, remarks. You spoke of the necessity of looking at the Russian danger anew, as early as 1950. I would
have thought: 1952–1955. (But surely even *before* Stalin's demise.) Of
course it was by no means certain that Stalin or his successors may
have been ready to renegotiate the division of Europe somehow. But
what is certain is that it was surely worth trying: and that the fearful
unwillingness of even considering that cost us and the world plenty, for
decades to come. And—perhaps you were a tad too generous about the
historical function of the Council on Foreign Relations. Of course the

occasion was the proper one; and that function has been, by and large, an honorable one. But only "by and large." They—even the excellent Ham Armstrong—* did not understand you in 1950 and for a good long time after. Not because of ill will; and not because of a lacking respect for you. But because of a complex mish-mash of all kinds of reasons, not necessarily dishonorable ones. Only—a kind of Wilsonianism has marked the Council and that American "elite" you spoke about eloquently—for seven decades, and the end is not yet.

I thought that Gelb's reference to your family as a "nuclear family" was somewhat silly—that phrase is current now, and it means just about nothing. . . .**

G.K. to J.L.

Institute for Advanced Study
Princeton, New Jersey
March 9, 1994

This letter is actually thought of as an appreciative acknowledgement of your letters of February 8 and 17. They both reached me in the midst of many distracting events, and I had not chance to reply to them at the moment.

You mentioned the fact that the time when we might have tried to talk to the Russians about Europe might better have been 1952–1955, rather than 1950. I freely concede that; and you may recall that I repeated the appeal for talks with the Russians in the Reith Lectures given in 1957. On both of these occasions, when I attempted to move things in that direction—in 1949 and again in 1957—I was many times confronted with the answer: "Why, the Russians will never agree to what you are suggesting." My answer to this was "Perhaps not, but you will never know whether they will or not unless you try to negotiate with them. What they put forward in advance of negotiations is only what you could call their asking price. They don't expect to get it in full; and you will not know what their real price is until they see what we are prepared to offer in return." After all, the fact that we might enter into

---

* Hamilton Fish Armstrong, editor of the council's journal, *Foreign Affairs*, from 1928 to 1972.
** Les Gelb, who became president of the council in 1993.

negotiations did not preclude our breaking them off again if they were unsuccessful; but my friend Llewellyn Thompson* taught us all that you should not despair of ultimately coming to an agreement with them just because their initial reactions seemed negative. Patience, coupled with polite firmness, sometimes paid off.

I was much struck by the reminder, in your letter of February 8 [not included in this volume] that some of the finest contributions of the intellect are made not in the centers but on the edges of the respective fields. How true, how true.

I will give you a ring when I return from the south. Meanwhile all the best *von Haus zu Haus*.

I sent him (either the manuscript or the proofs) of my Destinations Past, *a collection of my travel articles and journals, published by the University of Missouri Press in 1994.*

G.K. to J.L.

Kristiansand, Norway
August 1, 1994

I have been reading your *Destinations Past*. (Thank you, incidentally, for the kind inscription.) Parts of the book I had seen before; but I have re-read those parts, and the new ones as well, with undiminished pleasure. This is quintessential Lukacs. It is all there: the unfailing curiosity, and, in response to it, the fine powers of observation and of aesthetic, and social, and historical analysis, such as very few in our country, and probably none at all, could equal. And all of this founded on an erudition in European history, especially modern history, that is itself unique. Nothing seen or described in static terms—all correctly seen in motion, as part of an endlessly changing stream of civilization. In your case as in my own, things can be said, in and through the lines of travel accounts, which can be brought forward only with great difficulty in a purely theoretical treatise.

* U.S. ambassador to Austria from 1955 to 1957 and to the Soviet Union from 1957 to 1962.

I have another reason for writing to you at this moment. I recently received a very kind letter from our Secretary of State [Warren Christopher] telling me that he is setting up a visiting lectureship under the auspices of the State Department: one lecture each year, for which they hope to find lecturers of outstanding distinction and prominence, by no means only Americans—the topics to be related to current problems of international affairs that affect and engage American diplomacy. The lectureship is to be in my name; and I am asked, and have agreed, to give, in the coming October, the initial lecture.

I have naturally been giving thought to the question as to what I should talk about; and there is one possibility which I wanted to mention particularly to you. It is, in essence, this: Noting the extent to which my own life has coincided in time with the century now coming to an end (particularly if one accepts your illuminating observation that the century really began in 1914), I would review, in the first part of the lecture, the outstanding events in the life of what we might call western civilization, point out what a brutal and, from this standpoint, a self-destructive century it has been, and how many problems it has created rather than solved; and I would then turn around and ask what has been the relationship of the United States, in particular, to this series of disasters and the new problems emerging—problems that had not, at the outset of the century, been even widely perceived to exist. Out of this examination I would try to identify the points at which our behavior, as a country, had been helpful and those at which it had had an opposite effect, during the century just ended.

I would emphasize that with relation to what is now emerging as the 21st century, I can make no specific suggestions. It is not *my* century. I cannot even attempt to foresee its life, to sense its atmosphere, or to make suggestions as to how our policy-makers should behave. But since great peoples, like individuals, are creatures of habit, and in many instances the slaves of it, it might be interesting to note where, during this past century, American policies and actions have been useful, and where they have not. For we are apt, unless forewarned, to repeat errors that might, with a little foresight, have been avoided.

I shall try to write, and to attach to this letter, an outline of what

I would think to say about this past century. But if I find it hard to accomplish this without delay, I will omit it.

I invite your comments on the above, because of all the people I know, there is none that has looked deeply into this last century as you have. If you find what I have outlined above to be a poor idea, don't hesitate to tell me. If I did not want your honest opinion, I would not be writing to you. And my feelings toward you will not be in any way affected if you tell me that what I have described is a lot of nonsense. Or, indeed, if you have any ideas of what I might better speak about on a ceremonial occasion of this sort, I will be glad to have them.

J.L.to G.K.

15 August 1994

About your October address. It seems to me that you have moved from your original idea of a review (in the first part of your prospective lecture) of the main events of the new closed century, to speaking about the place of principle in American foreign policy. Well—here comes your grand sense of duty again—writing this will be more difficult than the first impulse; but, without knowing more about the eventual contents, I agree. (Honored and pleased as I am, too, for your asking my opinion.) Perhaps you will make the essential distinction between *ideas* and *principles*. There is this American tendency to elevate the former as if they were identical with the latter which, or course, they are not. Burke had made that distinction—throughout his life and work, if not philosophically—and so have you during your entire life. Contrary examples abound: Wilson, Eisenhower (and in his way, Reagan). I am confident that you can make the argument seriously and trenchantly, without necessarily naming such Presidents. I remember telling you some time ago what John Morley wrote about Burke, that B. changed his front, but he never changed his ground. It fits you to a tee, and it is also more profound than Palmerston's famous statement, that England has no friends and no enemies, only her interests. . . .

J.L. to G.K.

31 October 1994

First, in order—and also in importance—is my, now habitual, amazement at the muscular freshness of your prose. There is simply no difference between the *verve* (if that is the "mot juste") of your prose now,
and of your prose thirty or forty years ago. And by "freshness" I do not
only mean style, or felicity of expression, but also the fact that, after
all those years, there is really no real repetition (as distinct from a real
consistency) of your arguments. . . .

Going further, it seems to me that a further distinction ought
to be made between national interest and "Realpolitik"—which, I
mean the latter, cannot be simply translated to the United States from
European historical precedents. (Which is why I have been skeptical
of people such as [Hans] Morgenthau or Kissinger, etc.) Right now
in this country we have the further confusion between "government"
and "State." Those people—and there are many of them—who are so
vociferous against "government" are often the very same people who
favor the endless extension and funds devoted to "Defense." (Or, when
a Republican is in the White House, of the staffing and the powers of
the Executive branch.) But isn't that "government" too?

The troublesome matter is that no "definition" of national
interest will do. But then that is the case with almost every *principle* of the world. As Dr. Johnson said: "Definitions are the tricks
for pedants." (Try to "Define" history, beauty, decency, truth, etc.!)
Words are not fixed symbols of *things*; they are symbols of *meanings*.
And there is such a thing as national interest, whether we can define
it or not. . . .

G.K. to J.L.

Institute for Advanced Study
Princeton, New Jersey
March 15, 1995

You may wonder why you have not heard from me sooner about the
transcript of a book that you sent to me, if I remember correctly, some

two months ago.* Well, I have now read three fourths of it (280 out of some 380 pages). I intend, and hope, to finish the reading at some point, but there is something else to which I must turn for the immediate future. Yet I did not want you to wait too long for a reaction on my part. Hence this letter.

The reading, even to this point, took a great deal of time, partly because I read very slowly, but partly, also, for a different reason. You recently observed, with reference to another letter I wrote you, that it was "dense." Although in a somewhat different sense of the word, that is true of much of your own prose. I shall return to that presently. Suffice it to be said here, that the reading of it does not go rapidly.

Now, before I turn to the context of the book, and to avoid any misunderstanding, let me say this. The region that forms the center of your interests is, as I see it, primarily northwestern and central Europe, with its Canadian and U.S.-American extension into the new world. And a great deal of your interest in this region, as an historian, has centered on the 19th and 20th centuries. Within these limits, I can think of no one, worldwide, who has given a more searching attention to the development of modern civilization and culture, and who has a wider knowledge and understanding of it than yourself. What you have brought to it in these respects is unique and impressive. Please do not think that I do not have all this in mind as I write this letter.

If, on the other hand, I were to be asked: Will the publication of this transcript be a literary or commercial success? my answer would have to be that I am skeptical of that possibility; and I shall try to tell you why.

I have to distinguish here between the reviewers and the reader. So far as the reviewers are concerned (except for the *New York Review of Books*, which is always capable of surprising you), I need not waste space. They will not read it; they will give it at best a glance or two; they will not find what they are looking for, and they will dismiss it with a few words that reflect neither interest nor attention, and least of all understanding. All that is not very important.

A different situation will prevail in the case of the readers. But here, too, I doubt that the book will be appreciated and understood as it should be. And this is primarily for two reasons.

* This was the manuscript of *A Thread of Years*, published by Yale University Press in 1998.

The first of these is that the connections between the vignettes, on the one hand, and the significance of the dates and of the accompanying discussions are in many instances too subtle—sometimes hard to establish. This is true, in fact, even for the discriminating reader. For the undiscriminating one the connections will simply not be visible: Many people will not be able to understand how this particular vignette, and this particular discussion, fit with the year in question.

Secondly, much of the material in the discussions, as here presented, will be far above the average reader's head. Indeed, you overrate your readers in a number of respects. You overrate their knowledge of both the history and the culture of these last hundred years. Many of the references are to persons, events, and situations of which they have no knowledge whatsoever. Only a person whose range of reading is almost as wide as your own (and how many of these are there? I myself would not qualify) could be expected to follow comfortably along. I am aware that it is better to talk up to the reader than to talk down to him; and to a certain point I can go along with this. But when the atmosphere is too rarified, the reader, like the one who has climbed too high on the mountain, becomes light-headed, breathless, and uncomfortable, and longs to descend into the more comfortable atmosphere of his familiar valley. . . .

And now, a word or two about the vignettes. They vary extensively, it seems to me, in what they reveal and what they add to the force of the book. In some of them there comes to the surface the truly remarkable ability you have to evoke atmosphere in all its beauty and pathos—an ability that came so prominently and successfully to the fore in the book on Budapest at the turn of the century. Sometimes, when this *does* come to the fore, it adds to the strength of the vignette. In other instances, the remainder of the vignette comes as a let-down from it. And indeed, the endings of some of the vignettes seem like let-downs of themselves, because they sound so promisingly like the first pages of short stories or novels, which then fail to appear. . . .

J.L. to G.K.

20 March 1995

And this may connect with something that I had felt I ought to write you in a letter from Switzerland but then I didn't. My annual skiing vacation was spoiled, since three days after my arrival, I came down with pneumonia so that I could neither ski nor come home—feverish and agitated, I had to stay in my hotel ("Sie muessen nicht reisen" [You must not travel] the Swiss doctor ordered me). During my stay the value of the dollar fell to 1.10 Swiss francs. I was not thinking about my consequently increasing expenses—I had discounted those. But I was appalled by the remarks of the head of the Federal Reserve and the Secretary of the Treasury and of about all American economists that I read in the International Herald Tribune. They all said that this fall of the dollar "did not matter" (headline in the IHT: "Americans Shrug Their Shoulders About Dollar Decline"). Well they shouldn't. What this means, and what this has meant for some time, is the decline of the world's confidence in this country and in its people. When Nixon came in a dollar was worth more than four Deutschmarks or Swiss francs. Soon it will be worth one mark and one franc, if not less. And this is the true symbol of what is happening—not the Stock Market Index, not the Balanced Budget Amendment, not the Price-Earnings Ratio, not the Interest Rate, not the Gross National Product (what an obscene phrase *that* is), etc., etc—but a decline in the confidence and in the prestige of this country, something that will not recover, at least not in the foreseeable future. The idiot economists and the politicians, including the Republicans with their wide grin, do not know that. They ought to: because with all the numbers and figures spewed out by the computers, everything that is material in this world (including the value of money) depends (and has come more and more to depend) on things that are not quantifiable, for example, confidence, which is a matter of quality and not of quantity. And about that the computers can tell us nothing.

And there are other symptoms too: despite all of that empty prattling about International Trade and Supernational Corporations, etc., the American presence in Europe is slowly disappearing. . . .

G.K. to J.L.

Institute for Advanced Study
Princeton, New Jersey
July 10, 1995

I have wanted to tell you, in connection with Stephanson's mention of my pro-Catholic inclinations, that I have spent most of my spare time since arriving in Norway in the reading of the 250 page autobiographical portion (ten, that is, of the twelve "books") of Pusey's classic translation of the Confessions of St. Augustine. I thought you might be amused (and, I hope, not rendered too indignant) if I first quote from the entry I made in my diary upon completing something like the first 100 pages of the book. "I find myself," I wrote, "less interested in the conversion that the book describes than in the habits, the interests, and the personality of the man who wrote it: the humorlessness, the incapacity for enjoyment of the minor and innocent pleasures of life and of the more endearing absurdities of ordinary people—this all matched by the compensatory preoccupation with the most abstract questions of religious philosophy—a never ending preoccupation, extending over all the years of youth [and] early middle-age—a preoccupation that slighted life on this earth it the effort to solve the mysteries of a future life in another world.

I find a great deal—a stupendous amount, in fact, of attention given here to the relationship of man to God, but very little of the relationship of man to man. And this fails to satisfy me; for I find myself asking whether the greatest service the human individual is capable of making to God should not be seen in whatever service he can render, during the short time he spends on this globe, to his fellow-men.

"Also, I find myself disturbed by the extremely personal nature of Augustine's claimed relationship to God—by the demands, that is, that this relationship implicitly places on the concerns and attentions of the Deity for the situation of a single man—as though what God was being confronted with here was a drama of heroic significance, on the outcome of which the fate of vast numbers of others would depend. 'Well,' might not St. Augustine (or his enduring spirit) have said, 'did the dramatic development of my relationship to God not have precisely the quality you just mentioned? Is it not evident that my struggle was one of world-wide and lasting significance—evident in the very fact that here are you, sixteen centuries later, still reading the account of my spiritual struggle? And have my teachers not become one of the pillars of the great spiritual and ideological[1] edifice known, ever since, as the Catholic Church?'

"Yes, yes, is my reply. But still, you were only one among many. Even your faith could not entirely destroy your mortality and the unfinished quality—the tendency to error—that you share with so many others of us. God's mercy, and his understanding, are comprehensive, not exclusive; and there must have been countless millions of others who needed that mercy and understanding, and upon whom precisely because of their helplessness and insignificance, they also had to be expended. You, St. Augustine, were unquestionably a great man of your time. But it was not for you, as I see it, in advancing your claims on God's attention and understanding, to assume for yourself so high a place in his concerns and preoccupations."

I cannot avoid, in this connection, an irreverent memory.

On a placard affixed to a wall somewhere in England, and containing only the words "Jesus saves"; some irreverent person (and I suspect a young one) had added the words: "Jesus is tired. Save yourself."

Well, so much for the diary entry. Now, 150 pages farther into the reading, I could add to it, and this in a more serious vein, but I still have deep differences with the positions and attitudes of the saint. Yes, as I said in the diary, he was a great man of his time—great in the very depth of his intellectual penetration into the deepest meanings of religious faith. But the realm into which he was endeavoring to enter was one to be profoundly penetrated only at the cost of the abandonment of all participation—of all interest, in fact—in the affairs of this world any such participation is rejected as sinful and corrupting. For anyone who had achieved a complete entry into Augustine's nirvana—to anyone who had made his way completely (as Augustine himself seems to have been not quite able to do) into the "knowledge of God"—what

---

[1] I am using "ideological" here, in the original meaning of the term—not the modern one.

remained of life on this unfortunate planet could be seen only as a form of preparation for death, undertaken in the confidence that the purity of a man's detachment from the affairs of this world would assure him of a state of endless bliss in the arms of his Maker.

But this, it seems to me, makes no more sense from the standpoint of a benevolent Deity than from that of the human party. God, in Augustine's view, was the creator of all reality, including our present secular world. What sense would it have made for him to design this marvelous planet (the only one of the multitude of heavenly bodies known to us that has anything even faintly approaching its suitability as a seat of human habitation) only to regard it as a horrible and irredeemable vale of tears and corruption, through which one had to pass in order to come favorably into God's presence? I cannot avoid the thought that St. Augustine could have avoided a great deal of his agony of introspection and of his attempt to establish his relation-ship to God, had he been willing to accept the view put forward in my recent book; that the mysterious Primary Cause of our physical universe, to the nature of which we are obliged to accommodate ourselves, was and is, in its relationship to us, neither good nor bad, neither loving or unloving, supremely indifferent, in fact; but that there is another dimension to our existence: namely, the presence of a spiritual God, I believe, understanding the competing strains that come to bear upon us, will show to us, in the future life, a mercy no smaller than that which we ourselves have shown to our fellowmen in the present one.

In short, the objects of St. Augustine's great efforts were ones that over-reached the possibilities of both God and man; and the search for complete achievement of them was a form of extremism useful to none of us. His account of his travails and aspirations strikes me as an endless effort to arrive, in the spiritual world, at something that could only be called *le mieux*, ignoring the fact that such effort, carried too far and too ambitiously, is nothing less, as we all know, that *l'ennemi du bien.*

I find the Catholic Church of our day, mellowed by its great burden of experience and tradition, to be far wiser, more compassionate, and more understanding of God's needs as well as of man's, than the saints of so many centuries ago, who tried to play, and did indeed play, a part, but in my opinion an eccentric and unacceptable one, in its development.

J.L. to G.K.

30 July 1995

The only question I may raise is within your long—and beautiful— paragraph on page 3. There you seem—and perhaps only seem—to separate what you write as "the mysterious Primary Cause of our physical existence" from the "another dimension to our existence: namely, the presence of a spiritual God." To me at least, the Primary Cause and the spiritual God are the same: my belief in the spiritual God is inseparable from the Creator of the Universe—who of course transcends not only space but also time—and that the great gift of His Son to us was to incarnate and demonstrably show how a love of God without our love of human beings is worthless. But that you and I know only too well. . . .

J.L. to G.K.

25 August 1995

The interesting matter about Lenin's—so-called—"Testament."* It is now obvious that the text of the latter has been doctored, if not alto- gether falsified, by Trotsky who gave it to the American Communist Max Eastman. Consequently, Eastman who, of course, sympathized with Trotsky (and it may not be inadmissible to at least presume that the Jewish element was involved here) published a version more complimentary to Trotsky than to Stalin. And when Stalin raised hell and the trouble arose, Trotsky was a coward and a weakling (this 3 years before his expulsion from the USSR). And how many people in the West had moaned and prattled during sixty years that if only it had

---

* A—now questionably authentic—text of Lenin's "testament," accepted and cited by hun- dreds of historians, in which Lenin allegedly warned against the dangerous shortcomings of both Trotsky and Stalin.

been Trotsky not the unspeakable Stalin, who would have continued the legacy of Lenin. Even E. H. Carr in his three volumes did not *once* mention that a Jewish head of the party would have been unthinkable. . . .* And God writes straight with crooked lines. If a Trotsky (or a Zinoviev; or a Bukharin) would have governed Russia in the 1930's, Hitler would have had little or no trouble to upset them or to conquer them. What a profound irony is latent here. . . .

J.L. to G.K.

5 February 1996

As we were sitting on the sofa in our living room, you turned to me and asked a question that stunned me. How did I see, or what did I see as the future problems of this country. Stunned—but also honored—was my first reaction; and then I did not think I had sufficient time or even presence of mind to talk about that clearly and directly. But I have been thinking about your question ever since. Here is, surely inadequately, what I can tell you, whatever the worth of my thoughts and their expressions may be.

In the first place, I must concentrate on what I see as problems peculiar to this country now—and not to the world, or to the Western world at large. Unlike in the 19th century, many of the problems of this country involve conditions that are similar to those besetting other Western democracies. But I must attempt to sum up those that are especially relevant to the United States of America now. So, let me omit those wide-ranging problems of the pollution of nature, or the sclerotic character of most parliamentary institutions, or the inflation of expectations of the provider state, Etc., Etc. They are incarnated differently from country to country, but they are not uniquely American ailments or problems now.

I can see two large, and deep-seated conditions that endanger this country and its people, and that presumably will continue to endanger them in the foreseeable future—since it is now in the nature of our political as well as intellectual life that most problems are not merely ignored or wrongly treated but that they are wrongly recognized from

* *The Bolshevik Revolution, 1917–1923* (Macmillan, 1951–53).

the beginning. There can be no therapy without a half-decent diagnosis; and our diagnostic capacities are weak and sorrily wanting.

One of these problems is beginning to be recognized by some people, but almost always insufficiently so. Beneath and beyond the problems of Immigration and Multiculturalism there exists a wholly insufficient understanding of the English (more precisely: the Anglo-Saxon and the Anglo-Celtic) roots of American freedoms and laws. American freedoms incorporated in the Constitution, etc. were not abstract freedoms but English freedoms to which a large number of Americans in the 18th century were accustomed. They have been weakened and transformed and compromised and, here and there, corrupted since: but their protection and the procedures in American courts have remained in practice until very recently. This despite the fact that the portion of the American population of Anglo-Saxon or of Anglo-Celtic (and I include the Irish whose liberties and laws were, after all, inherited from England) origins has diminished for more than one hundred years now and now they amount to less than one-quarter of the Population. Still, American jurisprudence and the respect for law have, until very recently, differed from that of other countries (except for Canada) on this continent. But this, I fear, is no longer so.

(An example: the key to this horrible [O. J.] Simpson "trial" was, in my opinion, NOT race. It was the degeneration of American legal and courtroom practices—together with the cult of celebrity which makes a mockery of "Equal Practice Under Law.")

In "Democracy in America" Tocqueville wrote about lawyers being the real aristocracy in America. He thought that there were some bad consequences to that but that, by and large, it was a salutary thing. I know many intelligent and respectable lawyers in Philadelphia who are despairing and disgusted at what the practice and the procedures of law have become during the last thirty or forty years.

The second—and allied—danger may be summed up briefly. It has to do with the degeneration of democracy itself.

Democracy had *overestimated* the character and the intelligence of people. But confidence is still preferable to hopelessness, and illusions are still preferable to cynicism. Democracy has now led, cynically, to *underestimation* of the character and intelligence of people. This may exist elsewhere, too, but nowhere as much, and with as disastrous portents, as in this country. Its evidences are there not only in Hollywood products and "entertainment" but in all of our political practices and rhetoric, in publishing, "communications," and on all levels of American schooling. This cynical underestimation of people has now debouched into self-fulfilling calculations. The managers of our entertainment and politics and education and information, etc., find that it is easier to deal with people in that way. Yet this may lead to catastrophes whose consequences are unfathomable.

But there is the hope not only in Providence but in the unpredictability of history, that is, of people. There are still large numbers of people in this country to whom the cult of the lowest common denominator does not appeal—no matter what "market research" may say. And no matter what our so-called and self-appointed "conservatives" may say, since most of them are hopelessly shallow and puerile. Their cult of the "free market" (a myth), of "the bottom line," etc., is nothing but another cult of the lowest common denominator; and some time from now, when the English language is still revered and spoken and thought about, people will wonder how Conservatives had come to parade (and to see themselves as) Populists. . . .

J.L. to G.K.

25 March 1997

During our telephone conversation the other day you were interested in what I attempted to tell you about the 1956 documents. You asked whether I was writing, or planned to write, about them. I said no. But your questions whirled thereafter in my mind. They have stimulated my writing this to you.

My interests in historical research end, by and large, with 1945—which does not mean of course, that my general interest in history at large ceases after that period. And so I read, with considerable concentration, materials that were sent or given to me (in most cases not because of my request for them) about the events in October–November 1956, particularly concerning the Hungarian Rising at that time. These materials consist of documents as well as—rather intel-

ligent and insightful (in most cases)—analytical articles and commen-
taries based on them. They fall into two categories. One of them are
documents that are recently accessible in Moscow. You and I know that
the present Russian practice of allowing foreign researchers access to
Soviet documents is erratic and selective, whereby their value is sometimes compromised. This does not seem to be the case with these. There
are not very many of them, and some of them were released because of
a Yeltsin promise during his visit to Hungary that documents relating
to the 1956 events will be made available to Hungarians.* The most
valuable batch of these are stenographic records of the Politburo meetings from 23 October to 4 November 1956. The Hungarian translations
of these have been already published last year in a small volume; but
there are a few other Russian documents too.

The other category—which I, oddly, or perhaps not so oddly, find
perhaps even more interesting—are the American documents of the
same period (essentially of a wider period, some of them going back
to early 1956, the Khrushchev speech denouncing Stalin's crimes and
going as far as the end of November). Now: the actual status and the
provenance of these documents are more complicated than those of the
Russian ones. It seems that when the sequential opening and publication of FRUS [Foreign Relations of the United States series] reached
1956 many of them were published, but selectively: there were selective excisions and omissions of certain phrases too. Many of these
have become since (in the later 1990's) accessible to researchers but
White Spots still exist—for example in the CIA papers and the NSC
[National Security Council] memoranda. The mass of documents is of
course large: it includes records of [Secretary of State] Dulles' telephone conversations, for example (but how complete are they?). And
this brings me—even before I tell you what these documents reveal, to
me—to what I am inclined to call the serious historographical problem.
This is the complexity of the American government. The historians and
commentators (many of them native Americans) have been assiduous,
largely judicious, and precise. At the same time the phrase "Washington" appears and reappears. But "Washington" included such diverse
persons as Eisenhower and Dulles and [CIA director] Allen Dulles and

* Boris Yeltsin, Russia's first post-communist president.

[Joint Chiefs of Staff chairman] Admiral Radford and Herbert Hoover, Jr. (in charge of the State Department when Dulles was ill) and the NSC staff that wrote those memoranda and the CIA bureaucracy and even some influential Congressional figures—whose intentions and, more, whose process of thought were ever so often unsimilar. It is possible for a historian—by and large—to assess what decisions were taken, or what kinds of decisions were not taken. But the intentions behind these decisions (and even their timing) were not easy to ascertain: indeed, perhaps more complicated and Byzantine than the decisions taken in the Kremlin by a few men.

So: what is then interesting in these revelations? (Perhaps "discoveries" would be a better word.) On the Russian side: (1) that Khrushchev and Co.—and there were divisions within the Politburo—were upset and even helpless about what was happening, and that their communique of 30 October declaring a withdrawal from Hungary and a reformulation of their relationship with the Warsaw Pact satellites was genuine; (2) that those suggesting a withdrawal included not only [Soviet Deputy Prime Minister Anastas] Mikoyan but also [Soviet Defense Minister Georgy] Zhukov—while the latter was adamant not to give in to Poland, except for the domestic reforms and other matters represented by [Polish Communist Party leader Wladyslaw] Gomulka; (3) that until 30 October the Chinese—rubbing their hands when looking at Soviet troubles, by the way—were very much in support (indeed, vocal about it during their meetings with Khrushchev) of Russian concessions to Poland and Hungary; but by 31 October they (and also [Yugoslav leader Josip] Tito) changed their minds; the Chinese became adamant in asking for a Russian military crushing of the Hungarian rebellion; (4) that the contemporaneous Suez affair had nothing essential to do with the Russian decisions about Hungary;* (5) that—before 31 October—the very term "Finlandization" was muttered, here and there by some Russians as perhaps applicable to Hungary; (6) that the absence of any sign of a serious American willingness to negotiate about the rapidly developing Central European situation confirmed the resolution of Khrushchev & Co. to reoccupy Hungary militarily.

---

* They were agitated and deeply worried about East Europe, not about the Middle East.

More complicated and incomplete (what the Germans say: "lücken-haft") is the American record. (It confirms Tocqueville's remark that the history of democracies will be so much more difficult to reconstruct & write than those of aristocratic regimes.) Of course the American documentary mass is infinitely more voluminous than the Russian one. But that is just the problem. On the one hand Eisenhower and Dulles (and some of the NSC memoranda) still talk of "rollback" and "liberation." On the other hand, they make it clear—to themselves—that American military intervention is out of the question. (Except for Poland, where a NSC session as late as 15 November—incomprehensibly—includes a preparation of war with Russia, if the Russians would militarily intervene in Poland—this almost a month after the Khrushchev-Gomulka compromise.) Most of the commentators attribute these things to "inconsistency." I think it is more complicated than that. There is some evidence (excised from most of the even now reopened documents) that there was some covert CIA action—mostly reports by observers—in Hungary. At the same time the CIA and the NSC summaries reveal much shortsightedness about the Russian intentions. For example, both the extent of the uprising and the Russian decision to withdraw on 30 October strikes *everyone* in Washington as a complete surprise—but not because of lacking information or previous reports: to the contrary, because of an inability to free their minds from the categories of accepted ideas, many of them rather rigidly ideological. Finally, it subtly appears that the Russian military crushing of the Rising on 4 November actually pleased Dulles and Eisenhower. Now there was nothing they had to do: and the brutality of the event was a magnificent propaganda advantage. Eisenhower, of course, understands the dramatic quality of the situation less than does Dulles or Allen Dulles. At one of the NSC or Cabinet sessions, [Vice President Richard] Nixon mentions you: he says something to the effect that "we cannot accept the Kennan idea of not being able to do anything with the satellites"—which of course was *not* your idea at all. Also—in the earlier 1956 Cabinet or CIA or NSC papers there is nothing indicating that the powers in Washington, on *any* level, understood the significance of the 1955 Russian withdrawals from Austria or Finland, etc. That it might be worthwhile to at least consider the possibility of renegotiating the division of Europe with them: not a trace of that anywhere.

Now, to end this letter. I read this stuff with acute attention but I found *nothing* that surprised me in them. In 1960 I wrote an essay-kind of book, "A history of the cold war" (about which you then wrote me a wonderfully magnanimous long letter)* in which there was a short chapter about 1956, with tentative conclusions about the meaning of those events; these are the same now as they were then. I am not patting myself on my back: rather, the contrary. What all of this suggests is that history—that is, human beings—make documents, rather than documents "making" history. A modest knowledge of history and a modicum of "Menschenverstand"—these are not *always* sufficient but when they do not sufficiently exist . . . as indeed today they don't. . . . I only hope that I have not bored you with this. . . .

In 1997 Richard Snow, editor of American Heritage *magazine, proposed a long interview, or tape-recorded conversation, between Kennan and myself on the occasion of the fiftieth anniversary of the "X" article—what had led to it? We—both of us being addicts of the written word—then decided to do this in the form of three exchanges of letters. Later that year they were also published in book form:* George F. Kennan and the Origins of Containment, 1944–1946: The Kennan-Lukacs Correspondence, *with my introduction added, by the University of Missouri Press, including a bibliography and an index.*

G.K. to J.L.

Princeton, New Jersey
May 31, 1997
Handwritten

I have just finished reading the first 200 pages of your *Hitler of History*.** I should, I suppose, have refrained from writing you about it before I had completed the reading. But realizing that this letter should be

---

* G.K. to J.L., pp. 28–30.
** John Lukacs, *The Hitler of History* (Knopf, 1997).

reaching you just after your return to this country, I wanted you to be greeted, upon arrival, by this initial reaction to the book.

This reaction is one of real excitement—for you, as an author and historian, for myself as a friend. Words fail me to convey the full strength of my impression. I want to avoid anything that would suggest a comparison with your other writings, for each of these had its own purpose to serve, and each should be judged only on its own terms. Let me just say that I find this a superb work of historical insight and analysis, and probably in relation (again) to its purpose and its prospective readership, the most important book you have ever written.

I see this work (and I hope you do not too violently disagree) not as a biographic study, but as a profoundly thoughtful and discriminating critique of the treatment of Hitler by German and other historians— of the historiography, in other words, addressed to the reality of his person and to the relationship of that person to the emerging political patterns of this age. This is of immense importance for the future of Europe and of this country; for without a clear understanding of these things, the Germans will not come to terms with themselves or with their position in Europe, nor, for that matter, will we—nor will the other Europeans with them. . . .

G.K. to J.L.

Institute for Advanced Study
Princeton, New Jersey
November 21, 1997

The letter about England arrived yesterday or the day before.* I was too exhausted, upon returning from Philadelphia, to give it a proper reading, but put it off until today. I have now read it—twice in fact— with the attention that practically anything you write commands.

(Two days have elapsed since I started this note. The little dictating box I have before me has lapsed into a sullen inactivity. I must have done something wrong to it. It is trying to tell me: "For anyone else I would perform, but not for a dope like you.")

---

* Not included in this volume.

My first reaction to your letter takes the form of an exclamation. What a restless seething *Geist* (in the German sense) holds you in its power, particularly when you travel! Observations, impressions, insights, implications, and challenges to critical judgment cascade in an impetuous torrent across the mind, each one crowding and pressing the one before it, like waves in a heavy angry sea (if you've even noticed it), leaping on the other's back, disputing, clamouring for attention before the other has had its say! And what a strain it must be to accept the components of this torrent, to try to sort them out and make sense of them, and not give up!

I share, of course, your sensitivity to the abundant contradictions in English society. You might note the reasons on pp. 174–75 and 187–88 of my *Sketches from a Life*. These contradictions must be far more marked now than they were 40 years ago when I lived and lectured in Oxford. But I also share the reassurance you seem to find in parts of English life. Had I to live in any truly great city, the first choice, I think, would be London.

John, I must stop. I am trying to write in bed, and it is a struggle.

J.L. to G.K.

11 July 1998

I am now convinced that we are only *at the beginning* of the Democratic Age. All of the English and the American and the French, etc. Revolutions notwithstanding. That we are beyond the end of a century (the 20th century having been that short one, 1914–1989) is obvious, and what is also obvious (the realization of this *is* a somewhat new phenomenon, part and parcel of our evolving historical consciousness) that we are also near the end of the so-called Modern Age (a wrong term, but let that go here), a great age that began about 1500 and is closing now. And one great, perhaps the greatest, characteristics of that 1500–2000 Age has been the coexistence of aristocracy with democracy. A coexistence sometimes marked by fearful struggles but not always. So, during the last 500 years, aristocracy has been gradually (sometimes dramatically) declining, while democracy has been rising—politically as well as socially. And the greatest achievements of the last 500 years were the results or, rather, the achievements of their mixture, or compound:

that Democracy was not total; that socially, and even more, politically, majority rule has had its limits, respected and imposed by entire societies and by Constitutions.

All of this is, or ought to be, rather obvious. From Aristotle onward, the greatest thinkers observed that no total system of society can be good, that because of the frailties of human nature the best government is some kind of Mixed Government, that (and here Tocqueville enters) the frailty of mankind is such that once we push an idea, no matter how "good," to its extreme, it degenerates into its very opposite. And of course, it was Tocqueville (the Aristotle of the Modern Age) who saw history at a turning-point, perhaps greater than the great transitions between Ancient and Middle and Modern: that is, from societies and states governed by minorities to societies and states governed (or, rather, ruled) by majorities—and that perhaps *this* might be the greatest change in the history of mankind.

Well—in my opinion, we have reached this stage only *now*. That is: democracy having become the *absolute* acceptance of majority rule. (In some cases: democracy having become Populism.) But this goes beyond politics; it involves society, "culture," education, etc., etc.

That—eventually—new "aristocracies," that is, ruling minorities will appear is fairly certain. What is probable is that they will be crude, cruel, and barbarian, asserting their power and authority by force. (This is also one of the reasons why the present—so-called "conservative"—ideology *against* the *state* is dangerous nonsense. The state, as such, was a product of the Modern Age: a necessary structure of law and order and, yes, even of certain liberties. What we see in Russia today is the very opposite of what the anti-Soviet ideologues were preaching: the problem there is not the great *strength* of a state but its very *weakness*.)

But what preoccupies me is the (to me, daily more and more evident) condition that in this mass-democratic age—contrary to its promoters *or* critics—things are not becoming simpler. Just the contrary. For "the people" speak seldom. What is happening is that people speak in the name of the people—a step away from reality, indeed, toward abstraction. Yes, it was back at the time of Andrew Jackson that the original construct of the Founders had changed, that elections and politics became popularity contests. That (for a

conservatively inclined observer) may have been regrettable. But in
the 20th century came another, worse change, from Popularity Contests
to Publicity Contests. And this prevails now not only in politics, but
in every field of life, material, intellectual, spiritual. An intrusion of
complexity and corruptibility into the very structure of events, including,
of course, "news" and "entertainment" (the two hardly separable now).
What happens is inseparable from what people think happens; what
people think their choices are; indeed, what people "really" think—this
has now become an extremely complex process and, indeed, phenomenon, with results that I at least am unable to foresee.

However—at least at present—the managers of such "communications" and, of course, of Publicity, may be corrupt and insidious but
they are also *weak*. This is why I think that our social and financial
and economic structures are top-heavy, dependent on insubstantial
materials, and liable to something catastrophic—I hope not in the near
future. I am—at times—sustained by my belief—indeed, a conviction—
that because of God's great gift history *is* unpredictable. . . .

But that is *not* much consolation. . . .

G.K. to J.L.

Kristiansand, Norway
August 3, 1998

You are right, of course, in the belief that what is now dawning upon us
in the beginning of a new age. I find it questionable, however, whether
it will be correctly referred to as a Democratic Age. Let me expand on
both of those views.

This will indeed be a new age. The civilization that has marked the
last centuries of European life will not only be largely abandoned, but
also largely forgotten. For the abandonment of literature and poetry, in
what is now to come, will also undermine all, or most, sense of history,
which required literature for its pursuit and expression.

In place of this, there will now come what I would expect to be a
long period of virtual enslavement. For it occurs to me that all those
phenomena to which the people of the latter part of this passing
century, and particularly the Americans, have looked for one form or

another of freedom and liberation, have proved to be forms of self-enslavement. The automobile, television (including televised photographic, artificial visions of life), drugs, and now the computer culture, have become not the enlargers of life they were originally seen to be, but the restrictors of it—forms of entrapment, all of them, from which people no longer know how to extract themselves. In this condition of servitude, real creativity, even in fact the sense of language, will suffer suffocation and will tend to die out. And all this will represent an almost total break with the European civilizations even of the late 19th century and the fin de siècle by which it was followed. The Europeans may well be less affected by all of this. Older forms of civilization may have a stronger hold on some of them, but only, I fear, to the extent that they succeed in detaching themselves from American influences.

Now, turning from this to the political field: I must question the use of the term "democratic" to the life that is to come. The founding fathers of our country, if my memory is correct did not like the term, viewed it as signifying a danger rather than a hope, and seldom if ever used it to describe what they thought they were inaugurating.

There is, actually, no such thing as democracy in abstract. When used to describe a political system, there are as many democracies as there are countries that thus describe themselves. As Tocqueville wrote, it is not the political institutions but rather *les manières* of a people that are significant. And there are no two sets of popular manières that are exactly alike.

And if it is self-government, and particularly self-government by the mass of the people, that you have in mind, here, too, I have great reservations. Gibbon, I believe it was, said something somewhere, in his *Decline of the Roman Empire* to the effect that if political power is placed in the hands of the masses (of an "unwieldy multitude" was, I seem to recall, his term), it will be first abused and then turned over to the nearest and most likely candidate for dictatorship, to be used according to his liking. I would have no confidence in the success, or even the durability, of any attempt to make the vox populi the basis for political power anywhere. Our founding fathers understood that, I think, very well. And the only role they conceded to the popular masses was not the governing of the country but rather the choosing by election, and this for limited periods, of representatives by whom that was to be performed. And there was, in my opinion, very good reason for such an arrangement; for the average man is apt to be much more discerning about the qualities of individual fellow-citizens than he is about the intricate and extensive compromises that are bound to lie at the heart of most acts of legislation. And if, as is often the case, they are somewhat less than admiring for those that they choose to represent themselves, they at least value, and should have, the privilege, from time to time, of throwing "the rascals out," on the theory that it is undesirable for any one set of mouths to be too long at the trough.

If I thought that this—"representative government"—was to be the pattern for the new age, I would be less skeptical of its future. And something resembling it may be long maintained in the European governments with their responsible parliamentary majorities and ministerial governments. But in the U.S., I fear, the trends are in the other directions. I would be grateful, here, if you would glance, once more, at pp. 133–41 of my *Around the Cragged Hill*, which perhaps shows more clearly what I have in mind.

J.L. to G.K.

11 August 1998

We tend to see so many things alike. Alas, important things—whence our mutual pessimism of the near future. But there is one matter about which I am more optimistic than you are. You write that "the abandonment of literature and poetry, in what is now to come, will also undermine all, or most, sense of history, which required literature for its pursuit and expression." I agree with the *essence* of this profound and summary statement: that the sense of history is inseparable from a sense of language (Emerson: "The corruption of man will be followed by the corruption of language"—in many ways the reverse is true)— whereby the modern tendency to consider History as a Social Science is lamentable. But there are many signs indicating an opposite direction. There is an appetite for history—in this country, too—which is rather unprecedented. To illustrate it would require many pages. It includes— among many other things—the popular interest in all kinds of histories and biographies, at the expense of the declining interest in, say, novels. Of course appetite may be served by junk food. But the existence of appetite is, after all, a good and vital sign. I have for long believed—and some of my own works may be, perhaps indirect, indications of this— that eventually most of prose literature will be absorbed by history, in one way or another. That there are potential dangers in such a develop- ment I know. But the tendency is at least worthy of recognition. And that the overwhelming majority of intellectuals and professional histo- rians do not see it: so what? *Tant pis.*

A response to" A Letter on Germany" that Kennan wrote to Gordon Craig. It would appear in New York Review of Books *on December 3, 1998.*

J.L. to G.K.

16 November 1998

Your most splendid passage is when you write that it took "longer than it should have" for you to recognize that in governmental service "one is routinely forgiven for saying the wrong thing at the right time, but for saying the right thing at the wrong time—never." (You wrote about this in another splendid passage in your Memoirs, too, about 1946.) Well—this is more than an aphorism—it is alone sufficient to secure the reputation of a great philosopher and wit. . . .

J.L. to G.K.

5 December 1998

Many years ago, at least on one occasion, I suggested to you that your Diaries and Letters ought to be published—independent of the official biography now prepared by Gaddis—and that I am not only willing but desirous to edit such a volume.* We did not pursue this idea further. If I remember, you may have mentioned your commitment to Gaddis. (From what follows, you will see that I at least see no conflict between

---

* Yale historian John Lewis Gaddis.

your commitment to your biographer and such a potential volume suggested by me.) You also said, perhaps on another occasion, that at some future time your "Collected Works," including your correspondence will probably be published. (Permit me to question this impression. A *complete* publication of *Oeuvres complètes* or *Gesammelte Werke* belong to the 19th century. The volume of your published and unpublished writings, including the enormous mass of your correspondence, is such that such a "Collected Works of GFK," running perhaps to twenty or more volumes, is an impossibility. Even the current, and generally excellent, *Library of America* series does not aspire to completeness.). . .

What I see is a most impressive and substantial volume of your Diaries and Letters—which I am most desirous to work on, father, edit and select—and which Yale University Press is *very* desirous to publish in a *most* impressive large volume. But this brings me to a list of questions which I ask you to ponder at your leisure and to suggest your answer to me personally and verbally, not in any detail or in writing. . . .

G.K. to J.L.

Kristiansand, Norway
August 11, 1999
Handwritten

I thought I might try to tell you what, as among more important matters, has most preoccupied me in these summer weeks. First of all, Norway. Life changes very slowly in such a country; and I could, for this reason, refrain from looking at this one critically in each of these summers; but I do so look at it, and it saddens me to have to say that I find it more depressive than ever before.

Yes, life is (if you forget some of the urban youth) well ordered, and government is humane, but there is a difference between humanness and lax indulgence, and a little more of firm principle and conviction would do no harm. And what most greatly depresses me are first, the rank and pervasive materialism and secondly, the lack of challenge.

Is it not ironic that in a country that is rich beyond anything people even dreamed of up to some twenty or thirty years ago, where money

is easily available and accessible to anyone who wants to exert himself
to obtain liberal mounts of it—that in such a country it should be
primarily money that dominates the pages of the press and, we must
conclude, the interests and preoccupations of the mass of the people?
Prices, taxes, costs and revenues preempt at least the greater part of life
as reflected in the papers.

As for lack of challenge: the term is an inadequate one, but there
is something to it. I can think of no place that more deserves Gray's
reference to the place "where wealth accumulates and men decay."*
Tocqueville foresaw this, too. Here, one is taken care of from birth to
death insofar as this is possible at all, by the state. There would be no
excuse for anyone sleeping on the street. And no one does. On the
other hand, there is no dissuasion from sleeping, figuratively, anywhere
else—not even, if one prefers, at the work place.

Perhaps this view of Norwegian life is, of course, a narrow one.
Allowing for this, I can only say that what I most lack here is any preoccupation with the deeper mysteries of life, even among the youth. Is
this a generational phenomenon? Would this be true of our youth as
well? It probably would. But among students of my own at Princeton,
there was far more of an interest in various aspects of philosophy than
I see here even among the adults. There was then more curiosity about
the deeper understanding of beauty, of religious faith in any one of
the occasional and wholly unplanned meetings ("bull sessions" they
were then called) of undergraduates in the room of my friend Bernard
Gufler (a Catholic, incidentally) in Witherspoon Hall at Princeton in
1924—more than you could encounter in an entire year of social life
among either students or adults in the town of Kristiansand.

Particularly significant is the condition and role of religious life
in this place. Such of it as exists seems to find its location in the parts
of the lower middle class and in the dissident sects rather than in the
state-sponsored Lutheran Church; and the quality of it in theological-
philosophical depth is, I should think, about on the level with our own
"born-again" Southern Baptists. Among the upper classes, regardless
of educational level or wealth, there seems to be no religious faith at
all, or even interest in religion. People fall back, to be sure, on the great

* Actually from Oliver Goldsmith, "The Deserted Village."

ceremonial institutions of Christian faith—baptism, marriage and leave-take from the dead; they do, even in a state of bewildered helplessness, recognizing that these events demand some sort of solemnization and contenting themselves with what the church has to offer, even where they lack even the faintest knowledge of its philosophical and theological foundations. . . .

I began reading Kennan's diaries (my plan was to read and then select from his diaries first, and from his letters thereafter) in the first six months of 1999. His personal papers were deposited in the Mudd Manuscript Library of Princeton, where they (those before 1970) were still closed to researchers and the public. He also introduced me to work in his office in the Institute for Advanced Studies (which he now, in the 96th year of his life, still visited about every second day). I was stunned by the enormous quantity and by the rich quality of his diaries, beginning as early as when he was 20. I had got as far in my reading and selecting as the early 1940s when (for reasons unknown to me) his then newly appointed literary executor, a relative and an academic, surprised me by courteously suggesting that I not pursue this work. (Later his literary executor became his son Christopher.) I then chose to abandon this work (also as advised by my wife, Stephanie—in order to spare Kennan), and not to speak to him about it.

G.K. to J.L.

Princeton, New Jersey
October 11, 1999
Handwritten

I appreciated your note of the 5th. I trust you will bear with me if I refrain from comment on the present state of the matter about which you wrote.

I would like just to say that I am particularly unhappy about this recent unpleasantness because of my awareness that so much of it is attributable to the clumsiness of my part in the matter in earlier years.

P.S. My warmest congratulations on your *Five Days in London*,* an amazing work of careful yet imaginative scholarship. I am encouraged to hope that it is going to find the reception it deserves.

J.L. to G.K.

15 October 1999

Your letter came last night. Its kindness touched me *deeply*.
You must *not* vex or blame yourself about *anything*. . . .

J.L. to G.K.

25 October 1999

I must tell you something about Buchanan** (whose recent book I read, and even reviewed it for a right-wing, rather Buchananite, magazine, and critically indeed). He respects you; and it was a nice (though also politic) gesture of him to write you. There are many things about which he and you and I would agree. These from the first and the last chapters of his book where he proposes certain things for American foreign policy, including a few unusual and even radical departures from what exists in common intellectual commerce nowadays: propositions with which you and I would largely agree. Among other things, he feels strongly about the undue Jewish influence in American intellectual and political life; he is sensible about what American policy regarding Russia should be (of course he surely was not sensible about that in the past.) In his other seven chapters, his summary of the history of American foreign policy, he is also right—sometimes.

But when he is wrong, he is very wrong. That is why he must be regarded with a wary and perspicacious caution. Deep down—as a matter of fact, not so deep down, since this tends to bob up to the surface—Buchanan admires the German Third Reich and even Hitler (though, on occasion, he will deny that); while at the same time, he

---

* John Lukacs, *Five Days in London, May 1940* (Yale University Press, 1999).

** Patrick Buchanan, a conservative columnist and sometime presidential candidate, sent him a letter and a book.

despises England and especially Churchill. Much of this is probably due to his family origins: his father Scotch-Irish (*not* true Irish—the latter have largely abandoned their anti-British sentiments), and his mother German. Irish-German: not the best combination. The same thing was true of Joseph McCarthy, whom Buchanan admires and with whom he truly has much in common. (One crucial example: their excoriating the war against Germany, and yet immediately afterward preaching the need for a crusade against Russia.) I shall not go into his many errors, except perhaps to say that, as is the case of all nationalist demagogues, his hatred for his opponents is so much stronger than is his love for his country. Last night you and I talked about the German aristocrats and Prussian officers who tried to save the honor of their country and of Western civilization by eliminating Hitler. They were the finest tragic representatives of that civilization. Buchanan would consider them traitors. I thought that this would interest you. . . .

G.K. to J.L.

Princeton, New Jersey
January 28, 2000

Trying, this morning, to sift through masses of old personal papers, I find this copy of an article I published in FOREIGN AFFAIRS in 1951, even before the Chicago lectures.*

You asked me yesterday, I seem to recall, what I considered as the most important of my own books. I gave a shallow and, I fear, unconvincing reply. But had the query related to articles rather than books, this one, particularly from p. 355 on, would unquestionably take first place. I mentioned, in our talk, Forster's *Passage to India* and pointed out that almost [all] of what the author had to say was really said in the first chapter. Well—so it is with this article. It contained, as I now see it, the bulk of all that I have been trying to say in the ensuing half-century. If all my other writings should be destroyed or otherwise consigned to oblivion, this is the one which I would hope might be preserved.

---

* "America and the Russian Future," *Foreign Affairs* (April 1951).

J.L. to G.K.

7 January 2001

At the Second Coming, at the end of the world, what will happen to
Christians (St. John of the Apocalypse) will be what happened to the
Jews at the time of the First Coming of Jesus. They will divide. The
majority will follow the Anti-Christ (a smiling, handsome, seemingly
generous, telegenic personality). A minority will see through him and
follow the true Christ, to be saved. . . .

G.K. to J.L.

Kristiansand, Norway
July 18, 2001

We have now just passed the halfway mark in this, our summer's stay
in Norway. I had intended to write you sooner, but was held up by the
problem of finding a new ribbon for this ancient typewriter. And now,
in the meantime, my intention to write was much stimulated by the
discovery, in a long neglected drawer of one of the tables in this cottage,
your letters to me from the summer of 1992. I had, just before leaving
for Norway, sent you the typescript of the volume called *Around the
Cragged Hill*; and these newly-discovered letters were your response.
They were fine letters, the importance of which has been no whit
diminished by the passage of the intervening years. I shall send them to
you at a later date.

Although you spoke with appreciation of the first three chapters of
the book, it is clear that you were, in general, disappointed by it. And
with good reason. The book was in just about all respects a failure—a
term that I use not in the financial sense, but in its failure to meet the
hopes that had inspired the writing of it, that it would carry to the
readers a useful impression of my thinking on a considerable number
of public problems and would, in this way, enter the intellectual climate
of the time. We will, I hope, have occasion to talk further about this
when I get home.

I have been essentially house bound over all these weeks in Norway;
and the experience has not been for me a pleasant one. It will be a

great relief to me (or so I picture it) to become again installed in the
Princeton house and to have the devoted help of our two Portuguese
servants. Since only rarely have I had access to any good English or (if
the Herald Tribune can be called that) American newspaper. Faute de
mieux, I have given quite close study to the Norwegian ones, hoping
that I might find at least some evidence of a sensible and solid stability
of a modern civilization. But this, again without reassurance. Norway's
past, poor, hard, and sometimes desperately unsuccessful owing to a
population-growth beyond the country's meager resources, was, God
knows, no easy one. But it bred many strong, healthy, modest and
pious people. This, alas, no longer. The money from the oil rigs, and the
example of our country, to which so many Norwegians had emigrated,
have changed all that. Aside from the triumphant successes of the automobile with which we are so extensively acquainted, there has been the
usual massive stampede of what was once the rural population to the
few cities, particularly Oslo—a movement which I strongly deplore. . . .

J.L. to G.K.

17 August 2001

I am *deeply* vexed by the arrogant and thoughtless policy of this
dreadful administration toward Russia.* I will not detail its evidences;
you know them better than I do. The trouble is that the Democrats do
not really have a policy to counter it, since they are (1) afraid to say
anything that suggests that they are weak on "defense" (that stupid
term); (2) the American public seems uninterested in the rest of the
world, surely less interested than they have been for a long time.
History does not repeat itself, but much of this is reminiscent of the
1950's. what can one *do* about it? . . .

J.L. to G.K.

15 October 2001

I promised to tell you about my trip to Sweden . . .

---

* President George W. Bush entered the White House in January 2001.

I see beneath their pallid Puritanism (for their socialist democracy is, in its way, puritanical) a thick layer of moderate humanism which does not only govern their behavior but also their thinking. Sweden is a very civilized country—in the best sense of that adjective. It is also "modern"—well, we know that. But, in a way, it is also very bourgeois— and not at all in the often pejorative and dismissive sense of that adjective or category. There is an urbanity in Swedish cities that has now crumbled elsewhere, and not only in the United States. There is not much urban sprawl. People still live in some of their solid old houses; they are not abandoning them. Of course there are only eight million of them in a large country. But their landscape is humane, not disfigured by sprawling "developments." I kept looking at their countryside, again and again, on the three-hour train journey from Stockholm to Gothenburg.

They are also a nation of readers. (*Per capita* I, for one, may have more readers in Sweden than perhaps in any other country of the world.)...

J.L. to G.K.

3 February 2002

Of course, I re-read your letter from Prague to your sister, almost instantly.* I write "re-read" because I had of course read it in 1989; more, I remembered it rather well. Now all of it struck me, and rather deeply, again. The essence is the beauty of your writing. These are some of the most beautiful (and, given the theme and the place, some of the most poignant) pages you have ever written. You think that they illustrate your (and my) sense of historical consciousness. Of course they do: they breathe both the quantity and the quality of your very knowledge of history. But: I see something more, and perhaps even something deeper, in these pages. That is your sense of the futility of all human endeavors. I need not tell you that this is there in all of your writing and thinking, it is the essence of your view of human nature and human destiny. You know, I think, that I come very close to this, because of my (Catholic) belief and conviction of the Original Sin....

* He had sent me two letters he had written to Jeanette, his sister closest to him.

You did not know, how could you know sixty-one years ago that you will be allowed to live, with full mental and spiritual strength, to your present age; and together with your splendid wife; and surrounded by the affection of your children; that you will rise, for a short time, to a place where you will help set the very course of the history of your nation; that you will write a dozen books that soon after their publication will become American classics, studied by and inspiring to many thousands of young people; that people will see you—and without the slightest efforts of publicity—as an American sage, representing great and grave wisdoms? . . .

G.K. to J.L.

Institute for Advanced Study
Princeton, NJ
February 11, 2002

We come now to your suggestion that I should read the final pages of your book* and give you my reactions to it. I seem to have lost the page numbers you mentioned, but I suspect that what you had in mind were primarily the pages from 204 on.

May I first make one general criticism? I think that the following pages are overburdened by quotes of the words of others. These are excellent quotes, but their very abundance tends to carry the reader away from your own views as presented in your own words. Could you not dispense with the number of them so as to keep clearly before the eyes of the reader your own argumentation?

I think that the little passage (page 212) on the history of the word "world" might be omitted or shortened.

I welcome with real enthusiasm your reference to the miracle of our "warm earth."

But those are merely casual remarks. What I really feel obliged to comment on is the section beginning on page 213, with regard to "God." You begin by relating the concept of God to our consciousness. And that down to the middle of page 214, is coherent as an introduction

---

* I had sent him (only the last, philosophic chapter) of my *At the End of an Age* (Yale University Press, 2002).

to what you have later to say on this subject. But it seems to me that you get carried away from the final line of page 214 by quite different thoughts and continue with them until you return to the "contemplation of God," on page 216 and include in it at some length the quotation of your own thoughts of fifteen years ago. Valuable as are those thoughts, I have a feeling that somehow or other, and not because they have been invalidated by the passage of time (which they have not), but rather because the reader would like to hear you saying these things to him today, in today's language, which would never be exactly that of earlier years.

Now for the principal question raised by these final passages, namely, that if what we fancy to observe in normal life is, as you have so powerfully stated throughout your book, in large part the creation of our own consciousness, is this not also true of our relationship to God? Are we not, in other words, recreating God rather than recognizing his power as something quite beyond that of our own capacities of perception?

I do not mean to deny that our own consciousness properly contains what Wordsworth called "intimations of immortality." Christ himself said, on one occasion, that "the Kingdom of God is within you." Well this seems to have been another of the instances where Christ put forward his greatest and most divine thoughts in extremist terms. In any case, there are within us, to be sure, what I might call wisps of the Kingdom of God, but certainly not all of it or even anything that approaches such dimensions. It is not just that the essence of the Kingdom of God is beyond us. It is more than that: it is something that is, and must remain, beyond our powers of comprehension or judgement.

We know that we cannot look at the sun with direct and naked eyes. It blinds us if we try it. Just so, there are things about the nature of God which we should not, and cannot, attempt to envisage and understand. To suppose that we would be capable of such a thing would resemble in itself a form of blasphemy.

To explain what I mean, included are the final two paragraphs of a re-written version of the letter to my children about religion of which you once saw, I believe, some earlier versions. I will give them here as they stand at the new ending of that document.

So I will end this discussion only by a backward glimpse of a scene of my long-distant childhood. The second-floor bedrooms of our Milwaukee house then being occupied by more mature members of the family, I, as a little boy, was relegated for sleeping purposes, to a small and somewhat dreary room on the third floor. Its windows looked out over the roofs of a few more houses to the Milwaukee River, and on the further side of the river were the always busy railway sorting yards, so that all night you heard the whistles of the switch engines and the clicking of the freight cars being shunted from one track to another. And it was amid this ambiance that I, as a small boy, knelt down every evening beside my iron bed and directed to "Our Father who art in Heaven" the Lord's Prayer (not knowing then, as I do now, the most of the words were those suggested by Christ to his first disciples, when they asked him what a prayer was and what it should include).

While no doubt only dimly perceiving the meaning of the words he was pronouncing, the child, I am sure, never doubted that those words were part of a great and solemn mystery, unamenable of course to his understanding but deserving of his wonder, his awe, his deep respect, and his reverence. I cannot know how many of these reactions and perceptions of a kneeling child would be meaningful for sensitive adults of our present age. But I raise the question whether they would not still provide, in all their purity and power, a surer and more enduring foundation for religious faith than all the questionings and reasonings of the nine decades of conscious adulthood on my part that were destined to follow. And an affirmative response to that question would probably define better than anything else, I think, the nature of my own faith. . . .

J.L. to G.K.

18 February 2002

Your thoughts about God and our consciousness. Christ: "the Kingdom of God is within you"—well, that is enough for me. I *know* that that is not *all*. (As you say, "there are things about the nature of God which we should not, and cannot, attempt to envisage and understand.") I am satisfied—satisfied, rather than comfortable—with my understanding of the limits of our knowledge, and with the consequent sense that our

knowledge of these limits do not impoverish but, perhaps, paradoxically, enrich us. (I think that you will agree.) I also agree with you—
how can I not?—that both the existence of God and our consciousness
of Him contain an inevitable sense of mystery. But I have two thoughts
to add to that. One is that our relationship—more, with our sometimes conscious, sometimes vaguely and hardly conscious, sometimes
unconscious relationship with God (note that I write "with" and not
merely "to") inevitably involves participation: participation, rather than
observation. (This is what I may have meant in our telephone conversation when we talked about The Holy Spirit. Sometimes when I pray, I
sense that I am involved in something that is more than my talking to
God and hoping that He listens: for I also sense that God is suggesting
some things to me: and that this is something else than two living
beings talking and listening to each other, because my talking to (or,
more correctly, asking) Him are, mysteriously *simultaneous*.) The other
thought is my conviction that there is an element of mystery not only
within us but in this world also, all around us. Owen Chadwick, whom
I consider the greatest living historian, wrote that "all historical events
remain, in part, mysterious." (I quoted this in my book.). . .

J.L. to G.K.

1 April 2002

I am reading a book the contents of which may interest you. It is
published in the series of monographs of the Institut fuer Zeitge-
schichte, and I personally know one of its authors, [Hermann] Graml.
"Die Stalin-Note vom 10. Maerz 1952. Neue Quellen and Analysen."*
This is the note in which Stalin offered free elections in Germany and
the removal of all foreign troops within a year. You know all about
this—if I remember, the then Secretary of State [Dulles] failed to
inform you about it when you had set out for Moscow, if I remember
rightly. It now seems that one of the authors, Wilfried Loth, found a
mass of documents in the Russian archives about the preparations for
such a Russian-proposed peace treaty for Germany, eventually leading
to Stalin's four-power note on 10.3.1952. Some of the documents are

* Wilfred Loth, Hermann Graml, and Gerhard Wettig (Oldenbourg, 2002).

interesting—they indicate that the original impulse came from the
Foreign Ministry and not from Stalin, in the fall of 1951, and that it was
strongly supported by [former Foreign Minister Vyacheslav] Molotov
even though [Andrey] Vyshinksy was the Foreign Minister then. Of
the three authors, Wilfried Loth emphasizes that it was a definite
move for the eventual establishment of a Weimar-type Germany;
my friend Graml questions this, not always convincingly; the third
scholar, Gerhard Wettig simply repeats all the cold war propaganda
formulas. I regret that none of them see that what Stalin feared (this
is my view, of course) was the establishment of an American-West
German alliance; that he was NOT interested in the further extension
of Communism beyond the line that divided Europe and Germany but
what he strongly wanted was the definite consolidation and security of
his Easter European domains; and none of the authors notices in their
"Schlussfolgerungen" [conclusions] how the USSR recognized West
Germany in 1955 without requiring that the Western Powers recognize
the East German "regime." . . .

---

*Because of the temporary absence of the devoted Portuguese couple who cared
for the Kennans at home, in September 2002 they had to spend a fortnight in a
Washington "retirement" home, where he was desperately unhappy. (During this
time we had long telephone conversations.)*

J.L. to G.K.

26 September 2002

You return to your home today. Your Purgatory is over. I (we) think of
you both and cheer you on.

I am writing this because last time you had some trouble hearing on
the telephone. And of course, this note does not require an answer but
you did not hear me well. You said that you went out or were taken out
for a short time from the Purgatory Mansion and you suddenly remembered the people of the Washington you knew and that all of them
are gone now from that world. What I wanted and now want to say:
your life at your age is God's gift by itself, but there is more to it—your

mental and spiritual awareness of what has gone, a matter not gone out alive in your heart and mind. Your life—not only in the past but now, too—has much meaning. . . .

You too must be vexed by the tragic comic theatre that is going on in Washington now. Sooner or later the American people will be judged—will they accept this now present vile propagation of a universalist nationalism, or will they not? . . .

My wife, Stephanie, died on January 5, 2003. I had to dissuade Kennan, now bedridden, from being driven to her funeral.

G.K. to J.L.

February 14, 2003

I received, yesterday, the copy of my letter of December 22, 1950,[*] which you unearthed somewhere and kindly sent to me, asking me to tell you, by telephone, what I thought of it. This last I shall try to do, but not (for various reasons) by telephone.

The first two pages of the letter were, I see, on the stuffy side, and upon a first hasty reading of them by poor light, I said to myself: "Heavens, what a silly and pompous ass you were." But today, upon reading it all through, and that by good light, I saw why I had written it, and gained a different impression of it. Let me explain.

The real American Foreign Service was established in 1923 or 1924. Its establishment owed itself to primarily the interest of a small group of rather old-fashioned gentlemen of mature age, most of them men who had had first-hand experience with American diplomacy in earlier years. They agreed on the need for a permanent professional diplomatic service. And because they were themselves well known and generally respected persons in Washington, they found there the necessary understanding and support for what they were doing.

The new service was to be entered only by severe examination, both written and oral, in the administration of which several of the founders played a lively personal part. The further service of those admitted

[*] This letter he had written to Carlisle Humelsine.

was governed by a special personnel board. And the service itself, throughout their entire careers, was independent of all control from Washington other than by its own board. Its officers bore the title of "Foreign Service Officer"—and enjoyed a dignity roughly comparable to that of a captain in the Army.

The second World War, for reasons I have never understood, put an end to all that. The independence of the administration of the Service was abandoned, power over its affairs now falling into the hands of an official in one room of the State Department, the official occupant being a member of the now vastly expanded Washington bureaucracy. The name "Foreign Service" was retained for reasons also obscure to me, but the Old Service was simply and mutely abolished. Men who had worked themselves into higher positions in the Old Foreign Service were told, in effect, their status as officials of the government was no longer recognized, and that for their future relationship to the war-time government they should abide by the decision of the draft board of their particular place of residence in the United States. With this one decision, the entire structure of the old Foreign Service was mutely abolished and destroyed.

I had remained in the official service of the government during the war-time years, partly because two of them were spent in Germany and terminated by months of imprisonment by the Germans. After that, I was picked by [Ambassador W.] Averell Harriman and brought to Moscow as his senior assistant. I was still, then, in the employ of the government but actually in the position of a personal assistant to Mr. Harriman. When that service came to an end I returned to Washington, served as Deputy Commandant of the National War College in the first year of its existence, and was taken from there by General Marshall when he became Secretary of State and wanted someone to establish, as his immediate underling, a Policy Planning Staff, which I did, and did to his satisfaction. (This was the background of the Marshall Plan.) But then, when the Republicans came into office, I was, as you well know, in effect dismissed from this governmental service by the new Secretary of State, Mr. John Foster Dulles, whereupon I moved, in effect, to scholarly work at the Institute for Advanced Study, and to the establishment of a residence in Princeton in the year 1950.

Mr. Humelsine just then having come into occupancy of a position of the Department of State, seems to have asked me for an opinion as to what should be done with the remains of the old Foreign Service.

This letter was the response.

*****

I am sorry to have taken up so much time and space with the above. But I know of no other way to explain this curious letter. I suspect that Humelsine would have liked to restore the old service but found himself unable to do so; and vague memories tell me that he soon left government employment himself, to take up a new and prestigious position in Williamsburg, Virginia.

J.L. to G.K.

5 March 2003

Arriving home from England, I found two extraordinarily valuable letters from you: one about the long letter you had written to Mr. Humelsine 53 years ago, the other a copy of your letter to your nephew, written on 19 February.* You asked me to destroy it which I shall do in a few minutes. But I read and re-read it twice and may do that once more.

You have honored me by telling me some intimate matters about your youth and your stepmother, etc., and now much of this letter to Mr. Hotchkiss deals with such. Of course all that you told me or wrote about such things will remain in my mind and issue from it nowhere. But toward the end of your letter—and what a gift from God is the enduring marvelous power of your mind, evident in your ability to express yourself so tersely and clearly—you write about a condition that vexes me as much as it seems to vex you: the unprecedented puerility and presumptuousness of the present President and the largely tacit, confused, though uneasy, acceptance of his wish for war by the majority

* Partly quoted in my *George Kennan: A Study of Character*, 187, about the coming American invasion of Iraq. "I take an extremely dark view of all this—see it, in fact, the beginning of the end of anything like a normal life for all the rest of us . . . What is being done to our country today is surely something from which we will never be able to restore the sort of country you and I have known." This was the last written example of one of Kennan's profoundest convictions, first jotted down in his diary in Berlin in 1940: "No people is great enough to establish world hegemony."

of the American people, including men who ought to be his outspoken
opponents. There were other Presidents during two hundred years who
wanted to go to war: Polk, McKinley, FDR, for example. They were
convinced that the national interests of the United States dictated their
choice; and they hoped that the then enemy would fire the first shot
(this was also so with Lincoln and Fort Sumter in April 1861). That is
not so now. This president's mind (and character) is that of a 15 year old
American teenager who wants to remain the class president, a position
he had got through mere luck. Commentators are wrong when they
speculate that he wants to revenge what [Iraqi leader] Saddam H. had
planned for his father. No: George W. never liked his father; he wants to
show that he can do even better than his father. We know the immortal
warning of John Quincy Adams: "we do not go abroad in search for
monsters to destroy." This puerile president is worse than that: he
proclaims and pinpoints one monster for the sake of consolidating his
and his party's popularity. . . .

G.K. to J.L.

> Princeton, New Jersey
> August 27, 2003
> Letter from Betsy Barrett*

Mr. Kennan asked me to call you and just say a few words in explanation of his condition. He then proceeded to dictate what I might say,
and I have decided to type exactly what he said and send it to you.

   "I have had a real problem with how to fit into my own present
routine my friendship with him which has a number of unique aspects
and lends itself to no uniformities, but I would like him to know
that such has been the decline in my condition that I don't think any
meeting or unusual effort to communicate would be of any sue to you
[him]. But I hope that he will not hesitate to let me know of anything
he thinks that he would like brought to my attention, even in present
circumstances. Nothing will be forgotten from the years of our friendship and active communication. I put him in a category by himself."

* His secretary and nurse.

J.L. to G.K.

25 January 2004

I am leaving Thursday afternoon for Hungary and England. I shall be away for five weeks. This means that I shall not be here on the day of your one-hundredth birthday.* You will believe me when I say how much I regret this. . . .

I have not come to see you in Princeton these past few weeks and now I can no longer do so. I shall come very soon when I return (late on 7 March). That I think of you very often—very often—is but one inner manifestation of the affection and the gratitude for our friendship (which now goes back for so many decades), but it is not the extent but the quality of our affection for each other that has enriched my life. That God has allowed your loved ones to celebrate your one hundredth birthday is a symbolic marker; and how much more important is the condition that His endowment of your mind has been such that it continues living on, sensitive, knowledgeable, and often very vivid, till this day. You have much to be thankful for (and so am I, for your presence in this world and in mine). My heartfelt love to Annelise, and to you. "Omnia vincit Amor."

* About the last year of his life, see my *George Kennan*, 187–89. I last saw him in February 2005. He died on March 17, 2005, one year, one month, one day after his 100th birthday.

Calendar of the Letters

A SELECTIVE CHRONOLOGY OF WORLD EVENTS
THROUGH AND AFTER THE COLD WAR

1952
September 3   L. to K.   Kennan Ambassador to Moscow.
                                        Expelled by Stalin (October).
                                        Dwight David Eisenhower
                                        elected president (November).

1953
October 31   L. to K.   Stalin dies (March). Crisis in
November 6   L. to K.   Germany, riots (June).
November 18   K. to L.   Joseph McCarthy rampant.
                                        Secretary of State John Foster
                                        Dulles forces Kennan to retire
                                        from Foreign Service.

1955

October 28	L. to K.	Russia retreats from Austria
October 31	K. to L.	and Finland, recognizes West
November 9	L. to K.	Germany.

First Cold War "summit":
Eisenhower, British Prime
Minister Anthony Eden, French
Prime Minister Edgar Faure,
and Soviet Communist Party
leader Nikita Khrushchev
in Geneva (uneventful and
inconsequential).

1956

July 11	K. to L.	Khrushchev's speech denouncing
August 21	L. to K.	Stalin (February).
September 6	K. to L.	Polish resistance to Moscow.

Revolution in Hungary.
Eisenhower reelected
(November).

1957

January 17	L. to K.	Kennan's BBC lectures about the
February 25	K. to. L.	Cold War and the division of
December 2	L. to K.	Europe.
December 28	K. to L.	

1958

January 8	L. to K.	Moscow reopens the Berlin
March 11	L. to K.	problem.

1959

January 11	L. to.K.	Tension between Russia and
January 16	L. to K.	China.
April 5	K. to. L.	Khrushchev visits United States.

"Captive Nations Resolution"
passed by Congress.

1960

February 10	L. to K.	American spy plane (U-2) shot
February 26	K. to L.	down over Russia (May).
November 4	K. to L.	Failed "summit" in Paris.
		John F. Kennedy elected
		president.

1962

November 28	L. to K.	Kennan ambassador to
		Yugoslavia.
		Cuban missile crisis (October).

1963

May 12	L. to K.	Kennedy assassinated
May 29	K. to L.	(November).
		Lyndon B. Johnson president.

1964

April 30	K. to L.	Khrushchev demoted in
		Moscow; Leonid Brezhnev and
		Alexei Kosygin succeed him
		(October).

1966

| June 17 | K. to L. | Vietnam war escalates (1965). |
| July 13 | L. to K. | |

1967

October 4	L. to K.	Johnson meets Soviet Prime
October 19	K. to. L.	Minister Alexei Kosygin in
December 3	L. to K.	Glassboro, N.J.
December 7	K. to L.	6-Day War between Israel and its
		neighbors.

1968

December 3	K. to L.	Czechoslovak crisis, Soviet
		occupation.
		Richard M. Nixon elected
		president.

1969

March 27	K. to L.	Border fighting between Russia
April 13	L. to K.	and China.
April 20	K. to L.	
July 22	L. to K.	

1970

August 20	K. to L	American-German-Russian
November 15	K. to L.	agreement on Berlin and East
		Germany. "Détente" begins.

1971

April 14	K. to L.	Nixon's "opening" to China.
May 12	L. to K.	
May 20	K. to L.	

1972

| January 18 | K. to L. | Nixon reelected. |
| | | Armistice in Vietnam (1973). |

1974

February 7	K. to L.	U.S. retreat from Indochina.
March 8	K. to L.	Nixon resigns.
September 23	K. to L.	Gerald R. Ford president.
October 16	L. to K.	

1975

April 13	K. to L.	Helsinki "three-tier" accords.
August 24	K. to L.	
October 19	K. to L.	

1976

November 20	L. to K.	Jimmy Carter elected president.
December 11	K. to L.	
December 21	L. to K.	

1977

| February 6 | K. to L. | |

1978

| August 8 | K. to L. | John Paul II, from Poland, |
| August 15 | K. to L. | elected pope. |

1979

January 10	L. to K.	Russia invades Afghanistan
May 8	L. to K.	(December).
May 17	K. to L.	
August 10	K. to L.	
September 10	L. to K.	
October 28	K. to L.	

1980

January 7	L. to K.	Carter sends American
January 13	K. to L.	commandos into Iran.
March 9	L. to K.	Carter boycotts Moscow
March 13	K. to L.	Olympics.
		Polish "Solidarity" movement
		rises and gains strength.
		Ronald W. Reagan elected
		president.

1983

March 17	L. to K.	Reagan "Evil Empire" speech.
September 27	K. to L.	

1984

January 15	K. to L.	Mikhail Gorbachev becomes
February 23	K. to L.	Soviet leader.
March 5	L. to K.	Reagan reelected.
April 10	K. to L.	
July 8	K. to L.	
July 18	L. to K.	
July 27	K. to L.	
August 16	L. to K.	
August 27	K. to L.	
September 4	L. to K.	
October 22	L. to K.	
December 9	L. to K.	

1985

April 3	L. to K.	Gorbachev's openings: "glasnost"
May 7	K. to L.	and "perestroika."
July 28	L. to K.	Leaks across the Iron Curtain.
September 19	K. to L.	Reagan bombs Libya, invades
October (undated)	K. to L.	Grenada.
October 15	K. to L.	
October 20	L. to K.	

1986

February 17	K. to L.	American intervention in
March 27	K. to L.	Nicaragua.
April 7	K. to L.	Reykjavik "summit" between
April 15	L. to K.	Reagan and Gorbachev.
April 16	K. to L.	Reagan recognizes changes in
May 31	K. to L.	Soviet behavior.
June 1	K. to L.	
July 1	L. to K.	
August 8	K. to L.	
August 22	L. to K.	
September 23	K. to L.	
September 26	L. to K.	

1987

January 13	K. to L.	"Iran-contra" scandals.
February 7	K. to L.	Reagan visits Moscow.
February 10	L. to K.	Gorbachev in Washington
July 31	L. to K.	(December); at a reception he
August 7	K. to L.	recognizes and salutes Kennan.
October 4	L. to K.	
November 6	K. to L.	
November 13	L. to K.	
December 12	K. to L.	
December 20	L. to K.	

1988

June 3	L. to K.	George H. W. Bush elected
June 15	K. to L.	president.
June 30	L. to K.	
July 5	K. to L.	
July 24	L. to K.	
November 20	L. to K.	
November 25	K. to L.	
December 23	K. to L.	
December 30.	L. to K.	

1989

February 11	L. to K.	Breakup of Soviet sphere
May 7	L. to K.	in Eastern Europe. End of
June 11	K. to L.	Communist rule in Poland and
June 19	K. to L.	Hungary.
July 18	L. to K	End of the Berlin Wall
August 24	K. to L.	(November).
August 29	L. to K.	End of Communist dictatorship
October 4	L. to K.	in Czechoslovakia (November)
		and Romania (December).

1990

February 15	K. to L.	Germany reunified.
February 18	L. to K.	
March 19	L. to K.	
March 28	K. to L.	
April 2	K. to L.	
April 5	L. to K.	
May 5	L. to K.	
May 12	K. to L.	
May 18	K. to L.	
August 20	L. to K.	
September 5	K. to L.	
November (undated)	K. to L.	

1991

March 15	K. to L.	Boris Yeltsin replaces Gorbachev.
March 30	L. to K.	First (brief) Gulf war.
May 22	K. to L.	Baltic republics, Ukraine, and
May 28	L. to K.	Caucasian statelets declare
June 16	K. to L.	independence.
August 29	L. to K.	Beginning of Yugoslav civil war.
September 13	K. to L.	End of the Soviet Union
September 19	L. to K.	(December).

1992

April 13	L. to K.	War in Yugoslavia intensifies.
May 6	K. to L.	Bill Clinton elected president.
June 1	K. to L.	
July 27	L. to K.	
August 4	K. to L.	
November 11	K. to L.	

1993

January 4	L. to K.	(Disastrous) American
January 6	L. to K.	intervention in Somalia.
April 5	L. to K.	
April 14	K. to L.	
December 13	K. to L.	

1994

February 16 (K.'s poem at 70)		Rwandan genocide.
February 17	L. to K.	South Africa holds first
March 9	K. to L.	multiracial elections.
August 1	K. to L.	Clinton and Yeltsin sign Kremlin
August 15	L. to K.	accords, under which Russia
October 31	L. to K.	and the United States would no
		longer aim missiles at each other.

1995

March 15	K. to L.	Yugoslav civil war formally ends
March 20	L. to K.	(December).
July 10	K. to L.	
July 30	L. to K.	
August 25	L. to K.	

1996

February 5	L. to K.	Clinton reelected president.

1997

March 25	L. to K.	Extension of NATO and
May 31	K. to L.	American military presence into
November 21	K. to L.	Eastern Europe.

1998

July 13	L. to K.
August 3	K. to L.
August 11	L. to K.
November 16	L. to K.
December 5	L. to K.

1999

August 11	K. to L.	U.S. Air Force bombs Belgrade
October 11	K. to L.	(and other sites in Yugoslavia)
October 15	L. to K.	during Kosovo conflict.
October 25	L. to K.	

2000

January 28	K. to L.	George W. Bush elected president.

2001

January 7	L. to K.	Terrorist plane attacks on
July 18	K. to L.	New York and Washington
August 17	L. to K.	(September 11).
October 15	L. to K.	

2002

February 3	L. to K.
February 11	K. to L.
February 18	L. to K.
April 1	L. to K.
September 26	L. to K.

2003
February 14   K. to L.   Bush invades Iraq (March).
March 5   L. to K.
August 27   K. to L.

2004
25 January   L. to K.   Kennan's 100th birthday
                                       (February 16).

Index